The False Promise of Liberal Order

For Jane
For everything

And for Hugh Alexander Porter
Welcome aboard

The False Promise of Liberal Order

Nostalgia, Delusion and the Rise of Trump

Patrick Porter

polity

First published in 2020 by Polity Press

Polity Press
65 Bridge Street
Cambridge CB2 1UR, UK

Polity Press
101 Station Landing
Suite 300
Medford, MA 02155, USA

ISBN-13: 978-1-5095-3867-6
ISBN-13: 978-1-5095-3868-3 (pb)

A catalogue record for this book is available from the British Library.

Library of Congress Cataloging-in-Publication Data

Names: Porter, Patrick, 1976- author.
Title: The false promise of liberal order : nostalgia, delusion and the
    rise of Trump / Patrick Porter.
Description: Cambridge ; Medford, MA : Polity, 2020. | Includes
    bibliographical references and index. | Summary: "A radical critique of
    US-led liberal foreign policy"-- Provided by publisher.
Identifiers: LCCN 2019047003 (print) | LCCN 2019047004 (ebook) | ISBN
    9781509538676 (hardback) | ISBN 9781509538683 (paperback) | ISBN
    9781509538690 (epub)
Subjects: LCSH: Trump, Donald, 1946- | Hegemony--United States. | World
    politics. | Liberalism. | United States--Foreign relations--20th
    century. | United States--Foreign relations--21st century.
Classification: LCC JZ1480 .P664 2020 (print) | LCC JZ1480 (ebook) | DDC
    327.73--dc23
LC record available at https://lccn.loc.gov/2019047003
LC ebook record available at https://lccn.loc.gov/2019047004

Typeset in 10 on 16.5 Utopia Std by
Servis Filmsetting Ltd, Stockport, Cheshire
Printed and bound in Great Britain by CPI Group (UK) Ltd, Croydon

For further information on Polity, visit our website:
politybooks.com

Contents

Many writers have dreamed up republics and kingdoms that bear no resemblance to experience.

Niccolò Machiavelli

Acknowledgements

I am grateful to Louise Knight at Polity for talking me into this, and to Inès Boxman who helped steer it through. Likewise, I am grateful to Chris Preble for talking me into the first version, which the Cato Institute kindly published and permitted us to draw on. And for permissions to reproduce material, thanks are due to Taylor & Francis, *The Washington Quarterly*, Daniel Immerwahr and Josh Shifrinson. I am grateful, for everything, to my wife Jane Rogers and to Hugh, our first-born, and to my family Brian, Muriel, Emily and Patrick, and to Frances Rogers for keeping the fires burning.

This book grew out of many conversations with friends, colleagues and worthy adversaries. My gratitude goes to David Blagden, Jeanne Morefield, Robert Saunders, Joshua Shifrinson, Tanisha Fazal, Michael Mazarr, Rosella Cappella Zielinski, Ryan Grauer, Apratim Sahay, Justin Logan, John Bew, Lawrence Freedman, Jennifer Lind, Robert Kagan, John Ikenberry, Daniel Deudney, Kori Schake, Jake Sullivan, John Mearsheimer, Stephen Walt, Barry Posen, Charles Glaser, Thomas Wright, David Adesnik, Hal Brands, Gil Barndollar, Peter Hitchens, Malcolm Chalmers, Daniel Deudney, Matt Fay, Michael Lind, Rebecca Lissner, Mira Rapp-Hooper, Asaf Siniver, Jamie Gaskarth, David Dunn, Mark Webber, Tim Haughton, Adam Quinn, Mike Sweeney, Stephen Wertheim, Daniel Nexon, Tarak Barkawi, Jerrod Laber, David Edelstein, Daniel Bessner, Chris Preble, John Glaser, Eric Gomez,

Emma Ashford, Geraint Hughes, James Goldgeier, Jonathan Kirshner, Randy Schweller, Andreas Behnke, Mark Kramer and Dan Drezner.

Anyone writing about international order is in the debt of Hedley Bull and Robert Gilpin. I was never lucky enough to meet either, but hope they would have thought this book worthwhile. We are also intellectually indebted to two 'Johns' – Mearsheimer and Ikenberry – who, after the fall of the wall, built the theoretical floor on which the rest of us dance. The first John helped to hammer out the realist tradition that has inspired this work. And while I challenge the second John's arguments, this book would not have been possible without his seminal body of thought.

Lastly, a word about the United States. Much of what follows is wintry. That wintriness does not flow from hostility. To the contrary, it is offered in a spirit of tough love, in solidarity with Americans and their allies who sense that something has gone very wrong. And in this century, flattery has gotten the republic nowhere.

Introduction:
Nostalgia in an End Time

In Cormac McCarthy's noir western novel, *No Country for Old Men*, an honourable sheriff sees brutal, lawless days fall on his county, seemingly out of nowhere. He seeks solace by imagining a lost era of chivalry. He recalls an era when lawmen didn't bear arms, a world that never was. In the face of inexplicable evil, his dream gives him something to hold onto and affords him dignity. It also paralyses him, making him a hapless witness to the chaos. Substitute the violent frontier for the world and the sheriff for foreign policy traditionalists, and a similar reaction is now under way in our angry days. Aghast that the time is out of joint, with the rise of President Donald Trump, populist demagogues and dangerous authoritarian regimes abroad, a group of people lament a dying order and the passing of American primacy in the world. They look back to a nobler past. Like the sheriff, they sense an end time has arrived. And like the sheriff, their invocations of a lost era cannot restore it. Invoking an imagined past impoverishes history. And it damages our capacity to act effectively under a darkening sky.

This is a book about euphemisms. Euphemisms are nice-sounding words that enable us to talk about a thing while avoiding its brutal realities. In this time of tumult, a set of evasive and soothing images about the past has come together, to imagine a lost world, a so-called 'liberal order'. Pleasant words, like 'leadership' and 'rules-based international order', abound as a dispute grows over international relations. That

1

dispute concerns the most important questions: how did we get here? And what must we do? As I argue, the concept of liberal order is misleading, as is the dream of its restoration. 'Ordering' and the business of hegemony is rough work, even for the United States, the least bad hegemon. If we want to forge an alternative order to the vision of Trump, it cannot be built in a dream palace. Only by gazing at history's darkness can we confront the choices of today.

'Orders' are hierarchies created by the strong, to keep the peace on their terms. There have been many orders: Roman, Byzantine, Imperial Chinese, Ottoman, Mughal, Spanish, French and British. They are often also imperial in their working. After all, most of history is a history of empire, a form of power that exercises final control over its subject societies. The great powers that do the 'ordering' remake the world partly through institutions and norms, and partly through the smack of coercion. Orders encourage a politeness of sorts, but a politeness that ultimately rests on the threat of force. When lesser powers forget this, the dominant states quickly remind them, as in 1956 when President Dwight Eisenhower threatened Britain with an economic crisis if it didn't cease its military adventure over Suez. Supposedly, according to their creators, orders remake the world in ways that replace chaos with regularity, making international life more legible, peaceable and secure.[1] As they order the world around them, hegemons articulate that order in elevated rhetorical terms that soften the realities of power. Euphemisms reflect the dominant power's conceit that it is unique, serving only as the source of order, never disorder, and always for the common good. More predatory overlords, like Imperial Japan, gave their programmes of enslavement preposterous names, like the 'Greater East Asia Co-Prosperity Sphere'. The instinct to euphemize also infects the United States, the gentlest hegemon thus far: wars are 'police action', crushing revolts

2

is 'counterinsurgency', propaganda is 'information operations' and torture is 'enhanced interrogation'. Reflecting on order (*imperium*) in his own time, and the gap between form and substance, the Roman historian Tacitus put a speech in the mouth of a Caledonian king who said of Roman violence, 'these things they misname order: they make a desolation and they call it peace'.[2]

To most of its admirers, America's order, created around the end of the Second World War and now fading, was different because it was 'liberal', meaning that it was organized around freedom, consent and equality. To them, the ordering power was not an empire. It was a more benign 'hegemon', a word drawn from ancient Greek to mean 'leader'. For the first time, according to this orthodoxy, the most powerful nation on earth forsook imperial aggrandizement, instead using enlightened measures to make a world safe for market democracy in which people could find emancipation. America possessed vast and unprecedented power, the hard instruments of wealth, intelligence, military force and an array of alliances. Despite being a new goliath, though, Washington bound itself into an international system of its own design, constraining its might and thereby winning authority. Unlike earlier orders, this was a truly international world system. It was founded primarily on rules. It opened up a once-closed world. It provided public goods like freedom of the seas, and stable monetary systems. Like all past hegemons, America regarded its settlement as not only legitimate, but sacred.[3]

An international class of security experts and policy practitioners believes that there was such a benign dispensation, and that it lasted seven decades. In common, they believe America and the world are best served through an enduring marriage of liberal principles and American primacy, or supremacy. To its admirers, this new design was imperfect but noble. It marked a system of peaceful ordering – of hegemony without empire – to which we might return. The only alternative, they fear, is regressive chaos.

The apparent fall of this system is all the more distressing to its defenders, given that the ruin seems to come primarily from within. Rather than being conquered by an external aggressor, America's order self-destructs. Western citizens lose faith in the project and fall prey to false consciousness. Demagogues, aided by sinister foreign powers, whip them up into a backlash. As Donald Tusk, President of the European Council, warned: 'The rules-based international order is being challenged . . . not by the usual suspects, but by its main architect and guarantor, the US.'[4] Or, in the words of the idea's principal theorist, G. John Ikenberry, it is as though the citizens of an unsubjugated Rome are tearing down their own city. An unsettling analogy for a supposedly non-imperial superpower.

We can speak of an American-led order. But a liberal one? We should be wary. For every order, including America's, has a shadow. It is one of hypocrisy and the threat of force well beyond the bounds of liberal norms, be that threat brazen or quiet, astute or naive. Hegemons will have their prerogatives, whether this means insisting that others open their markets while protecting their own, demanding that their sovereignty be respected while conducting raids into others' backyards, or denouncing election meddling while practising it. Not for nothing did Hedley Bull define order as 'imperialism with good manners'.[5]

In all the yearnings for a restored order, and in the closeness of liberal ambition and empire, lies the ghost of President Woodrow Wilson (1913–21). Wilson, it will be recalled, sought to translate victory in the First World War into a new international order. He envisioned a world governed by laws and converging towards democracy, a 'community of power'. But he, too, typified the tendency of hegemons to set rules for others and play by their own, the better to remain in the ascendancy.

4

The new hegemon would supplant the old and exercise its prerogatives. 'Let us build a bigger navy than hers', he said of Britain in 1916, 'and do what we please.'[6] Like most great powers that boast of their mandate to bring peace to the world, Wilson made war often. Against weaker adversaries from Latin America and the Caribbean to post-Tsarist Russia, his commitment to enlarging liberty was imperial, even when he wasn't aware of it. When he drafted a speech claiming 'it shall not lie with the American people to dictate to another what their government shall be', his secretary of state added in the margin: 'Haiti, S Domingo, Nicaragua, Panama.'[7] In this respect, America as a great power is unexceptional.

To be clear, the target here is *not* the minimal 'baseline' claim that an American-led order was better than the alternatives. It clearly was. It was better for the world that America became the dominant power, rather than its totalitarian competitors, even if the exercise of that dominance varied in its wisdom. As hegemonies go, America's was the least bad by a decisive margin. It was a bulwark against twentieth-century totalitarianism; it won more than half the Nobel Laureate prizes, pioneered Jazz, helped rebuild Europe, invented the polio vaccine and took humanity to the moon. American hegemony was obviously less atrocious, and more constructive, than European colonial, Axis or communist empires. Some forget that America created this world through agonizing compromise. Its relative moral superiority, without power politics, cannot explain America's rise. It cannot prevent its fall. And the belief in one's indispensability can lead to the fall. Athenian primacy in the ancient Hellenic world was more open and free than Persian autocracy, but that did not prevent its self-destruction. To confine ourselves to the comfort that, at least, the *Pax Americana* was better is like retelling the national story with frontier massacres and the Civil War left out.

Rather, the target is a more ambitious proposition, that America

5

exercised hegemony without being imperial; that it oversaw a 'world historical' transformation in which rules about sovereignty, human rights and free trade reigned and defined the international system; that the USA voluntarily constrained itself in such a system; that the 'good things' that the order produced are attributable to liberal behaviour; and that the sources of the current crisis somehow lie outside the order. This version of liberal order is ahistorical about the nature of power relations in the world. It tells us little about how we got here. Wrong about the past, it is therefore a bad guide for the future.

Even America's most glorious achievements – with liberal 'ends' – were not clean pluses on a balance sheet, made by liberal 'means'. They relied on a preponderance of power, a preponderance that had brutal foundations. America's most beneficial achievements were partly wrought by illiberal means, through dark deals, harsh coercion and wars gone wrong that killed millions. No account of US statecraft is adequate without its range of activity. Coups, carpet bombings, blockades and 'black sites' were not separate lapses, but were part of the coercive ways of world-ordering. Prosperity generated pollution on an epic scale. Even today, when the USA is keener to limit its liability and is more reluctant to wade ashore into hostile lands, it bombs countries with almost routine frequency. And central to its repertoire are economic sanctions, a polite term for crippling economic punishment, at times even siege and 'maximum pressure', inflicted on whole populations and often not with liberating effects. Possibly one-third of the 'open' world's people live in countries under economic warfare of some kind.[8]

Conversely, the same America has a conscience. It has held genuinely liberal ideals. Such ideals are a pillar of the American diplomatic mind. For most of those close to power who hold these ideals, this is not a case of ulterior motives, or dressing up narrow material interest in

6

the cloak of universal justice. They are driven by a deeply rooted belief in America's singular duty to lead the world. But too often, sincerely held ideals had inadvertent and illiberal consequences. In this century, when external restraints were weak and a sense of power and ambition grew, the USA intensified its pursuit of armed supremacy, confident it could see further, and stepped up its effort to spread a system of ever more adventurous global capitalism. From the almost-forgotten capitalist shock therapy visited on post-Soviet Russia, to wars to remake the Greater Middle East, to the loosening of the global financial system, or the incitement of democratic revolution abroad, efforts to spread liberal light have provoked history's wrath. The very attitude built into the nostalgia, the assurance that one's international role is vital, that one's actions are the source of stability and peace, that the dangers of inaction are the only ones worth worrying about, helped lead to disaster, whether in Wall Street, Moscow or Baghdad. To rewrite this history as an 'arc' of progress, or an 'arc' of anything, is to repeat the hubris that got us here. The arc of history bends toward delusion.[9]

There is a poverty in the righteous storytelling that underpins the liberal order idea. The main move of nostalgia is to lament the order's fall, or call for its revival, while sparing the order any blame for its own plight. Somehow, while it was powerful enough to transform modern life, the *Pax Americana* remains innocent of its own undoing. It was the fault of other actors, or of leaders who didn't believe in it enough, or the masses who failed to keep the faith. Its error is to suppose that American power and its liberalism was not only good, but *essentially* good, that good and wise things are 'who we are', while destructive excess is an aberration, and failure must be due to something else. Nostalgia gives the lost order an alibi as wicked populists and a set of 'isms' – populism, authoritarianism, protectionism, racism – are to blame. It is also reductionist about the present, offering false binary choices like internationalism versus isolationism, leadership versus quitting, global domination versus isolation in a post-American world. This damages our ability to adapt today under constraints, when prudent statecraft will require some mix of power-projection and retrenchment.

These conceits have come together in the figure of former Vice-President, and presidential candidate, Joseph Biden. 'This too shall pass', he declared at the Munich security conference in February 2019, prompting a standing ovation.[10] The applause echoed 'a longing to return to a world order that existed before President Donald Trump starting swinging his wrecking ball'.[11] Biden presents Trump as a passing aberration: 'America is coming back like we used to be. Ethical, straight, telling the truth . . . supporting our allies. All those good things.'[12] 'Good things' suggests a cleansing of history. It holds out an assurance that Trump, and the revolt, are exogenous to the order, and thus can be swiftly hurled back into the night without an inquest. Keep the faith, it urges, and await the return of the sleeping king. This attitude is reflected in the Democratic Party more widely, where there is little contest over fresh ideas about foreign policy, and where electability overshadows questions of substance. What if Biden is wrong? What if the order itself was flawed, and drove these revolts? What if the political crisis cannot be undone by one ballot?

Not only did a liberal order never truly exist. Such an order cannot exist. Neither the USA nor any power in history has risen to dominance by being ethical, straight or truthful, or by supporting allies, not without a panoply of darker materials. To suggest otherwise covers over a bloodier, more conflicted and more imperial history, of a superpower driven both by ruthless power-seeking and messianic zeal, in a world shaped also by resistance. The hegemon imposed, stretched or ignored rules, built and bypassed institutions. By turns it coerced, cajoled and abandoned allies, to remain in the ascendancy. When overblown notions of its world-historical mission took hold, it led to unexpected chaos and unanticipated pushback, and damaged liberal values at home. At times, it was simply defeated. Euphemistic memory does not deny this history. It just refuses to linger on it. It loses sight of how our world was, and is, ordered – indeed, what 'ordering' involves, deflecting attention from its hard dilemmas.

If you share these doubts, read on. If you are a believer and are already irked, let me try to persuade you, in the spirit of liberal toleration.

The Context

Sudden and distressing changes have rocked the international system since the early 2010s. Hostile revisionist states are on the move, ranging from Russia's seizure of Crimea and its covert campaigns of subversion and terror; China's domestic repression, its expansion in the South China Sea, its bullying of foreign populations and its threats to Taiwan; and North Korea's acquisition of a deliverable nuclear weapon. There has been sectarian bloodletting in the Middle East, mixing war with humanitarian crisis and the flight of refugees, and intensifying security competition. Only recently, the black flags of the Islamic State flew above Mosul. There are the agonies of the Arab Spring revolutions, which lurched into despotic reaction in some countries, state implosion in others. Economic protectionism is again on the rise. Crisis also rises within, in the fallout over Britain's withdrawal from the European Union (EU), nationalist populist movements in Europe, Asia and Latin America, and the coming of authoritarian 'strongmen'. In particular, political tumult and the election of Donald Trump to the US presidency have driven anxious commentators to lament the collapse of a post-1945 universe of institution-building, rule-following and enlightened leadership. Growing discord makes more faceless but tangible terrors, like the climate crisis, even more daunting.

These disturbances draw a widening cast of transatlantic security officials, experts, scholars, politicians, military officers, mandarins, plutocrats and public intellectuals to offer nostalgic visions of the past, and to speak of a political end time.[13] They either warn that the survival of a rules-based liberal world order is at stake, or they write its obituary. We are witnessing the 'end of the West as we know it', the abandonment of 'global leadership' by its 'long-time champion', and a 'Coming Dark Age'. *Foreign Affairs*, the house organ of the foreign policy establishment, recently asked thirty-two experts 'Is the Liberal Order in Peril?'. Twenty-six agreed, confidently, that it is.[14]

The new disorder attracts grand claims. At the 2019 Munich Security Conference, former leaders issued a Declaration of Principles that underpinned the post-war order: 'democracy; free, fair, and open markets; and the rule of law'.[15] With a stroke of the pen, history's darkness is banished and a world of discrepant experiences is wished away, from the killing fields of the Cold War, to the centres of authoritarian power, to the long history of post-war mercantilism. This is history at high altitude. From a similar height come the manifestos of the World Economic Forum at the Swiss ski resort at Davos and its ahistorical 'exhortatory slogans'.[16] The funeral of US Senator John McCain in September 2018, which was likened to a 'Resistance meeting', called forth praise for the cause of armed liberalism, and lamentations for the order's passing, with McCain's death marking its recessional hymn.[17] A large literature has formed, praising the liberal order. With honourable exceptions, the liberal order version of the past is a panegyric, a speech of praise. With their ideals under strain, proponents of these views circle their wagons and tend towards a sectarian style. They celebrate orthodoxies – free trade, expanding alliances, order-enforcing military action, American global leadership – and denounce heresies, such as protectionism, military restraint, non-intervention and détente with enemies.

If the heart of liberalism is the promise of liberation from tyranny, then the panegyrics suggest that Washington achieved security in an enlightened way by reshaping the world – or large parts of it – in its liberal image. America's domestic norms flowed outwards, reproducing in the world the socioeconomic order that prevails at home.[18] Because of this liberal character, the victorious superpower exercised not mere power, but global leadership and deep engagement, creating peace-promoting institutions. America underwrote the system with its unprecedented power, while also subordinating itself to it. Instead of power untamed, the new order was based, above all, on rules and regularity. The *Pax Americana* repudiated the old statecraft that had culminated in total war and genocide, in imperial domination and cut-throat geopolitics, land grabs and spheres of influence, protectionist tariff blocs and economic autarky, and zero-sum, violent nationalism. Unlike the brute dominance of empire and its rule by command, it was American hegemony that allegedly presided, a type of power based more on rule by consent and legitimate authority, providing public goods and 'flexibly enforced rules'.[19] As first citizen among nations, America both subordinated itself to rules, structures and protocols, yet was also a new Leviathan, restraining itself and, by doing so, acquiring authority. The new order was imperfect, its admirers agree. Its institutions need reinventing. Still, it created unprecedented relative prosperity and prevented major wars. It is a world, they believe, worth fighting for, as the jungle grows back.[20]

These sentiments are also voiced by the professoriate. A July 2018 manifesto against Trump, an advertisement paid for by forty-three professors of International Relations in the *New York Times*,[21] resulted in an online petition signed by hundreds of eminences of the discipline.[22] More measured than other panegyrics, even this statement treats its claims as self-evident truths, advanced by appeals to authority, and offering a sanitized historical picture of the USA as dutiful global citizen, deferring to the institutions it created.

The thrust of these claims is that the world can again be ordered in the enlightened design of a global system, run for the common good by a far-sighted superpower that legitimizes its order by willingly constraining itself. Liberal order visionaries counsel Washington to restore a battered tradition, to uphold economic and security commitments, and to promote liberal values. To interpret recent disappointments as a reason for revising orthodox positions, they warn, is an overreaction. The literature explains in detail why various actors from Trump to Putin pose threats. Yet it is also notable for its presumptuousness about its referent object. The rules-based system, assumed a priori as a real thing worth defending, for instance, by Britain's Foreign Affairs Select Committee, is the axiomatic historical starting point.[23]

The rhetoric has become an incantation. It is all the more striking for being relatively recent, a new vocabulary for what is supposed to be a single unbroken project pursued by the Atlantic West for generations. 'The less the actual liberal international order resembled the conditions of its early zenith', one observer notes, 'the greater became the need to name it.'[24] The worse international conditions get, the more the incantations repeat, as though repeating them will somehow sing a lost world back into life. The UK's *National Security Strategy* of 2015, written in the glare of Russia's annexation of Crimea and the Islamic State's eruption in the Middle East, repeated the phrase 'rules-based order' thirty times, Australia's *Defence White Paper* of 2016 thirty-eight times.

Thus far, constant reaffirmation is not faring well. It is not easing the present disorder, nor converting alienated voters, nor dampening the ambitions of America's rivals. Cross-sections of voters report that the notion of liberal order baffles and underwhelms them, while the majority of veterans agree with the majority of the general public that America's wars in Afghanistan, Iraq, Libya and Syria were wasteful.[25] For those in the audience with doubts, it feels more like being 'preached at' than being informed.[26]

The claim that America's order was exceptional, and the hegemony/ empire distinction, echoes the exceptionalist claims of previous great powers. It is an old conceit. It dates back at least to nineteenth-century Britain, another time of dispute over the relation between liberalism and empire. The Victorian historian and banker George Grote projected the same fantasy, of non-imperial hegemony, onto classical Greece, distinguishing Athens's benign leadership of a coalition from oppressive Persian overlordship. The Greeks, however, used the terms 'hegemony' and 'empire' interchangeably.[27] They had a point. For even between 'friends' in the international arena, interests eventually diverge. When they do, even benign stronger powers have a habit of bringing their strength to bear.

Euphemizing the exercise of power, this worldview should not survive interrogation. It simply leaves out too much contrary history. It over-privileges the peaceful centres of the American order – Western Europe and East Asia – when the order defined itself also in the zones where power was most contested. It fails to account for the most consequential event in post-war American public life, the Vietnam War. Like all hegemons, Washington for long periods loosened its restraint, exerting itself violently to save face, project credibility and sustain authority, and ignored rules as it suited.

Yet talk of liberal order proliferates. It has become the *lingua franca* of the Atlantic security class. Such is the consistency and unity of their language, and so close is their social network through conclaves in Aspen, Davos, Munich, Harvard, the Brookings Institute or the Council on Foreign Relations, and the revolving door between think-tanks, government, foundations, universities and media commentary, that the coalition of those who call for a return to a liberal order can be regarded as a class in itself, with its own dialect.[28]

In our age of complex realignment, the question of order also cuts diagonally across old lines, creating new coalitions. Hawkish internationalist Republicans and Democrats make common cause against Trump and the order's enemies.[29] Neoconservatives, committed to heroic greatness, subdivide on the question of liberalism, some enlisting in bipartisan resistance against Trump, others joining his administration.[30] The question even divides the Trumpists. Secretary of State Mike Pompeo declared the pursuit of a new liberal order based on the principle of national sovereignty, after which there emerged a starker conception of primacy, defined as 'We're America, Bitch'.[31] A group of the president's ministers, who chafe at some elements of the liberal order – for example, adherence to institutions – have tried to tilt their erratic boss back into the orthodoxy of US hegemonic leadership. This is not a simple story.

Advocates of the 'liberal order' believe it was a good thing, and worth defending.[32] It was, they argue, a constellation of 'bargains, institutions and social purposes'[33] created under the leadership of the post-war USA. As the dominant state, with its favourable geography, economic and demographic size and military preponderance, America shaped 'the rules of the game by which international politics is played, the intellectual frameworks employed by many states, and the standards by which behaviour is judged to be legitimate'.[34] For admirers, this was a profound project that rewired the world. They periodize it as a more-or-less continuous set of arrangements that lasted for more than seventy years from the Allied victory in 1945. America created a constitutional order as opposed to unchecked power, a system that was fundamentally consensual, benign and open. The order's longevity, stability and attraction rested on these liberal ideological foundations. This system constituted a harmony of interests, in that it was both good for America and good for the world.

Traditionalists share a vocabulary, historical reference points and logic, though what they mean precisely by 'order' varies. Some use the term loosely as a proxy for the general benevolence of American primacy. Others make more specific and ambitious claims about how that world once worked. All defend liberal order as a historical creation that rescued a world from depression, totalitarianism, world war and genocide. Most propose it as a model for the future, if only others would share their vision. Their pessimism varies. Some argue that the order is collapsing with America's 'retreat' and the rise of barbaric forces at home and abroad, and that the best we can do is salvage what we can. Others hope that even as an internal schism divides the West, the order created by America can outlive its principal architect.

In opposition, there are sceptics.[35] Most of these argue that liberal order is a false promise, a master concept that will do more to hinder than to help us pick our way through the chaos. They note the gap between nostalgia and history, and that the post-war world was never 'whole'. There may be 'islands of liberal order, but they are floating in a sea of something quite different'.[36] Most favour a more restrained grand strategy – less militarized, more accommodating, less driven to expansion. Some are isolationists, favouring bringing America home from its overseas commitments. Many are not – including this author. In their shared opposition to centrist orthodoxy, sceptics derive from a mixed and overlapping grouping of academic realists, anti-war conservatives and progressive-leftist internationalists, though there is also a group of primacists who maintain that the USA should still pursue dominance abroad but without extravagant projects to export democratic capitalism. In common, they challenge visions of liberal order as a once-achieved fact to which we can return. Such memories are ahistorical, and therefore no answer to the present predicament. Indeed, they are part of the problem. As a 'mytho-history' that provides an account of origin and a guide to action, the false memory of liberal order obscures what power politics involves. And it turns attention away from where it can lead, especially when the powerful inhale their own mythology. The task should not be to adapt, reform, refresh, repackage or rebrand this vision. That vision put the USA where it is now: saddled by unsustainable debt, stifled by excessive and unaccountable state power, struggling through multiple failed wars, on collision course with rivals in Europe, the Middle East, Asia and Latin America, and helmed by Trump. The prudent response is instead to correct, or at least restrain, its flaws.

Beyond that baseline argument, sceptics are a more heterogenous lot. They disagree with one another about whether there really was a liberal order or whether there can be. Some argue there was, at least once the USA become the unipolar primate and, unfettered, ran amok. Others celebrate liberal progress but claim that American hegemony had little to do with it. Still others complain that there ought to have been such an order, but it was absent. They call on Washington to practise what it preaches and obey the rules it insists others obey, suggesting that we could have such an order if only the hypocrisy were to end.[37] Thus there are unresolved arguments within the sceptics' camp about whether liberal order is desirable or possible.

Ideas about order matter and have weighty policy implications. Just as material power enables or forecloses certain choices, so ideas condition and constrain a country's grand strategic decisions. Those who lament the fall of the liberal order are saying, in effect, that some ideas are illegitimate and should be off the table. They worry that populism and isolationism endanger traditional ideas that were once dominant, leading America to abandon its manifold commitments overseas. When they call for the reclamation of the old order, they also call for the perpetuation of American primacy. By contrast, I argue that the exaggerated notion of the liberal order and its imminent collapse is one of the myths of empire that helped create the current crisis.

Today's politics is restoration politics, the politics of promising to resuscitate lost orders. Strongmen, demagogic populists, seek authority by claiming to speak for the true virtuous people against illegitimate alien elites, vowing to bring lost orders *back*. They will 'make America great *again*', 'take *back* control', or return jobs, industries, sovereign borders and national pride.[38] And they are not the only ones to harken back. Proponents of liberal order see their cause as forward-looking and scold voters and political realists alike for being backward-looking.[39] Yet they too traffic in nostalgia. In George Packer's elegy for the late diplomat Richard Holbrooke, a curator of the *Pax Americana*, his hero weeps at the 1949 musical *South Pacific* for the loss of a 'feeling that we could do anything', an era 'when we had gone to the most distant corners of the globe and saved civilization'.[40] Cautioning against being 'backward-looking', such minds also call for the revival of a system that was founded in atypical and impermanent conditions seventy years ago, under a different distribution of power, an exceptionalism based on America's technocratic capacity 'to innovate and solve hard problems'.[41] Former Senator, Secretary of State and presidential candidate Hillary Clinton accused Trump voters of 'looking backward'. But she too appealed to a romanticized past, a 'long-standing bipartisan tradition of global leadership rooted in a preference for cooperating over acting unilaterally, for exhausting diplomacy before making war, and for converting old adversaries into allies rather than making new enemies'.[42] The history Clinton praises was far more mixed. Historically, the USA often acted unilaterally, waged preventive war – and considered doing so – before exhausting all options, including in Iraq in 2003 with Clinton's supporting vote, and sustained enmities from Cuba's Fidel Castro to the Iranian Ayatollahs.[43]

At times, self-identified liberal traditionalists are risibly nostalgic. The writings of hawkish public intellectual Max Boot exhibit the nostalgia's imperial turn. Boot champions 'liberal order', scolding fellow Republicans that 'nostalgia isn't a foreign policy'. Yet he also advises Washington to find wartime inspiration in historical campaigns to pacify frontiers, borrowing his title from Rudyard Kipling's poem urging America to take up the 'white man's burden'.[44] Boot's explicit reverence for empire and its thirst for vengeance, his insensitivity to the genocidal and racial character of his subject, is an extreme case. It also reveals an awkward truth, often only in the margins of other accounts. Namely, that this is a history not simply of benign leaders and the grateful led. It is a history of resistance and imposition, of punitive force. Frequent violence at the hegemon's discretion, to tame the world into order, is central to the history.

Many believers in liberal order do not share Boot's enthusiasm for bloody frontiers. They think of themselves as peaceable and law-abiding. When they advocate for force, they believe they are creating a better state of peace. Yet in practice, they exhibit the liberal order's proclivity to militarism of a kind. Our post-war order, embodied in the United Nations, was originally founded more to limit the use of force in principle – 'the scourge of war' – than to license it. As good Atlanticists, though, enthusiasts for liberal order often advocate military exertion under US leadership, and often without formal authorization from the United Nations Security Council (UNSC), to enforce some rules, effectively, by violating others, and in ways they probably would not condone from other states. In August 2013, the liberal *Economist* denounced the British parliament for voting down air strikes on Syria to punish a chemical weapons (CW) atrocity, a bombing that was urgently needed to enforce a taboo and uphold a rules-based international order.[45] Opponents of war, who worried that ill-conceived military action breached rules or due process, and could inadvertently assist Islamist rebels, were branded as insular reactionaries. The assertion that, in the established order, a CW taboo is supreme and must override other considerations is ahistorical, as suggested by Washington's earlier record in sponsoring a CW-armed Iraq against Iran. Once again, liberal consciences were persuaded that airstrikes should be used as a tool of affordable moral action, denouncing sceptics for their backwardness. Once again, they claimed a special prerogative and disregarded alternative conceptions of order. Once again, liberalism was not very liberal.

The debate over international order is difficult to have in a productive way. The issue mixes up fraught concepts: the question of liberalism, a rich and conflicted tradition; the question of the 'international' and how American power should shape it; and conflicting ideas of 'order'. Liberal order is a moving target. Often it expresses not a falsifiable hypothesis but an article of faith, aspirations about American internationalism that confuse means and ends. As Damon Linker notes, the concept gets caught between two contrary views:

> The liberal international order that encourages rule-following and negotiation while fostering peace and prosperity among nations is our handiwork, as is the democratic world we have

nurtured around the globe. Those who oppose us in defending this order are evildoers . . . and we'll seek to demonstrate this by pointing to every bad thing they've ever done as evidence of their inherent treachery and malevolence. We're idealists, in other words. Moral, well-meaning, law-abiding, leading by principle and example in everything we do.

But that's only one half of the equation. America might be unwaveringly moral, but we are also tough, ruthless, hard-nosed, realistic about the ugly ways of the world, like a sheriff toiling to establish a modest and vulnerable zone of order in a lawless land. In such a world, the ends often justify the means. When fighting our enemies, we need to be willing to do whatever it takes to prevail. We have no choice . . . unlike the bad guys, whose every unsavoury deed deserves to be treated as an exemplification of their wickedness, our seemingly malicious actions appear to be rare exceptions, wholly excused by the lamentable necessities that govern a fallen world.[46]

Precisely because of the unswerving belief in the order's decency and soundness, panegyrics offer shallow accounts of the crisis. They serve up glutinous reassurances, that the order has all the answers to its own problems, that what is 'wrong' with the order can be fixed with what is 'right' with it.[47] The order's defenders offer technocratic remedies: refined institutions, fresh messaging or creative new programmes. If the order is perishing, it cannot be due to its own internal flaws. It is being assassinated, after being made vulnerable through neglect. This dictates unpromising responses, whether to write the order's obituary, blame 'defeatists', or preach for its revival in the hope that the disillusioned will return to its banner. If the world is changing as profoundly as nostalgists believe, we need inquest, not exoneration.

The Argument

The target here is the proposition of liberal order. This is not the same as liberalism, a rich tradition that is continually remade. Liberal order is a suggestion about how a dominant power organized, and can organize, the world. I argue that the concept is a self-contradiction. The world is too dangerous and conflicted to be ordered liberally, and overstriving to spread democracy abroad will destroy it at home.As the historical record shows, as well as consensual institution-building and dialogue, there were illiberal and coercive parts. These dark parts – the hypocrisies of power – were not aberrations but helped constitute the system. The order was partly driven by an imperial logic, of hierarchical dominance, partly an anarchic logic of competition for security, as well as recurring liberal impulses.[48] It was mercantilist as well as 'free'. It rested on privilege more than on rules. Appeals to the myth of a liberal Camelot flow from a deeper myth, of power politics without coercion, and empire without imperialism.

These problems are rooted primarily not in American political culture, but in the tragic nature of international life. In an inherently insecure world, to order is an illiberal process, and a violent and coercive one, that invariably forces compromises between liberal values and brutal power politics. Even the most high-minded overseas projects require collaboration with illiberal forces, whether dictators, fanatics or criminals. Even the episode most fondly recalled in transatlantic memory as an unambiguous good, the defeat of the Axis in the Second World War, was made possible through an appeasement of Stalin's Soviet Union.

Ordering is an inherently imperial undertaking. By 'imperial', I mean the exercise of dominance over another state's domestic policies, whether in the foreground or implicitly in the background. American statecraft reflects both the desire to liberate and yet also to control, a 'Crusader State', setting others free while determining their course, on American terms.[49] This need not be formal or annexationist rule. In this case, it is a distinctively American, informal mode of empire, one that functions as

> influence, exercised routinely and consistently, becomes indistinguishable from indirect rule ... When actors believe that certain options are 'off the table' because of an asymmetric (if tacit) contract, or consistently comply with the wishes of another because they recognize steep costs from noncompliance, then the relationship between the two becomes effectively one between ruler and ruled.[50]

Ordering the world requires that others be led, and, if not responsive to coaxing, more forcibly herded. The ordering power that demands compliance and rule-following from others will also reserve its prerogative not to be bound, on the basis that it is 'special'. As Ikenberry frames it, this is what we mean by an imperial logic. Complaining about the foreign policy of President George W. Bush, Ikenberry noted that 'it offered the world a system in which America rules the world but does not abide by rules. This is in effect, empire.'[51] So it was. That also, however, describes US hegemony since its inception.

The liberal order proposition, supposed to help develop trust and mitigate the forces of anarchy, underestimates the problem of the security dilemma, the paradox of taking steps to increase security only to heighten insecurity. Even the most well-intended, benign project to order the planet will appear hostile and threatening to rivals and potential adversaries. What looks to the ascendant power like a harmony of interests and a morally obvious set of arrangements, derived from self-evident timeless principles that serve the common good, will look to some others like the enforcement of self-interest, dressed up as moral universalism. Rivals and adversaries with a history of predation, and being preyed upon, fear that beneath the hegemon's insistence on an order of rules, it reserves a self-anointed right to enforce its preponderance by bending or breaking rules, routing around protocols and striking at will. Through the eyes of adversaries with long memories, it is too hard to distinguish American benevolent hegemony from a threatening preponderance of power. The hegemonic power may genuinely believe its own claims – that it doesn't practise the ugly power politics of 'spheres of influence', expansion or trade protectionism. This makes the problem worse, for it will practise aggrandisement without awareness, being shocked when its obviously benign actions result in resistance.

Liberal order also has a problem with war itself. Its founding conviction is that 'autocratic and militarist states make war; democracies make peace ... this is the cornerstone of Wilsonianism and, more generally, the liberal international tradition'.[52] This conviction tends towards belligerence. Making a world safe for democracy easily merges into making the world democratic. It slips readily into the further conceit that as 'our' actions are peaceful in their essence, the source of belligerence lies externally with other forces. Problems come not from tragic interactions but from malign external forces arrayed against a virtuous American hero-state. In turn, that logic supplies a warrant for applying righteous force. A commitment to permanent world-ordering strictly on one's own terms then entails regular military action, occasionally rising to violent crescendos. Those in favour of a return to liberal order usually demand more power projection, greater alliance commitments, more military presence, not less. Yet while such enthusiasts have much to say in praise of military arrangements – alliances, joint exercises, doctrines and capabilities – and in criticism of failures to apply military force, they are notably shy about the process of wars conducted in the name of their ideals, and what they lead to. Projecting power to achieve international order has had domestic, illiberal consequences like the increase of state power and the unbalancing of the constitution. Two decades of war have frayed American liberties, institutions and solvency.

While the proposition of singular American 'leadership' as a world-ordering hegemon has become a self-evident value amongst traditionalists, this derives from nostalgia for a temporary and unsustainable moment in world politics, and one that its admirers romanticize too much. The extravagant vision – of America as a world-ordering superintendent with an appetite for unrivalled 'global leadership' – overstates the country's power and knowledge. Historically, this has driven the USA into avoidable waste and misfortune. At its least reflective, the dream of liberal order produces a warlike righteousness, the instinct that chaos must be due only to a lack of power projection, ruling out the prudent consideration of retrenchment or adjustment. It serves to narrow rather than enlarge our imagination and choices, to reduce foreign policy to a dualistic contest between 'leadership' and 'isolation'. For them, the lessons of history are clear and unambiguous, and derive almost entirely from a single atypical case, the failures of inter-war isolationism and appeasement. By casting itself as a liberal Leviathan with an exceptional global role and historical mission, the USA inadvertently makes itself a Jacobin state, forever seeking expansion of its sphere and promoting regime change and revolution. All the while, it attributes problems to 'not enough' American dominance. If we need an alternative banner under which to mobilize against Trump's seductive promise of a return to greatness, that banner does not have to be just a refined version of what came before, an order that many experience as remote institutions, borderless, inhumane capitalism and war without end.

If the ultimate purpose of US statecraft must be to secure the republic – its institutions, its free way of life and its limited and constitutional government – as a good thing for itself and an exemplar to the world, other practices, drawn from a tradition of American realism, are a better bet. These too must be handled with care. Just as the targets of this book are vulnerable to nostalgia, so are we all. In observing the politics of nostalgia, we cannot presume to step outside consciousness of the past as a guide to action. Rather, the process of mining history for guidance should be richer, and open to a wider field of possibility.

Critique of liberal order also comes from the Marxist, critical and postcolonial wings of scholarship.[53] In particular, Jeanne Morefield argues that literature proposing and defending liberal order has, at its heart, the contradictions of empire that deflect attention from its inconsistencies by insisting that whatever errors, crimes and disasters liberal projections of power lead to, there is always a pristine essence to which America can return.[54] Morefield's critique parallels my own, though in different terms, against those who advocate order without paying enough attention to what 'ordering' historically actually involves. Critical literature strives for emancipation. By exposing the affectations of 'order' arguments, Morefield seeks to add intellectual fire to the movement so as to turn the world away from imperialism and *raison d'état*, and to build a new humanist order.

By contrast, this book does not. In the tradition of classical realism, by stripping away euphemism, it seeks less to transform than to reveal the hard-wired realities and constraints of an anarchic world, the hard trade-offs it imposes. If emancipation is impossible in this pessimistic tradition, if some hypocrisy and brutality is inevitable, if states and their rulers cannot be 'good', they can at least be wiser and more self-aware. They can develop a prudential capacity to practise a more restrained and self-aware power politics, to husband power more than waste it, to practise intrigue and competition without excess brutality, and to wage war without it destroying the state, or, in America's case, the republic.

In Chapter 1, 'The Idea of Liberal Order', I attempt to pin down the liberal order hypothesis as precisely as possible, to test it, and to bring its assumptions to the surface, arguing that liberal order rhetoric betrays an attraction-repulsion to empire. Chapter 2, 'Darkness Visible', forms the empirical spine of my argument. This chapter lays out a critique based on a review of the order's history. I demonstrate that order-creating is a necessarily imperial, coercive process that is not amenable to the kind of consensual, consistent rule-enforcement and rule-following that its proponents are nostalgic for. Chapter 3, 'Rough Beast', argues that President Donald Trump is more a culmination of the order than an aberration from it. While subjectively, he and his opponents cast him as the antithesis of post-war foreign policy traditions, Trump embodies two long-running tendencies, towards permanent war and oligarchy. Chapter 4, 'A Machiavellian Moment', turns to the future. Washington must reckon with the survival of its institutions in an increasingly hostile world, but by realizing that, contrary to liberal order claims, it cannot domesticate the world to its liberal values. As before, the USA will have to make hard compromises, to prevent a more competitive world from destroying its republic.

We turn first, though, to liberal order as a hypothesis about the past, a complaint about the present and a prescription for the future.

1

The Idea of Liberal Order

Hegemons are vain creatures. Having risen to power, they are easily afflicted with 'middle kingdom' syndrome, the fancy that they possess superior wisdom, standing at the centre of the cosmos with little to learn from others.[1] Far from being an American peculiarity, self-centric worldviews are an ancient conceit, from Persia's King Darius I, Spain's Philip II, China's Ming dynasty, Ottoman Sultan Suleiman the Magnificent, to Napoleonic France. The assumption of their own specialness encourages hegemons to identify their interests with those of other states, to see success as the sign of the cosmos's favour and adversity as a test of faith. In turn, this loosens restraint and makes them war-prone. They practise what medieval China called 'barbarian management', without suspecting themselves of being the source of belligerence. They give themselves permission to pick and choose among rules in ways they would not tolerate from others, to stand outside their system the better to sustain it.

When American power climaxed around the turn of this century, policymakers spoke as lords of the horizon. 'We're an empire now', said a senior presidential advisor in 2002, 'and when we act, we create our own reality.'[2] The attitude that America could make the world anew, with triumphant finality, was on display on 1 May 2003 when President George W. Bush descended from a Viking jet onto the USS *Abraham Lincoln* to declare the end of major combat operations in

Iraq. Bush spoke of free-market democracy as humanity's destiny, of America's divine appointment, reworking biblical quotations to substitute 'America' for 'God'.[3] Ensuing military and economic disasters failed to extinguish American leaders' confidence in the meaning of history. Even President Obama, who positioned himself against imperial hubris, returned to the same waters. He declared that the 'arc' of the moral universe 'bends towards justice', presuming that history is directional and that he knew its destination.[4]

This is not to say that all hegemonies are equivalent, or identical, 'black boxes'. They are not. A Chinese-dominated Asia would not simply replicate the American Century. Details would vary in important ways: the scale of brutality and repression, the willingness to intrude on other states' internal way of life and constitutional systems, and the level of ambition to reach beyond their own region. A Chinese hegemony would probably be both more brutal yet less prescriptive domestically, except when demanding obedience. These details matter. For millions, those differences are worth fighting and dying for. They matter for those who are on the receiving end, and for those who exercise power. And they matter regarding the sustainability of the project. Some hegemonies overreach further and destroy themselves more quickly than others.

Rather, the claim here is that most hegemonies share an underlying set of characteristics: a sense of their own 'specialness' and singularity; a selective attitude to rules; a proneness to war; and an elevated sense of themselves as a source of order and light. Hypocrisy – organized or casual – tends to reign. With growing power, these characteristics tend to increase. Those who articulate liberal order resist this claim. They argue that American hegemony was different, not only in degree but in substance. It was not just a new order, they say, but a new kind of order. This time, order was not just another word for structure or empire, but something qualitatively different, an organization of power defined and redeemed by liberalism. In the tradition of Hedley Bull, it established a sense of common interests, rules prescribing behaviour, and institutions that make those rules effective. To say this, however, is to speak like a hegemon.

This is not an arcane debate. It is linked to fundamental questions about how our world should be. Panegyrics to the pre-Trump order are an intervention in present political struggles. They are fashioned in an hour of emergency, as their creators fear the night is falling. They are uttered in order to affirm a sense of American mission, to warn the superpower against the temptation to narrow its horizons or retreat or give up its role as moral tutor. As a theoretical and historical proposition, liberal order is remarkably recent. While liberal internationalism has an old pedigree, the consensus that Washington presided over an order where liberal means served liberal ends with liberal results is only a few decades old. A genealogy is needed, the tracing of its origins and development as a concept. For with genealogy – the excavation of the roots of an idea – we can learn why the vocabulary and mytho-history of liberal order appeals to a certain caste of mind. By digging into its prehistory, we can identify what historical shifts and problems gave rise to it. And we can uncover the silences, contradictions and evasions that bodyguard the concept.

Closer inspection reveals problems. Liberal international order does not deal adequately with what it is supposed to be defined and organized against. What is illiberal order? The concept of liberal order distinguishes the American Century from other kinds of domination, ones that were based on arbitrary power and imperial diktat. This is not just historically suspect. Something more fraught is going on among the devotees themselves. A closer look suggests that the visionaries of liberal order are also attracted to empire and the privileges of hegemony. They desire what amounts to a world monarch. Proponents of liberal order hold up the idea of a world hegemon that voluntarily binds itself in constraints through an enlightened settlement 'after victory', thereby winning legitimacy and international concord. Yet they also cut against this, either underplaying the history of continuous great power rule-violation, or arguing openly for superpower privilege without attempting to reconcile it with the claim of a rules-based order. Time and again, they call for the USA to exercise discretion beyond the rules, justifying illiberal means in pursuit of liberal ends. Thus, liberal order visions lose sight of a longstanding dilemma in American arguments over foreign policy, for which there is no easy resolution – namely, that a republic continuously pursuing dominance and expansion abroad assumes the form of an empire. And this, in turn, threatens liberty at home.

Before we explore these problems, it is important first to set out the idea of liberal order, as clearly and as fairly as possible. This is not easy. For the idea itself, as it is articulated and defended, is a slippery one. Looking to express an aspiration, it projects it back into history. Like the order it valorizes, it is a moving target that ducks and weaves against close scrutiny. It floats like a butterfly, even if it rarely stings like a bee.

The Order in Theory

There are many moving parts to the liberal order hypothesis. The genre appears in numerous forms, from op-ed and academic articles to manifestos and book-length studies. At the core of it is a mytho-history. It claims that the USA in its hour of mid-century triumph rescued the world. It created a new system of international relations, and subordinated itself to it. The new order was fundamentally sound. It was so successful that its beneficiaries have forgotten its benefits, and will learn to miss it.

The hypothesis proceeds as follows. It begins in the mid-twentieth century with the coming together of two forces, the precipitate rise of the USA as a result of a world war that devastated competitors, and the ascent of liberalism. The story arc typically begins around the 'Truman moment', President Harry Truman's 'blueprint for a rules-based international order to prevent dog-eat-dog geopolitical competition'.[5] The order's intellectual roots lay in a body of ideas that were anticipated earlier. Partly, it can be traced to the philosopher Immanuel Kant's vision of universal peace, whereby nations subordinate themselves to principles and institutions that make it possible. It was anticipated also, decades before, by President Woodrow Wilson, and his doomed commitment to cooperative internationalism in the wake of the First World War. The idea was then hammered out into achievable form, in the matrix of the Second World War and through the tough-minded idealism of President Franklin Roosevelt and British Prime Minister Winston Churchill. Centre stage were their wartime pronouncements about the world to come, the 'Four Freedoms' speech, the Newfoundland Declaration and Atlantic Charter of 1941, the United Nations Declaration, as well as the creation of new institutions, such as the Bretton Woods financial settlement. The emerging order – and the wider cause of lasting American internationalism – was then consolidated by Washington (with encouragement from London) through celebrated words and deeds, Churchill's 'Iron Curtain' speech at Fulton, Missouri in 1946, the Truman Doctrine of 1947 and the creation of NATO in 1949. The new security system was anchored in formal collective alliances in Europe, and bilateral ones in Asia. The new political economy was anchored in global institutions like the World

Trade Organization (WTO), the World Bank, and the International Monetary Fund (IMF).

In accounts of the post-war liberal order, many or all of the following features appear, though with varying emphasis: the rule of law and the supremacy of 'rules', humanist globalism and humanitarian development, free trade, multilateral cooperation, and the security provision of the USA, principally through its permanent alliances, and a commitment to liberal progress through the advocacy of democratic and market reform. Its institutions span the United Nations, NATO, the North American Free Trade Agreement (NAFTA), the Trans-Pacific Partnership (TPP), the General Agreement on Tariffs and Trade (GATT), then the WTO, the IMF and the World Bank. Overwhelmingly, the emphasis falls on the edifying, consensual side of world-ordering, on its continuity and coherence, rather than on its interruptions, contradictions and killings.

The order's admirers claim, on its behalf, a large share of credit for the good things that followed. These include the absence of major war, economic growth, the reduction in trade barriers and successive waves of democratic and free market reform. Liberal order stood for transcendent values. It is the 'single most consistent theme' in American statecraft over seventy years, standing for 'political liberalism in the form of representative government and human rights; and other liberal concepts, such as nonaggression, self-determination, and the peaceful settlement of disputes'.[6] In their visionary world-making, the order's founders were heirs to the enlightenment tradition, seeking out and advancing a common interest among nations, realizing its promise for the first time through effective mechanisms of governance – and power projection – abroad. The order, proponents argue, embodied also a pattern of behaviour, a 'system of norms, institutions, and partnerships' whereby, under the hegemon's stewardship, collective cooperation trumped competition for relative advantage, significant shares of sovereignty were ceded for the benefits of collective action, as global consensus spread.[7] The order has also been described as a system of 'embedded liberalism',[8] with open markets, institutions, cooperative security, democratic community, progressive change, collective problem solving, shared sovereignty and the rule of law. It provided valuable public goods, like the freedom of the seas and the global commons. It created an 'open, rule-based international economy'. These were 'world historical advances'.[9] Such an amalgam of power and social purpose reduces insecurity, inhibits self-aggrandisement and discourages bids for hegemony. The ultimate logic is one of pacification through benign expansion. A world 'with more liberal democratic capitalist states will be more peaceful, prosperous, and respectful of human rights'.[10]

To say 'liberal' is not to mean 'soft-headed'. According to proponents, the founders were not utopians but hard-headed idealists, pursuing enlightened self-interest. The liberal order as it is offered is not the same as the pre-war abstract and pacifistic idealism that was assailed by realists such as E. H. Carr. In fact, its theoretical foundation is part liberal, part realist. Today's defenders argue that the pragmatic application of power is a necessary foundation of effective institutions, which in turn redefine relations between states.[11] The order was premised on the ambition that countries could cooperate as rational states operating under conditions of anarchy, and, through collective effort, turn 'anarchy' into 'society'. Because American hegemony offered leadership without overbearing dominance, it created 'a consensual order undergirded by some mixture of rationalist calculations of material self-interest and convergent values, affinities, and identities'.[12] Liberalism does not preclude coercion or violence. But minimally, a liberal order constrains and alleviates violence, so that those who wield force do so reluctantly, infrequently and with great self-restraint, striving to make their violence as consistent with liberal principles as possible.

As well as America's unprecedented level of material power and reach, what were the alleged sources of the order's stability? One answer is that the institutional framework itself took effect. Another version of the liberal narrative, reflecting the 'bottom-up' emphasis of the new liberalism, is that the superpower's domestic political and constitutional character was the decisive element.[13] It was liberal because its chief maker, America, was liberal. If a stable hegemonic order requires authority, which legitimises hierarchy, liberal powers are better at acquiring authority because of their own domestic constitutional limits on abuses of power, which make them more trustworthy international rulers. Here in the American Century was an order flowing from its own liberal political essence, of hegemony as distinct from empire, leadership as distinct from imperial domination.[14] Or in the words of one admirer, the modern 'rules-based order' is an 'an attempt by a community of like-minded democratic states to "domesticate" the international system in such a way that it becomes more like an international society, based on a clear set of rules, to try and prevent revisionist behaviour'.[15] This apparently succeeded until recently. The USA gave other states an equity stake in the order, reshaping interests to create a progressive equilibrium. Optimists believed – or hoped – these qualities would make the order robust against the rise of new rival powers.[16]

So this was, allegedly, a new kind of dispensation. It worked through a synthesis of benevolent internationalism and a preponderance of power, one that was post-imperial yet ordered, anchored in institutions yet relying also on a superpower's coercive strength. Thanks to the institutional depth and reach of American power, major war was taken off the table in traditionally belligerent power centres of the globe, specifically, continental Europe and Northeast Asia. Favourable settlements – concerning trade, diplomacy, alliances and patterned 'summitry' – locked in enduring patterns of consensual behaviour. Diplomatic access and 'voice opportunities' were extended to weaker states. For all the different shades of opinion, all unite in some general propositions. The USA, they argue, as global leader used its power and its sapience to create a new dispensation after the Second World War. It created institutions, permanent alliances, open markets and a general condition of consensual and cooperative behaviour, regularity and rules and rule-following. In turn, this system bore fruit. It transformed international life in ways that were fundamentally good, relative to an earlier more violent history of cut-throat power politics. They credit it with every significant benefit of the post-war years: the absence of major conflicts, the slow and limited proliferation of nuclear weapons, economic growth, freer trade, more recently increased life expectancy, and the retreat of poverty in the Global South. They argue that to remain civilized, the world permanently needs what arose in the late 1940s, a level of American power, unrivalled and unmatched, but carrying the mission of world leader, even if they disagree on whether this is still possible.

This all raises the question: what would an illiberal order look like? Liberalism itself is a contradictory and multisided tradition that only draws coherence from what it is said to be against. The liberalism recalled today was developed between the 1930s and the 1950s as the 'constitutive ideology of the West', especially through struggles with Axis then Soviet totalitarian menaces, against which it was framed as their ideological antithesis.[17] It came to be associated with democracy and freedom from tyranny. Undergirded by American power and direction, the new order worked towards a democratically inspired and commercially linked world, one of openness, cooperation and regularity. It marked a great, deliberate turning away from the older world of colonial empires, trade blocs and spheres of influence, which had in turn given rise to totalitarianism and genocide.

An illiberal order would presumably be the opposite of these things: politically and economically divided and closed, authoritarian, uncooperative, coercive beyond liberal boundaries, and disrespectful of rules and norms. It would be a system of oppressive overlordship. A clue to its shape, it is said, lies in today's hostile authoritarian powers, which are bent on revising world order, driven primarily by a malign ideology. They are led by Russia principally, by China and Iran, and include designated 'rogue' states like North Korea. Illiberalism advances, too, within the world's democracies in the form of domestic insurgents. Together, they make up a counter-enlightenment that is on the march. But what do they all have in common, apart from hostility to American leadership? A unifying theme, it is said, is the contrast with the nineteenth century as the historical antithesis of the liberal order, the world it claims to have repudiated and dismantled. Here there is an ill-defined enemy, loosely termed 'geopolitics'.[18] Proponents claim that the new liberal order supplanted not just power politics, but an older form of power politics. Statements of US officials give some clues about the outlines of the pre-liberal order that Washington believes it replaced. According to presidential candidate Bill Clinton in 1992, 'the cynical calculus of pure power politics . . . is ill-suited to a new era'. Or, in the words of President George H.W. Bush as he announced military action in the Persian Gulf War, the USA sought 'a world where the rule of law, not the law of the jungle, governs the conduct of nations'. The features of that old world were territorial spheres of influence, imperialism or economic protectionist blocs. Spheres of influence, or the division of the world into zones dominated with a free hand by great powers, is a particular focus as an antithesis of liberal order. While encouraging Georgia's eventual accession to NATO, pledging support to its territorial integrity and rebuking Moscow's claim to a 'zone of privileged interests' in former Soviet lands, Secretary of State Hillary Clinton averred: 'The United States does not recognize spheres of influence' and President Obama insisted that 'The days of empire and spheres of influence are over'. Secretary of State John Kerry criticized Russia's seizure of Crimea in similar terms: 'You just don't in the 21st century behave in 19th-century fashion.' In some way, there was a fundamental systemic change, in shared assumptions of what behaviour is legitimate and conceivable, reflected for instance in a supposed post-war norm against territorial annexation.[19]

Gideon Rose offers a similarly neat encomium about the 'team sport' that was 'the liberal international order that the United States has nurtured over the last seven decades':

[America's mandate was] to consolidate, protect, and extend the liberal international order that the United States helped create after World War II. Reflecting on the nightmares of the interwar period, when unregulated markets and uncoordinated behaviour led to economic disaster and the rise of aggressive dictatorships, Western policymakers in the 1940s set out to construct a global system that would prevent such problems from recurring. They ended up doing a masterful job, weaving together several components of domestic and international affairs into a unified, expansive, and flexible structure that has proved more durable and beneficial than they could ever have imagined.[20]

Because it is rhetoric of praise, the literature tends towards ambitious generalization and, at the same time, shields its subject from blame.

Disasters that accompanied the same system of hegemony, like the War on Terror, free market 'shock therapy' in Russia or the global financial crisis, are explained away reassuringly as departures from the same masterful system that was designed to prevent dangerous adventurism or unstable finance.

To preserve and enforce the order, the panegyrics advocate the continuation of US armed supremacy. If the order was a security system created and underpinned foremost by American might, then it requires sustained US military preponderance, striking power and a 'global footprint',[21] reflecting a consensus among primacists that the USA self-evidently needs far-flung military power beyond challenge. In a representative collection of essays, including by Samantha Power, Francis Fukuyama, Robert Kagan, Niall Ferguson, John Ikenberry and Charles Maier, the authors agree that 'the United States should be a leader in the international system', and that 'none of the contributors propose to reduce the military spending significantly or allow US superiority to erode'.[22] Even a system organized around cooperation, it seems, ultimately rests on one state's overwhelming capacity to kill people and break things. This is an observation we will return to. For if, like all other hegemonies, this one relied for its authority on the implicit potential for it to be imposed by force, and if this was in fact exercised often, then its uniqueness is in doubt.

If the liberal order hypothesis were to hold up as an account of US statecraft, how would we recognize it? What are the tests or 'observables'? We would expect to see, first, regularity. Washington would bind itself by its obligations under international law and according to the will of international institutions. It would not only do so for most of the time; crucially, it would do so even when it was reluctant, when its interests pointed in a different direction. We would expect to see Washington dismantle barriers to free trade. It would do so even to the point where it did not suit America's desire to remain economically preponderant. Washington would consistently strive for a level playing field for foreign industries and commerce. We would also expect Washington to use force, but reluctantly, discriminately, under careful scrutiny, in deference to liberal humanitarian norms and the laws of armed conflict. We would expect that Washington would regard its allies as an ideal-typical hegemon would do, picking up the bill while refraining from coercion, and as 'autonomous, coordinate units enjoying juridical equality (status, sovereignty, rights, and international obligations) regardless of differences in power'.[23] In sum, if liberal order is to mean something historically, it cannot be just a matter of convenience but one of inconvenience. The superpower would mostly submit itself to the demands of liberalism in circumstances where it would prefer to do otherwise, and behave differently than it otherwise might. If this all sounds ambitious, it is. For the most part, it is a test that liberals have set themselves.

Other Than That, Mrs Lincoln: Silences, Omissions and Ruptures

For its enthusiasts, liberal order is designed primarily to serve a political need in the present, just as this critique is. To engage with it is to contend with a series of potted histories about American power in the world. These histories skate over some obvious historical problems.

Those in favour of liberal order tend towards the reverential and the absolute, regarding an order as sacred and aberrant behaviour as profane. In doing so, they write out large swathes of history. Until recent irruptions, we are told, America stood for 'open borders and open societies',[24] built by Americans who 'are less interested in ruling the world than they are in creating a world of rules',[25] even though the latter presupposes the former. Ivo Daalder, former academic, President of the Chicago Council on Global Affairs, and former Permanent Representative on the council of NATO, made a typically absolute claim, uncluttered by historical detail: 'For 70 years, the United States has led the global effort to promote democracy, human rights and the rule of law.'[26] That there was variation, to say the least, in the extent of Washington's humanist commitment goes unmentioned. It would be instructive to try this argument out before a Latin American audience.

This is history served up to bolster a sense of mission. As Secretary of State Hillary Clinton recalled in 2014:

> After the Second World War, the nation that had built the trans-continental railroad, the assembly line and the skyscraper turned its attention to constructing the pillars of global cooperation. The third World War that so many feared never came. And many millions of people were lifted out of poverty and exercised their human rights for the first time. Those were the benefits of a global architecture forged over many years by American leaders from both political parties.[27]

In this milk toast version of the past, the darkness of history recedes. Only two wars are mentioned: the victorious world war of mid-century, mentioned as a book-end rather than a process, and another world war that wasn't. Other wars, also central to ordering, are pushed to the margins. Maximum emphasis lies on cooperative leadership and peaceable acts of creation. Minimal emphasis goes to coercion, to the point of near silence. On two frontiers, continental and then global, the rough power politics of history, from genocide of native Americans to the brutal struggles of the Cold War, are erased. Other possibilities go missing in action: that major war was averted by the terror of nuclear threat and still came close to erupting, that international institutions, the expansion of capital or aid programmes entrenched as well as alleviated poverty, or that deadly competition continued to define international politics. The rise of the USA is neatly simplified into a benign engineering project.

It is not just politicians who offer these cleansing summaries of history. It is also a standard credo of accomplished and decorated public intellectual figures. Reacting to the election of Trump, the diplomatic historian Jeremy Suri offered a similarly upbeat prehistory, charging that Trump is plunging the world into a great regression, by 'launching a direct attack on the liberal international order that really made America great'. The elements of this order include 'a system of multilateral trade and alliances that we built to serve our interests and attract others to our way of life'. 'The North Atlantic Treaty Organization (NATO) in Europe and a web of alliances in Asia and the Middle East', he explains, 'contained aggressive states, nurtured stable allies, and promoted democratic reforms when possible.' 'Other institutions', such as 'the European Recovery Program (the Marshall Plan), the General Agreement on Tariffs and Trade (now the World Trade Organization), the International Monetary Fund (IMF), and the World Bank', enabled the USA to lead 'a post-war capitalist system that raised global standards of living, defeated Soviet communism, and converted China to a market economy'.[28]

Like Clinton's tribute, Suri offers a strangely bloodless retelling of history. It is a euphemistic rendering of the Cold War and the actual practice of anti-Soviet containment by the superpower and its proxies. Napalm, Bay of Pigs and the Contras fade to the background. Repression all but disappears. Missing too are the anti-communist purges of Indonesia's General Suharto in 1965, a massacre of perhaps one million people, with the active help of CIA and US embassy staff. Regarding Latin America, support for death squads and revelations about Operation Condor go unmentioned, the US training programme for security forces in torture and blackmail techniques for twenty-five years. Washington, it would be fair to say, often chose to prioritize other interests above democratic reforms. The enormities of the War on Terror also disappear, such as rendition and torture. Unstable allies go missing in action, from Saddam Hussein to General Yahya Kahn to the Afghan Mujahideen to Prime Minister Benjamin Netanyahu to Mohammed Bin Salman al Saud. The corruption and protectionism of China's conversion to a market economy – its intellectual property theft, massive subsidies for state-owned enterprises, and barriers to market entry – here disappears. That this retelling should come from a distinguished historian of American diplomacy suggests how seductive the vision of an earlier and better order has become.

There is a problem of time and historical memory in liberal order discussion. A stock-standard periodization of the order's life is 'seventy years' or 'seven decades'. It harmonizes with NATO's recent anniversary and hints at a biblical completeness. This suggestion of an unbroken unity in the *Pax Americana* from 1949 until the recent past is appealing. It gives added sanctity and a sense of stability to the order. By heightening a sense of stability and continuity, it portrays the Trumpian interruption as a great and wrenching intrusion of time into paradise, like Anglo-Catholic memories of a tranquil Christian England thrown into chaos by the stripping of the altars. Today, the foreign policy establishment reveres global partnerships and institutions as almost sacred. NATO was 'the core of an American-led liberal world order'.[29] At times, the literature borders on a state of rapture. Former Secretary of Defense Ash Carter likened a joint news conference of presidents Trump and Putin to 'watching the destruction of a cathedral'.[30] With Trump in the White House, liberal order enthusiasts hope the torch will pass to other allies, as figureheads of enlightened internationalism. At the 2019 Munich Security Conference, Daalder hailed German Chancellor Angela Merkel as 'The Leader of the Free World', whose speech on the need for solidarity in upholding the rules-based order deserved 'thunderous applause'.[31] Only now, 'for the first time in its history', claims former diplomat and professor Nicholas Burns, is NATO threatened by 'the absence of strong, principled American presidential leadership'.[32] What Burns makes of the forceful critiques and browbeating of NATO allies made by most presidents from Eisenhower to Obama is not clear.[33] If the main difference now is that Trump berates allies in public while still materially reinforcing NATO, then the order's bedrock is fragile indeed.

Despite depictions of NATO as a moral community built around shared liberal values,[34] and hyperbolic claims that US coercion of NATO allies is unprecedented, the reality is that hierarchical imposition and demand have been part of transatlantic relations ever since the alliance's founding. In 1954, Secretary of State John Foster Dulles threatened Europe with an 'agonizing reappraisal' of alliances. In 1963, with threats of abandonment, President John F. Kennedy coerced West German Chancellor Konrad Adenauer into supporting US monetary policy and offsetting the balance of payments deficit created by America's deployments in Europe.[35] In 1973–4, President Richard Nixon and his National Security Advisor Henry Kissinger suspended intelligence and nuclear cooperation with Britain to punish non-cooperation over a US-initiated Declaration of Principles and the privacy of bilateral and UK–EEC discussions. The 'special' Anglo-American relationship has featured multiple episodes of arm-twisting. In 1982, when President Ronald Reagan slapped sanctions on foreign companies, including British ones, that constructed a Soviet pipeline through Poland, Prime

Minister Margaret Thatcher was 'deeply wounded by a friend'.[36] Despite Britain spending blood and treasure in Afghanistan and Iraq to support the War on Terror and cement its standing in Washington, President Obama bluntly threatened that departing from the EU would place the UK at the 'back of the queue' when seeking a bilateral free trade agreement. And the USA used the threat of abandonment to persuade allies and clients to cancel their nuclear programmes, including West Germany, Japan and Taiwan.[37]

That transatlantic solidarity leads easily into hierarchical demand is demonstrated by the fact that even some of today's leading admirers of NATO have also explicitly issued transactional demands against its members, cautioning that failure to contribute sufficiently will (and should) result in its extinction. The avowed Atlanticist Anne Applebaum laments the unravelling of the transatlantic alliance and Trump's demand that its members dramatically increase their contributions under pain of possible American withdrawal. For her, 'security and defence organizations' are 'special and inviolable', without which the USA 'ceases to be a force in Eurasia. The US military will have trouble projecting military power into the Middle East or Africa', leaving China to predominate and set the terms of trade. Security organizations were 'the basis for American military power, as well as for American wealth and prosperity'.[38] Yet only four years previously, Applebaum argued that President Obama 'does have the power to relaunch the Western alliance. He has all of the cards – the USA contributes three-quarters of NATO's budget – as well as the ultimate argument: if the Western alliance, as currently constituted, no longer wants to defend itself, America can always leave.' Significantly, this was at a time when Russia had already seized Crimea and was at war in Ukraine, so it was probably not a growing eastern threat that drove Applebaum to alter her stance. Rather, the confusion of this critique reflects a tension in American transatlantic order-building, to regard the alliance as sacred – or 'eternal', in Obama's words – while coercing its members with conditional demands. It could be objected that Obama and Applebaum, unlike Trump, would only make such explicit threats in order to preserve NATO. Yet for such threats to succeed, they would need to be credible, beyond bluffing. Having urged the White House to change European behaviour by explicitly using the threat of abandonment, Applebaum recoiled when it actually did so.[39]

Consider also two leading advocates of liberal order, Ivo Daalder and Robert Kagan, who in the age of Trump champion the cause of NATO's endurance and Germany's special place within the Euro-Atlantic community. Fearing its unravelling, Kagan spoke of the 'democratic alliance that has been the bedrock of the American-led liberal world order',[40] while Daalder argued that 'Allies need reassurance. They want to hear, as President Obama said in Estonia following the Russian invasion of Ukraine, that Article 5 "is a commitment that is unbreakable. It is unwavering. It is eternal".'[41] It was not ever thus. In 2004, when Berlin refused to send troops to Iraq to support a war it had consistently opposed, Kagan and Daalder sounded if not a Trumpian note, certainly a coercive one, in their joint denunciation of allies' recalcitrance.[42] They referred to NATO members in shudder quotes as 'allies'. They asserted that if European allies didn't pull their weight – and the Iraq campaign was not even a NATO operation – Americans should doubt NATO's value: 'There is the question of whether there is any meaning left in the term "alliance" . . . If France and Germany are intent on saying no, then future American administrations, including Kerry's, will have to reconsider the value of the alliance.' With the superpower confronted by growing civil strife and resistance in Mesopotamia, the two Atlanticists did not characterize the alliance as they do today, as the bedrock of the American-led liberal world order

45

that deserved eternal American commitment. They wrote at the height of the War on Terror, when the initial confidence of the Bush II administration was giving way to anxiety that the ambitious bid to reorder the Greater Middle East would be more costly and difficult than realized, and that internationalizing the burden would be needed. Growing pressure on American power revealed even among enthusiasts for liberal order the closeness of ordering with hierarchical coercion. Trump's subsequent public denunciations of the alliance on similar terms, and his insistence that US commitment was conditional, was a dramatic shift in style but not in substance.

NATO's history itself involved bargains with authoritarianism, even as its presence in Europe was a vital pillar of anti-Soviet containment. For decades, it included authoritarian regimes like Portugal and Greece. And while the membership of Spain under the repressive regime of General Francisco Franco was vetoed against Washington's preference, it was still informally linked to the actual transatlantic defence structure through the Pact of Madrid and a basing agreement. Turkey's increasingly authoritarian regime is a standing embarrassment to the suggestion of a liberal, democratic club. Expansion in Eastern Europe has demonstrably not liberalized Poland or Hungary. NATO's own military campaigns have not always enhanced liberal values. In Libya, the revolution facilitated by NATO's airstrikes led to the collapse of the economy, rival parliaments, the proliferation of torture and open-air slave markets. In the Balkans, intervention against genocide inadvertently led to counter-atrocities. As reported by the Independent International Commission on Kosovo, established in 2000 in the aftermath of the Kosovo war, NATO's international presence failed to prevent reprisal ethnic cleansing by the Kosovar Liberation Army.[43] The various forces that brought NATO together – anti-Soviet communism, liberal values, the European desire for cheap security and the US desire for transatlantic primacy – were not always in harmony. So the beguiling claim of seventy continuous years of order organised around liberal principles, and enshrined in institutions like NATO, does not hold up. The world before the invention of the term 'liberal order' was a foreign land, where they sometimes did things differently.

A glance at the genealogy of liberal order raises a further difficulty, that this is a largely retrospective construct being imposed upon a historical era, in order to intervene in present struggles. While its proponents trace it as a concept from the post-war era, the *Pax Americana*, and regard that order's value as transcendent and universal, as an article of faith its provenance is relatively recent. As Adam Garfinkle cautions, there is a distorting temptation in *post hoc* naming of a thing that seems threatened, to 'exaggerate the virtues of what is being named, and to round off any pesky dissonant edges from it'.[44]

Using 'Google Ngram', Joshua Shifrinson[45] created a graph llustrating the usage of the phrase 'liberal international order' from 1800 to 2008. As Shifrinson observes, the increasing use of the term coincides closely with the late years of the Cold War. It then takes off dramatically. Similar patterns emerge from searches based on other variants of the phrase. For example, usage of the phrase 'liberal order' rises, while the spike in usage of 'rules-based international order' is even more sudden and recent (see Figure 1).

So 'liberal order' as a phrase, and as complaint against departures from it, can be backdated to two historical intellectual moments. The first significant increase took place in almost exact correspondence to the rise in anxiety over US decline and the coming of multipolarity. In fact, two of the leading purveyors of 'liberal order' as a concept, Robert Keohane and Joseph Nye II, also led the debate over whether a liberal

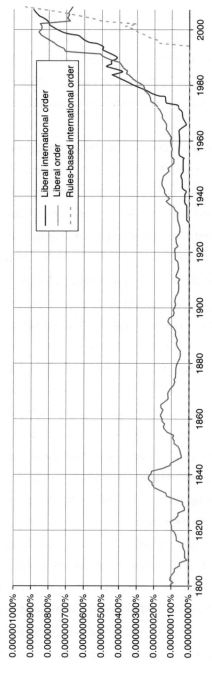

Figure 1 Usage of the phrases 'liberal international order', 'liberal order' and 'rules-based international order', 1800–2008

Source: Chart produced by Joshua Shifrinson on Google Ngram Viewer, reproduced here with permission.

international system would endure even after American hegemony waned.

The more recent episode involved critiques of the Bush II administration and the War on Terror, and a desire to reclaim the word 'liberal' as an honourable and American tradition, rather than the dirty word it had become in conservative politics. The critique, spearheaded by Ikenberry, was provoked by the Bush presidency's swaggering unilateralism, contempt towards allies, abrogation of international agreements and recourse to extraordinary rendition and torture. Those critics relied upon a sharp distinction between liberal and imperial orders. It was then the War on Terror, not Trump, that was the great interruption. This in itself contradicts the later claim that there were seventy years of order, whole and integrated, until the unprecedented Trumpian lapse.

One pronounced difference separates 'world order' literature of the Cold War and post-Cold War eras. Rhetoric about American security strategy in both eras shared a common commitment to a 'free world' and the exceptionalist assumption of a USA with a unique mandate. Yet statements about an American-led world order during the long security competition with the Soviet Union were both distinctly religious and enemy-centric. It made explicit references to God, to divine will and to a historical mandate handed down from heaven, and to a dangerously evil opponent. It deployed a wider language of faith, long before the Cold Warrior President Ronald Reagan courted the evangelical Right. Dean Acheson, one of the principal architects of post-war diplomacy, was the son of an Episcopal bishop with a keen missionary sense of America's responsibility, just as two of his successors as Secretary of State, John Foster Dulles and Dean Rusk, were sons of Protestant ministers. The intellectual architect of anti-Soviet containment, George Kennan, spoke of the need for a 'spiritual vitality'.

The signature Cold War strategy document NSC 68 exhorted the USA to mobilize a 'spiritual counterforce' against the fanatical creed of communism. The influential Secretary of State John Foster Dulles in explicit religious terms advocated a unifying American mission of belligerent anti-communism. Cold War authoritarians such as Senator Joseph McCarthy and FBI Director J. Edgar Hoover justified their actions around the cause of patriotic Christianity against atheistic communism. Cold War liberal hawks, too, drew on the language. Running for president, Senator John F. Kennedy spoke of 'a competition of ideologies, freedom under God versus ruthless, Godless tyranny'.[46] Even Henry Luce's clarion call for an American Century, a rationale for world-ordering that comes much closer to today's paeans, promoted religious revival as central to victory in the Cold War.[47] The rhetoric of spiritual battle, and the contest for Christian civilization against atheistic barbarism brought its own demagogic excesses. It also had sinew. As rhetoric and as an agenda for action, it brought effective mobilizing power. The referent object being offered today, the abstraction of liberal order, may not prove as stimulating. As Stephen Wertheim cautions, 'confronted with a choice between "America First" and "the post-war international order", voters will opt for what they understand and identify with, what evokes a better future. Does anyone really think "the order" will win?'[48]

By contrast with the era of blood, fire and judgement, the panegyrics of our time are highly secular. International politics rages under an empty sky. This is not to speculate about the personal theologies of the 'liberal order' faithful. Rather, it is to note a remarkable retreat of overtly pious language from their public offerings about America's global mission. It may be that this shift is largely due to the changing sociology and manners of the US security establishment, towards greater heterogeneity, for whom religious justifications of American statecraft are irrelevant or best kept private. Ostentatiously devout worshippers are no longer as numerous amongst the establishment as they once were. The socially narrower and more pious world of George Kennan, the religiously observant author of the doctrine of anti-Soviet containment, would be rarer now. Indeed, at times they define liberal order itself as the antithesis of obscurantist religion and blood myths. Some versions of the literature move so far in this direction that they present world order in mechanical and bloodless terms, that play down or even deny active power struggle. Assistant Secretary of State for East Asian and Security Affairs Kurt Campbell, for instance, framed American primacy in Asia as an 'operating system'.[49] The language of god and struggle is replaced by a computer metaphor, with the USA retaining authority as the supreme technician. Such an image appeals because it naturalizes American power, imagining the world re-organized around elevated principles, stressing the commonality of values, the harmony of interests and the obvious goodness of the design. Who could object to a well-functioning operating system? Yet who would fight for it?

As well as replacing an intense cause of spiritual struggle with a less compelling one, foreign policy minds lack another source of coherence and mobilization: a defining super-enemy. While China is richer and materially stronger, not even it poses the kind of universal ideological challenge of Soviet Marxism-Leninism. The Manichean worldview historically led to egregious errors, for instance in long denying the possibility of a Sino-Soviet split in the communist world. It also held out the advantage, though, of recognizing the reality of violent struggle and justifying awkward coalitions. It offered the equation of necessary illiberal means in pursuit of liberal ends. The USA could take part in compromising geopolitics, with the assurance of an ultimate moral end. With its specified adversary and eye for what anti-communists had in common, it offered a certain geopolitical coherence. With the defining enemy and single global struggle gone, it is more difficult for liberal order proponents to rationalize the linkage of means and ends. Cold Warriors could appeal to compatriots to focus on what they were against, and could rationalize illiberal behaviour as a necessary lesser evil, which could eventually reform authoritarian client states.[50] Religious anti-communism supplied the rationale for intervention in the Italian democratic election of 1948, the kind of detail that escapes more recent encomiums to the order. The CIA helped the electoral defeat of communists by funding anti-communist parties, forging documents to discredit the communist party, and warning Italians who publicly supported that party that they would be barred from entering the USA. For the sake of liberalism in the long term, the USA exercised its privileges. If the deliberate subversion of a democratic election abroad by means of fake news, bribes and coercion represents the antithesis of liberal world order, as Trump's critics now suggest, then Washington attacked that order in the period of its creation. If Washington in practice accepted that noble ends warranted illiberal means, that rationale assisted the creation of coalitions with illiberal forces, like the papacy.

Similar means-ends rationales also enabled more ironic alliances. One embarrassing counterpoint for the mytho-history of liberal order is America's long post-war tradition of collaboration with Islamist militants who are driven by medieval nostalgia, from President Dwight Eisenhower's welcoming of the Muslim Brotherhood organizer Said Ramadan into the Oval Office, to Brzezinski's 'arc of Islam' to contain the Soviets from northeast Africa to Central Asia, to US-sponsored jihads against Russian clients from Afghanistan to Bosnia, and its inadvertent support of Islamist militias in Syria.[51] At least on earlier occasions the USA knew in advance who it was supporting. This is not a commentary on the wisdom or folly of such measures. It is to suggest that a ruthless and more focused mindset, which at least confronted the problem of bargaining with necessary evils, has yielded now to a muddled one.

The purveyors of liberal order panegyrics realize, in their asides, that there are historical and conceptual difficulties with the global design that they advance. Many have served in government. They know that even the simplest things are difficult. There are, they admit, other mechanisms of order that lurk at the edges of the US-led one. There were, they admit, hubristic blunders, like wars of liberation or market fundamentalism that were somehow causally unrelated to the order, even if policymakers regarded them as central to world-ordering and a liberalizing mission at the time.[52] The world had its imperfections and errors – the limits of the UN's capacity and the hegemon's writ – and there were 'mistakes' like Bay of Pigs and Vietnam.

As soon as such difficulties surface, however, they are promptly separated from and in quarantine in the order's essence. The most self-aware panegyrics do not deny the negative parts of history. Rather, they separate them, like defence counsel excluding things from the pleadings. Darker behaviours were aberrations from liberal order, not features or pathologies of it. When things went wrong, a world-historical transformation, suddenly, was bounded and constrained, and errors under the order could not be linked to it or its epochal ambitions. Things that happened outside the West are marginal, suddenly, because it is a story really about what happened inside the West, despite proponents' other claims about global leadership and despite emphasis on a global military footprint, or on invigilating the Middle East, or on the vital importance of humanitarian effort or military strikes outside the West. With throats cleared, the core story proceeds undisturbed. Large parts of post-war history that don't fit the narrative are quickly dispatched – yet return to haunt the retelling. John Ikenberry claims that in order to keep Europe, Asia and the Middle East open to trade and diplomacy, empire was repudiated, and 'with some important and damaging exceptions, such as Vietnam, the United States has embraced post-imperial principles'.[53] There is an 'apart from that, Mrs Lincoln, how was the show?' quality to this argument. Vietnam was one of the USA's most intense and sustained post-war undertakings abroad, waged to preserve a system across seas and continents. As we will see, it is better understood not as an atypical lapse from the order into atypical, imperial excess, but as a sincere attempt at world-ordering to uphold that very world, a project driven by both liberal and imperial impulses, and one that reflected the tensions between them.

Occasionally in the literature, the narrative is ruptured, only for the order as a noble cause to reassert itself. In an attempt to apply sober measurement to the world order debate, Joseph Nye argues:

The mythology that has grown up around the order can be exaggerated. Washington may have displayed a general preference for democracy and openness, but it frequently supported dictators or made cynical self-interested moves along the way. In its first decades, the post-war system was largely limited to a group of like-minded states centred on the Atlantic littoral; it did not include many large countries such as China, India, and the Soviet bloc states, and it did not always have benign effects on non-members. In global military terms, the United States was not hegemonic, because the Soviet Union balanced US power. And even when its power was greatest, Washington could not prevent the 'loss' of China, the partition of Germany and Berlin, a draw in Korea, Soviet suppression of insurrections within its own bloc, the creation and survival of a communist regime in Cuba, and failure in Vietnam. Still, the demonstrable success of the order in helping secure and stabilize the world over the past seven decades has led to a strong consensus that defending, deepening, and extending this system has been and continues to be the central task of US foreign policy.[54]

To his credit, Nye acknowledges the danger of ahistorical romance. At the same time, the order's supporting mythologies prove resilient. Illiberal behaviour and what appear as 'cynical, self-interested moves' (even in what he calls a 'rules-based system') are lapses that are separate from ordering rather than inherent to it, and so hardly bear on the overall appraisal. The statement concludes with a ringing confidence that his caveats and qualifiers do not warrant. American hegemony is only a recent development, not a seventy-year 'system' of power, as Nye observes, and world order since 1945 was defined partly by the checking of America's bid for dominance. Its sphere was limited to the democratic, capitalist rimlands; it could not even prevail over smaller determined adversaries and its writ was circumscribed by large outside actors. Yet this leads to a non sequitur, that the record of curtailed hegemony and active resistance from rival powers is evidence for the need to extend hegemony further, in a world where multipolar competition is again returning. And, tucked into euphemistic phrases that almost slip past the eye ('did not always have benign effects on non-members', 'a draw in Korea') is a world of war and counterrevolutionary suppression.

Robert Kagan offers an important, and distinctively different, variation of the argument that serves as a point of entry into these problems. He makes an admission rare in the literature:

When it came to the application of force, in particular, there was a double standard. Whether they admitted it or not, even to themselves, American officials believed the rules-based order occasionally required the exercise of American power in violation of the rules, whether this meant conducting military interventions without UN authorization, as in Vietnam and Kosovo, or engaging in covert activities that had no international sanction.[55]

Exactly so. But with this acknowledgement, Kagan effectively concedes that by reserving the right to exercise illiberal means as a privilege, the hegemon was sometimes imperial. This points to an underexplored difference within the hegemon's camp: while some insist on the order's regularity, in means and ends, others are aware that the world is a conflicted place and defend the exercise of irregular methods for the greater good.

For war itself – as a bloody and illiberal process – fades from most of these visions. While the arguments regard America's hegemonic military power and its alliances and far-flung presence as foundational to the order, they mostly avert their eyes from hegemon's actual historical exercise of violence. Nuclear weapons are recognized as fundamental to the order, but it was their actual use against Imperial Japan in 1945 that demonstrated their destructive, genocidal and revolutionary power, arguably necessary to establishing deterrence in the first place. The absence of major war is credited primarily to American ordering, less so the fact that the USA was constrained in its capacity to order others by its adversaries' own nuclear arsenals. Indeed, the constraining effects of nuclear deterrence depended on the failure of some of America's non-proliferation efforts.

Panegyrics show a similar incuriosity towards how the USA acquired the very platforms for military power projection. Maintenance of the order is typically ascribed to a global military presence. Parts of that apparatus were created through decidedly imperial means. An awkward fact about the structure of planetary military power that enforces rules-based liberal order is that the archipelago of defence facilities was partly created through colonial dispossession.[56] It involved the eviction (or duress) of native islanders in order to use territories, from the Chagos Islands to Guam, along with other annexed territories like Puerto Rico, the US Virgin Islands, the Northern Mariana Islands and American Samoa, whose indigenous peoples remain unenfranchised. The Obama administration went to some lengths to isolate Prime Minister Yukio Hatoyama, the only Japanese premier to challenge the US military hold on Okinawa, isolating him with stony silence on the issue.[57] Likewise, in Diego Garcia Britain expelled the population of 2,000 Chagossians to make way for a US airbase after London forced Mauritius to sell the territory in 1965, as a price of decolonization. The UK has continued to hold on to the territory, despite a non-binding motion from the UN General Assembly and an advisory opinion from the World Court that the dispossession was wrongful.[58] The development of nuclear capability, too, took place through irradiating tests on the Pacific Proving Grounds, such as the Marshall Islands and Bikini Atoll. The order is supposed to have demolished the practice of land grabs. Yet such territorial annexations were also prior steps in the creation of a system of armed supremacy. It is awkward, too, because those enforcing the order insist that rising powers like China forgo the kind of colonial behaviour towards real estate that they themselves used in order to project power.

As the dark parts of war are marginalized in the story, note that there are also very few references to drones, and the recent creation of an armature of extrajudicial assassination. There is little reference either to the conduct of drone strikes, as part of what one military commander called 'almost an industrial scale counterterrorism killing machine' worldwide.[59] Given the intent, violence and scope of this raiding, it can hardly be separated from the order. With the arrival of the standoff technology and the desire to liquidate terrorist threats without the burden of casualties or live captives, drone strikes became a prime method for taming and bringing unruly frontiers back into order. Yet the rapidly expanding extrajudicial assassination programme hardly appears in appraisals of the Obama presidency, the last administration credited with being, in principle, a liberal order builder, or in appraisals of the state of the order under Trump. While gallons of ink have been spilt on the levels of disharmony within alliances at summits, the actual practice of applied violence in the shadows almost disappears from the accounting. Type in 'drone', 'assassination', 'killing' even into lengthier assessments of the liberal order's health – for example, the RAND study, the Aspen Policy paper, the CNAS report – and the return is either silence, or an anxiety that the technology is proliferating to dangerous adversaries. One of the few exceptions to this silence is the advocacy of US journalist and military historian Max Boot. For him, there is no painful trade-off. To defend the lofty values of cosmopolitan enlightenment, he advocates regular pacification by force, modelled along the lines of Britain's North-West Frontier and America's frontier wars.[60] This at least is clear.

It is not just an aversion to bloody details that explains these omissions. It is an aversion to the contradictions within ordering. The notion of an order with complimentary and reinforcing parts is also suspect. In the immediate post-war period the paramount security of sovereign states was a defining principle, at least in word. The principle of non-intervention is at the heart of the United Nations Charter, and the General Assembly has reaffirmed and clarified it on multiple occasions. Yet more recent doctrines have stretched or upended it, advocating in certain circumstances the subvertion of state sovereignty. Coalitions without a mandate from the United Nations have arrogated the authority to pronounce an offending state's sovereignty forfeit, in the name of humanitarian liberation. Again, some advocates of liberal order argue for a revival of the Reagan-era programme of financing electoral bodies, political parties, legislatures, independent media and labour unions, a programme that was directed in particular at hostile regimes.[61] In truth, liberal order could be taken to prize either project, a revolutionary commitment to democratic expansion, or a system of global governance that provides reassurance to sovereign states, in the hope they will convert them in the long run.

In this picture, the causal claims and the relative weight to be given to power and ideas are not always clear. The exact relation between ideas, institutions and material capabilities shifts between and sometimes within the arguments of each panegyric. At times, the literature accords prime causal weight to a 'package of ordering ideas and rules', suggesting that those things bear a decisive force in creating a lasting and attractive order, independent of the distribution of material power and US advantage in other forms of power such as nuclear weapons. At other times, these ideas and rules must be underpinned by the material power of hegemon, ordering others by giving them rational incentives through institutions. As proponents of liberal order assume their conclusions and assert what they ought to prove, the power of institutions and norms is asserted but hardly demonstrated. As one critic asks: 'Why are norms necessary to account for peace when US power preponderance would make it very difficult for any state or plausible coalition of states to match US capabilities in the near future; and when the nuclear revolution allows major powers to enjoy abundant security despite US hegemony?'[62] The boundaries of the order are not clear either. Rather, we are offered different versions of a world of overlapping, shifting zones of liberal order, at times confining itself to the Euro-Atlantic, Australasian and Northeast Asian spheres in a world of contention, at others times claiming to have integrated Russia and China into global governance – indeed, creating a unitary 'global system' – and a worldwide market economy. The Middle East hardly intrudes, except as a fatal region where American credibility and honour are at stake, and America's illiberal authoritarian client regimes in that troubled neighbourhood only occasionally enter the stage. The profoundly draconian Saudi bloc, in America's orbit, is strangely absent in the indictment, as is its array of activities, from imprisoning and torturing feminists, to sponsoring Wahhabist incitement, to practising indiscriminate bombardment in Yemen. We are asked instead to worry about whether the Gulf monarchies find Washington an unreliable patron. Strikingly, the War on Terror – which has persisted for almost two of the seven celebrated decades, which was in itself an attempt to reimpose order, which consumed the lion's share of the time and energy of the national security state – either goes largely unmentioned, or somehow lies outside the order.

All this ambivalence is partly a matter of many people sharing one tent, as the order appeals to theorists of different strains of theoretical orientation. It is also, though, due to a problem with panegyrics. The genre is primarily intended to affirm, celebrate and warn rather than rigorously establish cause-and-effect, or specify the sequences and weighting of causes. It is also, at root, political. Orders seek legitimacy and credit, while deflecting criticism and blame. The intellectual eulogists of those same orders typically are not writing to make the object of reverence falsifiable. When they do, for instance in the RAND diagnosis, troubling realizations flow that the same order could be complicit in its own undoing:

The order is in the most danger in areas where it has been pushed to the far edges of plausibility. In such areas as liberal interventionism, the reach and extent of European Union bureaucracy, and the speed of global trade integration, the data suggest that overly ambitious efforts to advance liberal elements of the order could be destabilizing.[63]

Confronted with demonstrable failures beyond (and sometimes within) its own heartland, the rhetoric of order runs up against the difficulty that liberal missions can be self-defeating, and that ambitions should therefore be tempered. Most versions, therefore, do not dwell on such problems, preferring to focus on evil agents, barbaric forces outside the walls or fifth columnists within.

The realization that the world is becoming less hospitable to schemes of visionary world-making, whether due to a relative power shift away from America's international pre-eminence or a domestic shift away from the orthodox consensus in favour of benign hegemony, has led to an intramural dispute about whether liberal order can outlast the profound changes that are under way. Accounts of the past, present and future of liberal order vary in their judgement about whether the order will survive. Some argue that it is durable and can regenerate through reform, though with increasing unease. Others are more fearful in the age of Trump, and write its obituary with warnings of what is to come. Others stake out a more open ground. Still others suggest that with the superpower abdicating its 'global leadership', it falls to other democratic, capitalist states to shoulder the burden and revive the order. As the paramount champion of the progressive middle powers, Germany emerges as the alternative leader of choice, or at least steward and keeper of the flame of liberalism, as the USA lapses into a dark Trumpian age of illiberal barbarism. Germany appears social democratic enough to adopt the programme, and large enough in relative size to count. Its governments, like the leading officials of the EU, appeal to the ideal of rules-based order. So far, this search for a liberal hegemon substitute has not been unduly detained by the possibility that rule-violating *Realpolitik* also drives the behaviour of Germany and the dominant states within the EU.

Ready for a Master: The Illiberalism of Liberal Order

Paradoxically, liberal order has an illiberal tendency. That is not because its architects secretly intend to do the opposite of what they intend. Rather, it is because liberal expansion is a missionary project that looks to extirpate rival alternatives. Ever since the founding of the USA, the impulses to liberate and to dominate have coexisted. George Washington led the insurgency against the British empire and to the creation of a constitutional republic. He also held slaves and supported the dispossession of indigenous peoples.

As it has been articulated, liberal order demands the perpetuation of American dominance and, effectively, a free hand. In the words of the Princeton Project of 2006, America's goal should be to secure itself by bringing foreign governments up to PAR, or 'Popular, Accountable and Rights-Regarding'. Frustrated that legacy institutions are increasingly inadequate to get the job done, the project advocated a loosening of restraints in order-building: ending the veto on UN Security Council resolutions authorizing 'direct action' in a crisis, and assuming a responsibility to protect on the part of the international community.[64]

When visions of a world transformed by a benevolent leader along liberal lines run up against resistance, the responses to dissent are revealing. When gainsaid, the order's supporting arguments, its intellectual integuments, can turn notably illiberal. The more forceful champions of liberal order treat dissent or revolt with incomprehension. Assuming the obvious rightness of their cause, they regard dissidents not merely as wrong, but as psychologically disordered or morally defective. Rebellion against the order is 'a pathology to be diagnosed, rather than an argument with which to engage'.[65] They insist that 'if you don't accept the value of alliances and free trade you are a primitive'.[66] Those from the 'stagnant pool' of people who want less immigration, we are told, 'should get out'.[67] Those alienated by the evolution of American capitalism have been made ungrateful and decadent by wealth and luxury. They are 'spoiled'.[68] Others dismiss wayward voters as 'a basket of deplorables',[69] 'introverted little Englanders',[70] 'angry old men' who will soon be 'freshly in their graves'.[71] At its worst, the discourse suggests a classist disdain for flyover country. Former Ambassador to Moscow Michael McFaul says the order's nemesis, Russian President Vladimir Putin, champions 'populist, nationalist, conservative ideas' that are 'antithetical' to the liberal order, thereby excommunicating the conservative nationalists who helped create and defend American power.[72] Rather than serious self-scrutiny, some of the order's most outspoken champions explain away a wave of democratic revolts by dismissing millions of people as backward, provincial racists manipulated by diabolical foreign powers. Officials who represent traditional order – like the IMF – congratulate themselves on being 'the adults in the room', an old slur that sets established authority and orthodoxy against infantile dissent.[73] This leads to the question of how 'adults' managed to allow things to get so bad in the first place. These flashes of intolerance, or pity, reflect the ideology's central tendency. It assumes attraction, but when it encounters resistance or critical fire, it tends towards coercive imposition. Liberalism in any form is supposed to value openness, pluralism and a sense of fallibility. Married to the capabilities of a superpower, it readily becomes a dogma that is jealous, messianic and intolerant, leading to its own illiberal opposite.[74]

Other advocates of liberal order offer more benevolent sympathy. They too assume that, as the order's fundamental workings cannot be the root of the problem, people revolt because they are misinformed or irrational. The order is eroding, they fear, not because continued unrivalled dominance is an inherently flawed ambition, but because it has not been properly tried. It needs to be done better. Heterodox elites or disaffected masses have been gripped by bad ideas or bad faith. Or just bad marketing: those who manage the order have poorly sold it. It might need fresh messaging or a 'reboot' or an 'updating' or 'renovation' or even 'new and urgent conversations',[75] and its defenders should find 'new ways to articulate their goals to those who feel left behind'.[76] The word 'feel' is suggestive. Alienation is *not* because they are left behind. It is a subjective error and a product of false consciousness, according to defenders of liberal order; it is not linked to objective social fact. They commend new programmes to win people over, yet only for 'preservation and adaptation, not disruption'.[77] Problems abroad are attributable to exogenous devils who are malign actors, such as Russia or Iran, whose hostility is rooted in forces unrelated to the order.[78] Other primacists find that domestic politics poses the greatest threat to the order, and that for the old order to reproduce itself, it must make a new economic settlement with the American working class, one that does not intrude on the order's fundamentals. Yet such a settlement would demand some revision of the economic order abroad that has prevailed.[79] If some change is needed in order to redress current difficulties, the order's foundations remain sound and must endure.[80] Linked to this mindset is a stark corollary, that there is no alternative model for liberal order in any case, only a regression to inter-war isolationism and/or appeasement.

A principle that worried the creators of the American republic was the damage that a permanent state of war and the creation of overseas empire could do to the republic. That did not preclude violent continental expansion at home or frequent imperialism in its Latin American neighbourhood. Yet, the anxiety that imperialism threatened the republic and that exporting liberty abroad threatened it at home still constituted an important part of the American argument about the extent and nature of commitments, especially beyond its declared Monroe territories.[81] A major defect in much of the liberal order literature is that it hardly addresses this historical problem. Rather, proponents of liberal order suggest that the USA can (and often did) domesticate the world according to its own values and virtues. That the planet pushed back, so that the project of world-making actually did more to reorder America than the other way round, hardly upsets the picture. Indeed, recourse to the language and tropes of 'liberal order' works as a way of deflecting troubling questions about the relationship between liberalism and imperialism. This deflection ultimately fails, however, as the domestic consequences of a near-permanent state of war are getting harder to overlook.

For in lamentations about Trump and the end of the liberal era, there is a troubling tendency. Namely, the appeal for a hegemon ordering the planet suggests a most unrepublican desire for a global monarch. And, in turn, this accompanies an uneasy attraction/repulsion to empire and its trappings. Richard Haass, among others, warns of a disastrous American 'abdication' of its international responsibilities. 'Abdicate' is how monarchs step down. It is no accident that Haass has also called for the USA to become an empire, serving a similar function to that of the British empire.[82] Bill Kristol too, who today speaks of a 'liberal international order', once argued that 'we need to err on the side of being strong. And if people want to say we're an imperial power, fine.'[83] The distinction between liberal hegemony, rule by consent, and empire, rule by command, collapses.

Along similar lines, French Atlanticist and war hawk Bernard-Henri Lévy laments America's supposed 'abdication', calls on Washington to recover its 'liberal vocation' and 'moxie', and deploys overtly regal language in an artful title, *The Empire and the Five Kings: America's Abdication and the Fate of the World* (2019). A monarchic and imperial aesthetic can also be seen. The grandeur of the *ancien régime* attracts Bruce Jackson, founder and president of the US Committee on NATO from 1995 to 2000, who championed NATO expansion and complains of American 'abdication' of world leadership, urging Germany to take up the role of 'enforcing appropriate behaviour in diplomacy'. Jackson expressed hope that his eighteenth-century Bordeaux estate would one day be the site of an international treaty.[84] He claimed that 'someday we'll write a treaty here on something . . . And actually, the "Treaty of Les Conseillians" has a nice ring to it.'[85]

One of the most suggestive manifestos comes from Ivo Daalder and James Lindsay. Their title, *The Empty Throne: America's Abdication of Global Leadership*, explicitly invokes a regal account of authority. The front cover depicts an empty chair at the head of a corporate executive table – a most Trumpian image of the world. The underlying presumption is clear. The increasingly disorderly, multipolar world is like a corporation awaiting its CEO to reorder and direct it with its disciplinary hand. Monarchism and commercialism come together. The same authors, like Haass and Lévy, once advocated empire in the pages of the *New York Times* in May 2003, at the apogee of US unipolar dominance that also marked the point of decline, when 'empire' speculation and sympathy for America's imperial mission were briefly in intellectual fashion, and before 'liberal order' returned to replace it as a less provocative euphemism.[86] Like many enthusiasts, they exalted empire without looking closely at the process of imperialism. Their argument for American 'empire' in 2003 anticipated closely their argument for 'liberal order' in 2018. They claimed that, given its 'power' and 'reach', the USA was an empire, one that was eminently sustainable 'on the cheap' (these were early days, before the expenses of 'global leadership' became a burden to be solemnly shouldered). They exalted in America's exceptional and gargantuan capabilities, reminding us that only the USA can float twelve '*mammoth* aircraft carriers', each housing an 'air *armada* larger than the entire air force of most countries'. They pointed keenly to the scale of imperial exertion, with American forces 'deployed in a grand crescent' across the Middle East, with American forces bearing 'absolute authority in Iraq', which was reassuringly in a state of mere 'reconstruction' (again, early days). Having effused grandiloquently over the superpower's military might, they then reminded Americans that they must exercise a more restrained type of empire, wherein Washington constraints its interests through multilateral institutions, alliances and law. In a nutshell, they want it both ways: the majesty of empire, with awe-inspiring military strength and untrammelled authority in Iraq, and the legitimation conferred by juridical legality and legitimacy of democratic sovereign states, and under an international law that prevails above power.

'Empire' as a concept attracts endless amounts of literature, reinterpreting the complexities of the term, to the point where we can overlook a core truth.[87] Imperial orders are built by command and conquest, and reconquest – not necessarily in the form of formal annexation – through the exercise of dominance, in ways that deliberately constrain the sovereign independence and domestic policies of their subjects. Empires also require emperors. That is the corollary of the longing for an occupant on a 'throne'. At a minimum, empires involve imposition, given the ruler's forceful intrusion into the domestic life of the ruled. Imperial methods go beyond formal international processes of consultation and dialogue, involving brute force as well as the manipulation of proxies, divide-and-rule and unscrupulous clients. Historically, they also spark uprising and defiance, often after underestimating resistance. The closeness of dreams of liberation and a demand for domination is suggested in the writings of conservative intellectual Jonah Goldberg. Today, he calls on Americans to uphold the liberal order against primitive regressions into romantic nationalism. In 2000, a more optimistic time, when American relative power was vast, Goldberg advocated the invasion of the whole continent of Africa in order to bring civilization and enlightenment.[88] And when, three years later, Washington took dead aim at an old adversary in Iraq, he adapted an ancient cry for a war of annihilation: 'Baghdad Delenda Est.'

Proponents of liberal order occasionally admit that the problem concerning what is sometimes framed straightforwardly as a rules-bound order is in fact a system of imperial power and vigilante privilege exercised by a hegemon. This explicit acknowledgement of an imperial quality was more frequent when the War on Terror and the effort to reorder the Middle East were first under way, when the sense of America's unconstrained power was greater. Robert Cooper, former diplomat and advisor to then UK Prime Minister Tony Blair, argued that if the world had a civilized core that deserved lawful conduct, there was also a barbarous periphery that warranted 'rougher methods of an earlier era'. 'Among ourselves, we keep the law but when we are operating in the jungle, we must also use the laws of the jungle.'[89] One-time advocate of an American empire, Canadian academic Michael Ignatieff admitted that being an imperial power 'means enforcing such order as there is in the world and doing so in the American interest. It means laying down the rules America wants (on everything from markets to weapons of mass destruction) while exempting itself from other rules (the Kyoto Protocol on climate change and the International Criminal Court) that go against its interest.'[90] At the height of the War on Terror, jurists advising the Bush administration used a similar logic to justify the suspension of the rule of law and Geneva conventions.[91] One can defend these inconsistencies as necessary, or not. That they continually recur suggests that liberal world-ordering is an inescapably compromised process. It is an awkward point for the liberal order hypothesis, which emphasizes the binding and regular (rather than the permissive and arbitrary) functions of the system America created.

In defining US hegemony to distinguish it from empire, John Ikenberry adopts a more careful and different descriptor, yet one that still points back to the original problem. The USA, he argues, became the world's 'first citizen'.[92] In American fashion, this borrows from the Roman republic. Its etymology is revealing. First citizen (*Princeps* or 'principate') was the Julio-Claudian dynasty's carefully chosen euphemism for absolute power. As the last of the warlords standing in 31 BC, Octavian with his aggregation of material power, patronage, wealth and executive office sought not to mask but to soften and legitimize what all knew was effectively an autocracy, by deferring to the phraseology of republican tradition and thereby placating a sensitive Roman audience. As the classical historian Ronald Syme noted:

To secure the domination of the Caesarian party, the consolidation of the Revolution and the maintenance of peace, it was necessary that the primacy of Caesar's heir should be strengthened and perpetuated. Not, however, under the fatal name of dictator or monarch. On all sides prevailed a conspiracy of decent reticence about the gap between fact and theory. It was evident: no profit but only danger from talking about it. The Principate battles definition.[93]

To rename the order, then, by clothing imperial power in the garb of republican tradition, is a similarly polite exercise in evasion.

There are also moments when euphemisms give way to blunt acknowledgement of imperial relations. In his vision of American primacy across the global chessboard, geostrategic mind and former Carter advisor Zbigniew Brzezinski opted for terminology that harkens back to the more brutal age of ancient empires: 'The three grand imperatives of imperial geostrategy are to prevent collusion and maintain security dependence among the vassals, to keep tributaries pliant and protected, and to keep the barbarians from coming together.'[94] This is stark language for concepts that liberal order cherishes in different terms, American primacy and reassurance keeping allies dependent and peaceful, and American preponderance preventing dangerous bandwagoning and hostile concentrations of power. For his part, Max Boot, who now champions liberal order, once approvingly called for an 'American-led, international regency in Baghdad', urging the USA to take up the mantle of the British empire. Later, he explicitly advocated the turn to euphemism, urging the state not to use the word 'empire' for its 'historical baggage', while maintaining the 'practice'.[95] Underscoring the logic of liberal empire, Boot inadvertently reveals the contradiction: 'We shouldn't hesitate to impose our democratic views.'

It was the unadorned and direct language of Julius Caesar's bragging of conquest, rather than the euphemism of Octavian, that sprang to the mind of Hillary Clinton, then Secretary of State, as she sat down for an interview in Kabul, Afghanistan, on 20 October 2011. Informed suddenly of the death of Colonel Gaddafi, Clinton's gleeful response was revealing: 'We came, we saw, he died.'[96] For a time, the intervention that led to Qaddafi's overthrow was described by enthusiasts as a strategic and moral triumph for NATO, 'smart power at its best', a 'triumph', a 'textbook example of the [responsibility to protect] doctrine working as it was supposed to', and a 'model intervention'.[97] Given what ensued, it was decided that the model intervention should not be celebrated, or even mentioned, on the occasion of NATO's anniversary eight years later. The enforcement of liberal order had violent consequences. Libya's fallen dictator was sodomized with a bayonet, before being summarily executed in his hometown of Sirte, without a rules-bound judicial court in sight. Disorder at the gallows foreshadowed the tumult of the ensuing revolution. Regime change led to the chaotic meltdown of the country. Clinton's triumphalist reaction revealed how easily the gravity of high-minded world-ordering could yield to imperial swagger. Excited at apparent victory, the Secretary of State celebrated the liquidation of an enemy and the demonstration of the hegemon's power, leaving chaos in her wake.

In these different versions, the articulations of liberal order rest on a set of contradictions and oversights. They denounce the recrudescence of virulent nationalism in our time. At the same time, they assert an ambitious form of American nationalism and exceptionalism. Washington emerges as the world's sole sheriff, an arbiter of rules, which, on inspection, remains ascendant by exempting itself from them. High-minded ordering comes dangerously close to, and presupposes, an imperial will to power. Or, in Roman terms, two supposedly different modes of rule turn out to be quite close, the velvet-gloved Principate and the nakedly assertive Dominate.

So, we have seen that nostalgic accounts of liberal order are caught in the contradictory impulses, the desire to emancipate and the desire to control. While they claim that America's willingness to constrain itself under institutions and rules makes its order distinctive, they also betray an attraction to the exceptional privileges (and at times, the majesty) of a world monarch. If, historically, visions of liberal order rest on a contradiction – namely, that projecting power imperially is necessarily an illiberal act – then, as Jeanne Morefield argues, those who articulate and defend the order tend to look elsewhere, '*anywhere* – but at the contradiction'.[98] It is time to look.

2

Darkness Visible:
World-Ordering in Practice

Think of America's greatest post-war achievements. Any list would include the transformation of defeated Axis states into proud democracies in Asia and Europe; the containment of the Soviet Union without a major war; the opening up of dialogue with China to assist the Sino-Soviet split, and China's later entry into international markets; and the termination of the Balkan conflicts of the 1990s. Each triumph was made possible by dark bargains with illiberal forces. To transform defeated Axis powers, and strengthen new regimes, Washington protected surviving elites of the defeated order. It outcompeted the Soviet Union with coups, election meddling, alliances with authoritarians. It avoided major war through the mutual threat of nuclear genocide, and through tacit spheres-of-influence agreements. Dialogue with China, trumpeted in the Shanghai Communiqué in 1972, was purchased at a steep human cost in Bangladesh, outlined in the Blood Telegram. In Asia, wealthy democracies first evolved as protectionist states governed under martial law. The Dayton Accords that terminated the Balkan wars in 1995 locked in tribalism and disenfranchised minorities. Each compromise can be defended. None can usefully be summarized as 'liberal order'. On the occasions when America did try to create a liberal order, and remake the world in its liberal image, its ambitious projects had inadvertent, illiberal consequences. The struggle for power, against resistance, meant that a hegemony supposed to be marked by rules and regularity instead broke the rules, and dominated through caprice.

An Illiberal World

Ordering involves inconsistency because we live in an illiberal world. The day after 9/11, Prime Minister Tony Blair wrote privately to President George W. Bush: 'These groups don't play by liberal rules and we can't either.'[1] Blair's words reflect an ugly truth. Ordering involves contestation, resistance and suppression. There are actors and interests abroad that do not wish to be ordered, or liberalized, on American terms. In suppressing resistance, hegemons step outside their rules. And because power is limited, hard choices arise that compromise liberal ideals. America defeated each of its main adversaries, from the Axis to the Soviet Union to Islamist terrorist networks, by cooperating with atrocious actors. To prevent dangerous imbalances of hostile power, Washington made common cause with authoritarians. At the height of the Cold War, court historian Arthur Schlesinger Jr. reminded National Security Advisor McGeorge Bundy that the 'free world' led by America included dictatorships in Paraguay, Nicaragua and Spain: 'Whom are we fooling?'[2] Even for well-intentioned rulers, constraints, scarcities and trade-offs create constant struggles between means and ends. Liberal norms are themselves in conflict, between law and justice, sovereignty and human rights, free trade and workers' protection. A haunting question for US diplomacy is how to promote liberalism abroad. Press for it urgently? Or sacrifice it now for the longer term, hoping that alliance with despotic regimes served the ultimate cause of liberty? Liberal ordering can therefore be taken to mean promoting democracy, accepting it when it emerges, or supporting friendly dictators.[3] There is 'evil in all political action', warned Hans Morgenthau, so the best we can do is minimal harm.[4]

Consider the Arab Spring, the wave of revolutions that struck the Middle East from 2010. Washington was torn about how to respond. Lacking a clear compass, by turns it supported, abandoned or toppled dictators. In Saudi Arabia the USA supported its client; in Egypt, it guardedly supported a revolution then helped reinstall a military dictatorship; in Libya, a US-led coalition overthrew a regime by force. Cover-all liberal concepts offered little guide to the choice between the risks of supporting revolutionary change versus sticking by illiberal allies. In an unstable moment in a volatile region, there was no strong-enough 'vital centre' with compliant democratic parties that Washington could embrace. As the region erupted, with its epicentre of violence in Syria, the commentariat itself, warning of a 'post-American' order, struggled to advise how to translate those principles into action.

Similar problems struck the earlier Bush II administration (2001–9).[5] In his second inaugural address, Bush called for Americans to embrace the promotion of global democracy and the end of tyranny as the path to security. This served only to alarm authoritarian Gulf allies. The administration veered between a 'freedom agenda' and reassuring its clients of Washington's support. The militant organization Hamas triumphed against a US-backed Fatah authority in the Palestinian parliamentary elections of January 2006, elections that America encouraged. A realization returned – that the popular will of foreign populations could threaten, not bolster, US interests. Shortly into Bush's second term, a consensus formed that US interests were too varied, its partnerships with despots too important, to prize liberty over stability.

Order as Hypocrisy

'Order' is sometimes spoken of as rule-following, the antithesis of rule-breaking. Double standards, though, lie at the core of ordering.[6] To preserve their supremacy and their free hand, rulers will stretch, ignore or reinvent rules at will. Believing they shoulder the burden of serving humanity, and therefore a duty to remain dominant, they will not – when pressed – be bound by deference to the codes they demand of others. One organization that trumpets its rule-oriented quality is the EU. In November 2003, France and Germany flouted the Stability and Growth Pact, the binding agreement between EU member states to help stabilize monetary union, and its rules on the ratio of deficits to GDP. Finance ministers blocked the European Commission's attempt to fine both states, but the transgression went unpunished, against the Commission's protests.[7]

Like EU heavyweights, Washington claims privilege. In February 1998, Secretary of State Madeleine Albright proclaimed: 'If we have to use force, it is because we are America; we are the indispensable nation. We stand tall and we see further than other countries into the future.'[8] For Albright, because of America's clairvoyance, half a million child deaths under the chokehold of international sanctions were a necessary price for disarming Iraq. Though accusations of mass infanticide were false,[9] her calculus was revealing. Washington could take up illiberal means in the service of liberal ends. Luminaries who laud liberal rules, like President of the Council on Foreign Relations Richard Haass, prove to be flexible. Haass urged Washington to treat Russia as a rogue state for violating Westphalian norms of sovereignty. Months later, he called for a US-backed coup in Venezuela.[10]

To remain in the ascendancy, the USA at critical moments exempts itself from rules and norms, even while preaching them. Consider the history of espionage. The USA has historically been a purveyor of mass, covert surveillance, including against allies. Even in the mythologized moment of creation, at the San Francisco conference that brought the United Nations into being, President Harry Truman had international delegates spied on, clandestinely intercepting their cables.[11] Such contradictions echoed through Obama's final presidential phone call with German Chancellor Angela Merkel in early 2017. They agreed on the need for 'a rules-based international order'. It was ironic that such affirmation happened by telephone. In 2013, the US National Security Agency (NSA) had tapped Merkel's mobile phone from a listening post atop the US embassy in Berlin. For Merkel, this was an affront. Germany withdrew from an intelligence-sharing agreement with Washington, denounced the violation of friendship, dispatched envoys to Washington to demand a 'no spy' agreement, and initiated a federal investigation. Transatlantic hierarchy reasserted itself, however. The NSA gave scarce cooperation to Germany's federal prosecutor. Germany judged it better in an hour of international upheaval to ensure intelligence cooperation by being a 'good ally'.[12] The provision or denial of intelligence is part of America's repertoire. When it did not suit the superpower, something other than 'rules' defined the system. Coercion quietly was brought to bear, partly by implicit threat of punishment, and partly by the ally's internalized realization of the possible consequences. Under the internationalist show, an older power politics endured.

Like great powers before it, the USA demands that its own sovereignty be respected even as it trespasses on that of others.[13] America launched coups, including against democratically elected governments (Iran in 1953, Guatemala in 1954, Brazil in 1964, Chile in 1973 – all the way to the democratically elected Muslim Brotherhood in Egypt in 2013), or treated electorally defeated oppositions as legitimate governments-in-waiting, from Palestine to Venezuela. Between 1946 and 2000, America engaged in eighty-one 'partisan electoral interventions'. In sixteen cases, Washington influenced foreign elections by covertly funding, advising and spreading propaganda for its preferred candidates. Between 1947 and 1989, it attempted seventy-two times to change other countries' governments. At times, this was done to frustrate land reforms or industry nationalization in other countries. The ordering hegemon allowed itself a different standard, compromising democracy abroad to forge a world safe for its own.

A similar pattern can be seen in the creation of international institutions. The USA helped create the International Criminal Court (ICC) in 1998, but exempted itself from the court's jurisdiction. The Clinton administration advocated a world criminal court, while striving to limit its writ, 'to shape a court that would not pose a threat to US citizens'. The State Department declared that it would require immunity from prosecutions, as 'American armed forces have a unique peacekeeping role', and, as agents of the superpower, in 'hotspots' 'stand to be uniquely subject to frivolous, nuisance accusations . . . and [the USA] simply cannot be expected to expose [its] people to those sorts of risks'.[14] Washington strong-armed and bribed other states into Article 98 bilateral agreements, to commit not to extradite US citizens.[15] In August 2002, the American Service-Members' Protection Act (ASPA) was introduced, banning military aid to countries that ratified the Rome Statute, the treaty that established the ICC, and placing sanctions on countries that failed to sign Article 98 agreements conferring immunity on US citizens. The coercion was explicit. In the case of aid-seeking Lesotho, a 'blunt' meeting with the US Ambassador indicated that Lesotho's profile as a non-signatory nation jeopardized its prospects of receiving aid.[16] The ASPA also authorized military force to free US nationals detained by the ICC, and became known as the Hague

Invasion Act. Amongst the 'yea' votes passing the act were Democrat champions of liberal order: Senators John Kerry, Hillary Clinton and Joseph Biden. To uphold order, the superpower sought immunity from the ICC, reserving the right literally to attack its institutions.

A Warrant to Strike

The problem of making and breaking rules becomes more intense with regard to the use of force. It resurfaced in September 2013, in debates over whether to conduct punitive airstrikes against Syria for its murderous use of chemical weapons. British Prime Minister David Cameron's government talked emphatically about a rules-based international system. Against the threat of a Russian veto, however, Cameron discovered reasons to set rules aside. To insist on a UNSC resolution for military action would be 'contracting out our foreign policy, our morality, to the potential of a Russian veto',[17] a 'misguided approach'. Some countries, this implied, were entitled to unilaterally suspend rules for the greater good. This pointed to a conflict within international order. An unauthorized attack on Syria, as some observed, 'might uphold the norm of CW non-use, but it would surely undermine the norm against interstate uses of force without UN Security Council authorization except in cases of self-defence'.[18] Would Cameron support non-Atlantic powers if they exercised the same discretion, to uphold a humanitarian norm by violating a rule? If not, he thereby claims a privilege, revealing that rules are not paramount.

Not all practitioners of order go to the trouble of developing a theoretical basis for rule-exemption. Former Secretary of Defense Ashton Carter, who invoked a 'rules-based order',[19] a decade earlier joined with former Secretary of Defense William J. Perry to advocate bombing North Korea's nuclear weapons programme to disrupt Pyongyang's ballistic missile tests 'before mortal threats to US security could develop'.[20] This went beyond a prudential 'pre-emption' option. A stationary North Korean nuclear-tipped missile, without other indications of aggression, would not in itself constitute evidence of an imminent threat and would not permit 'anticipatory self-defence' under international law. They were arguing for preventive strikes, to destroy a more distant threat, an illegal act of aggression based on the *Caroline* case of 1837 and under the United Nations Charter. Without spelling it out, Carter and Perry asserted a privilege, permitting the superpower to discard rules to neutralize an unacceptable threat. They would hardly allow other sovereign states, including North Korea, to exercise that prerogative. The sheriff retains a warrant to strike at will.

Frustrated by veto players in the multilateral forums whose creation they celebrate, traditionalists seek to create alternative doctrines and institutions to authorize the hegemon's actions. In the Princeton Project she co-convened with John Ikenberry, Anne-Marie Slaughter, sometime Director of Policy Planning in the State Department, argued for 'A World of Liberty under Law'.[21] Yet in two cases where Washington applied force without seeking a mandate from the UNSC, against Serbia in 1999 and Iraq in 2003, Slaughter discovered a rationale for benign vigilantism, a doctrine she described as 'illegal but legitimate',[22] finding that 'insisting on formal legality in this case may be counterproductive', though later she lambasted the Bush II administration for rejecting treaties, and flouting rules and the norms of global governance. In the case of Serbia, her doctrine invested NATO, a collective security system, with the authority to supplant that of the UN. In the case of Iraq, she hoped legitimacy would derive from success, replacing process with conquest as the determinant. We have, then, a doctrine of expediency that improvises a basis for rule-relaxation. The

Princeton Project proposed the creation of a concert of democracies as 'an alternative forum for liberal democracies to authorize collective action, including the use of force, by a supermajority vote'. If the international system will not confer legitimacy or enable action, the superpower should not submit itself, but instead invent other seats of authority, and new rules. When institutions threaten to block American action, those in favour of unauthorized action develop alternative rationales, go 'forum shopping', or simply press ahead, advocating implicitly for a privilege without explaining.

That does not mean Washington cares little for international institutions. To the contrary, it invests effort in their maintenance and functioning. Institutions and rules serve a purpose, not to constrain but to legitimize the hegemon's preferences. The pattern of post-war practice was that other states sought to bind the USA to institutions, that the USA mostly agreed with reservations, but then refused to be bound behaviourally. When they played any role at all, institutions were 'used by US policymakers to project and enhance the unilateral exercise of American power'.[23] Washington repeatedly went against those institutions that supposedly checked its power as it acted unilaterally, from the repudiation of the International Trade Organization Treaty in 1947 to the adoption of a flexible response nuclear posture to the termination of the Bretton Woods financial system.

International order, then, is not 'based' on rules. Like a spider's web, it is strong enough to catch the weak, yet too weak to catch the strong. Rules exist but do not define the system. Powerful states adhere to them only when they serve their self-defined interests at acceptable costs.[24] The fact that, in March 2019, there were fifteen cases before the ICC, and all the accused were African, points to de facto great power immunity. By contrast, 'when American staff sergeant Robert Bales allegedly shot dead sixteen civilians in Afghanistan, including nine children, he was quietly spirited away to a military prison in the US, despite the demands of Afghan President Hamid Karzai to try him in the country where the massacre took place'.[25] Every major power has significantly violated international law, rejected the rulings of international courts, or denied their authority. President Jacques Chirac's France, like Chancellor Gerhard Schroeder's Germany, opposed the invasion of Iraq in the name of upholding UNSC authority. Yet France flouted the same rule, participating in NATO's unauthorized bombing of Serbia in 1999 to rescue Kosovo Albanians from genocide. In 1985, following the sinking of Greenpeace's *Rainbow Warrior* by two French secret agents, the French government agreed to allow an arbitration process but refused to submit evidence to the ICC. In the 1980s, when Nicaragua successfully sued America before the International Court of Justice (ICJ) over the mining of its harbours, Washington refused to pay reparations or recognize the court's authority. America's then UN ambassador Jeane Kirkpatrick pronounced accurately that the ICJ is a 'semi-legal' body that 'nations sometimes accept and sometimes don't'.[26] The world's emerging counterpower, China, shows a similar attitude. In the summer of 2016, it defied the unanimous ruling of the Permanent Court of Arbitration that found against its territorial claims, continuing to seize disputed waters, islands and shoals in the South China Sea. Washington appealed to China to respect the 'legally binding' verdict, yet had not ratified the convention it urged China to observe.

Great powers, then, transgress rules with impunity. Faced with this simple truth, liberal order proponents respond with intellectual gymnastics. Some reply that at least offending states offer public legal justifications for their actions, reflecting the order's normative power.[27] Since such gestures are mostly costless rhetorical ones, that consolation is weak tea. Others offer protective clauses: 'Liberal international order is built around open and at least loosely rule-based relations . . . general principles and arrangements, as opposed to those built around regional blocs, spheres of influence or imperial zones.'[28] If rules are only 'loosely' the basis for relations, then great powers can abandon them at will – and they do. Others apply easier tests, looking to formal and official behaviour as a metric of the liberal order's health. For instance, one RAND study uses the frequency of the passage of UN Security Council resolutions as a measure.[29] This neglects incidents of the 'closet veto', whereby permanent members privately threaten use of the blocking prerogative to limit the UNSC's agenda and kill off unfavourable resolutions, preventing discussion of taboo issues. Thanks to hidden veto threats, the UNSC never debated the Algerian war or the partitioning of India, failed to classify the Rwandan atrocities as a genocide, and declined to name Vietnam, Afghanistan or Chechnya as armed conflicts. Others just lower the bar, claiming 'rules-based' just means 'whether the norms affect state and state actors' behaviours'.[30] But many things affect state behaviour apart from rules, such as greed, or the desire to maximize power. If rules only apply sporadically among other variables, then the system cannot be 'based' on them. To assimilate the disagreeable fact of great power rule-violation, the claim of rules-based order needs so many caveats that it dissolves in a sea of qualifications.

The Order at Birth

At the moment of its creation, the order was not intended to work along the lines for which it is now revered. Multilateral institutions were meant to legitimize hierarchy in a negotiated universe of major powers, without constraining its most determined acts. For the

Roosevelt administration, as it created new international architecture, the new system would lock in the privilege of the four great powers – the USA, the UK, the Soviet Union and China – while offering a sop to smaller states to feel included. For Roosevelt, the Big Four would make 'all the more important decisions', the United Nations working as a safety valve to let small countries 'blow off steam'.[31] And nor would the ruling quartet be equals. Roosevelt presumed a relatively weak China, and an Anglo-Soviet standoff in Europe.[32] The founding state intended the UN to bolster American primacy, reconciling the principle of universal participation with the reality of great power control. It would appeal to international organizations when convenient, and bypass them when necessary.

During the Second World War, voices within the US government, such as Secretary of State Cordell Hull, argued for a 'stable and enduring' order, which would prevent regression to 'economic conflict, social insecurity, and again war'.[33] Yet the desired pathway to these goals differed significantly. American power was to make that world through coldly calculated coercion, as well as attraction. Assistant Secretary of State Dean Acheson's wartime accusation against the Treasury Department exaggerated a basic truth about US war aims, 'a victory where both enemies and allies were prostrate – enemies by military action, allies by bankruptcy'.[34] During wartime, America created economic instruments to weaken the economic sinews of British international power. Sentimentality and blood ties only went so far. Asserting itself as the new colossus, Washington dismantled Britain's imperial preference trading arrangements and the supremacy of the pound, which was supplanted by the dollar as the key international currency. It attached not a heavy interest rate, but heavy conditions to its post-war loans. It went back on wartime commitments, forcing Britain to drop import controls and accept currency convertibility, and withheld promised nuclear-sharing arrangements. America had two aims in mind: to weaken and take receivership of an exhausted British empire, while keeping it strong enough to endure as a supportive satellite. The net result, after Britain's wartime sacrifices, was to turn it into a subordinate power and a financial supplicant.

A defining episode was the Suez crisis of 1956. In that hinge event of the Anglo-American relationship, the US Sixth Fleet stalked and harassed British ships in the Mediterranean, fouling their radar and sonar, menacing them with aircraft and lighting them up at night with searchlights. With the pound and oil supplies under pressure, President Dwight Eisenhower coerced Britain with the formula of 'no ceasefire: no loans'. Patronage could be rapidly withdrawn, regardless of recent history, blood ties or shared visions of order. Rules, norms, values, institutions – the new liberal order – did not prevent Britain from trying to maintain a colonial possession. And it did not stop the USA from arbitrating the matter by targeting its ally's vitals.

The post-war world before the term 'liberal order' came into being was a foreign country. If there were general principles that underpinned the UN at its founding, they were at first self-determination and sovereignty, selectively applied, rather than democracy and human rights. Recall that two of the permanent five of the UNSC were totalitarian communist states. Two of the democracies held colonial empires. The USA itself covertly assisted France in its campaign in Indochina (1946–54) and its colonial order in Asia. A major feature of the post-war order was the Cold War, the long security competition with the Soviet Union, which gave a particular shape to the calculation of ends and means. We can observe the interplay of sameness and difference in the rhetoric of order, then and now, in the Clifford Memorandum of 1946.[35] It bridged the earlier Long Telegram by George Kennan of September 1946 and the later guiding template NSC 68 of 1950, as a consensus formed for anti-Soviet containment. The Memorandum spoke of a 'decent world order'. Yet in contrast to recent statements about liberal order, the memorandum advocated preparation for biological war – outlawed by the 1925 Geneva Protocol – as, along with nuclear weapons, it 'may be the only powerful deterrent to Soviet aggressive action'. Roosevelt had already authorized a secret biological weapons programme that would last decades. The Memorandum cautioned against arms control measures, as 'proposals on outlawing atomic warfare and long-range offensive weapons would greatly limited the United States strength'. And it de-emphasized direct military commitments, prioritizing favourable trade agreements, loans and technical missions to demonstrate capitalism's strengths. Evidently, attitudes to what lay within or beyond the bounds of liberal order, what instruments were optimal, legitimate or taboo, were historically unstable.

The order also took root in America's handling of defeated adversaries, whom it looked to remake as subordinate allies. Important in the literature are the 'bargains' between the USA and the states it garrisoned and rebuilt: West Germany and Japan. Those bargains involved compromises with the old orders, whose help the USA sought. West Germany, like NATO, retained officials who had been security elites in the Third Reich. Former Nazi mandarins stuffed the highest levels of government. Several former Nazi generals would later become senior commanders in the Bundeswehr. By suppressing the record of their complicity in war crimes, the USA helped former Nazi scientists, engineers and technicians to emigrate, to assist its ballistic missile, aerospace and other weapons programmes.[36]

In Japan, the creation of a new order involved the exoneration of an emperor complicit in war crimes. To bolster the post-war settlement through the Showa throne as 'symbol monarchy', in 1946 General Douglas MacArthur's staff helped Emperor Hirohito rewrite the history of his reign and shift blame, exculpating him of responsibility for his country's disastrous imperial onslaught that had killed more than twenty-three million people, reinventing him from meddling ruler to blameless ceremonial monarch. Carefully managed war crimes trials wrote out the Emperor's complicity in arms expansion, militarism, emperor-centred nationalism, and his destabilization of the party cabinet system.[37] Japan could be remade into an anti-communist bulwark, then coerced into signing a bilateral treaty with Taiwan in 1952 and conceding a US presence in Okinawa and the Bonin Islands.

Similar predicaments confronted US diplomats again decades later, as they oversaw the reconstruction of states after shooting wars were terminated, such as the Balkan nations after the bloodlettings of 1992–5. To purchase an end to fighting, the Dayton Accords locked in ethnic divisions and partition. The insistence on democratization within the framework of the status quo meant that the main group affiliations (Bosnian, Serb or Croat, corresponding to confessional affiliations) dictated the distribution of government posts, institutionalizing divisions in the new constitution. Ethnic cleansing was effectively rewarded with the creation of Srpska. With the predominant groupings entrenched, seventeen of the country's officially recognized minority groups were prohibited from running for high office. The choice was a painful one between two illiberal poisons, either a settlement organized around a presumption of separate ethnic groups rather than transcendent individual citizenship, or continued killing, with the prospect of defeat for the Serbs. An illiberal world constrained even the superpower, as it brokered peace.

Political Economy

As the USA rose to international pre-eminence, it strived to reshape the international economic environment, to establish and exploit the dollar as the reserve currency, to open markets on its own terms, to make a world safe for the penetration of American capital. How far did that process, that longstanding commitment to the 'Open Door', represent a liberal drive for free trade? According to admirers, a great deal. Not only was a commitment to free trade allegedly a core component of the US order; it also holds out a general lesson, that free trade leads to peace and prosperity, while protectionism drives war and poverty. At times, proponents point to China's entry into the WTO, and the global economy, as a major dividend. The practical inference is that the USA ought to expand free trade, eschew protection and join rather than reject free-trading compacts such as the Trans-Pacific Partnership.

As we will see, the notion that America rose to power through a post-war political economy of unfettered capitalism on a level playing field is in fact ahistorical. Note, though, that this false memory played a central part in the way a triumphant America treated post-Soviet Russia. After communist rule collapsed in 1991, at the urging of and pressure from the US government, Moscow embarked on a programme of 'shock therapy', to restructure Russia around the principle of market exchange, adopting accelerated privatization of state industries, deregulation, fiscal discipline and the shedding of price controls.[38] This experiment was a major effort in the project to enlarge the order at a rapid pace. It had the support of the leading institutions of global capitalism: the IMF, World Bank, and US Treasury Department. Harvard academic Jeffrey Sachs, one of Russian liberalization's architects from 1991 to 1993, set out the programme's logic: 'To clean up the shambles left by communist mismanagement, Eastern Europe must take a swift, dramatic leap to private ownership and a market system.'[39] 'Swift, dramatic leap' – a vast programme grounded in classical liberal economics took on the tempo and zeal of the revolutionary communism it aimed to replace. These rapid reforms replaced an oppressive and failed communist system. They did so at the continual insistence of Washington that Russia must reform itself on 'our conditions'. The results on many measures were disastrous: capital flight and deep recession, slumping industrial production, malnutrition, a criminalized economy, a corrupt oligarchy enjoying a concentration of wealth, and the decline of health care and an increased rate of premature deaths.[40] By eschewing the more gradualist path of Poland or China, the consequences were profoundly illiberal.[41] 'Liberal order' visionaries are quick to give their ideas credit for the prosperity of nations from Western Europe to the Pacific Rim, finding causation in correlation. They deny such a direct link between their ideas and the problems of post-Soviet Russia.[42] Yet it is hard to accept that measures like sudden privatization and the rise of monopolies in a corrupt country were not related to asset stripping and capital flight, or that eliminating housing and utilities subsidies that millions of poor families relied upon did not play a major part in the social ruin that followed. Western technocrats, diplomats and politicians were deeply implicated in the new order's design.

What about the earlier history of political economy? Historically, great powers do not become great powers via free trade.[43] Countries tend to preach the doctrine of free trade only after becoming economically dominant. Ascending powers typically rise through the deliberate intervening hand of an activist state. They tend to shield their infant industries with bans, tariffs and other controls, while imitating or stealing innovations and technology abroad. This applied to Britain in the eighteenth century, and it applied to the USA of the nineteenth century, which had grown through a mercantilist policy under Founding Father Alexander Hamilton. It also applied to post-war America. The USA resolutely imposed restrictive measures when it suited, with non-tariff protectionism a persistent feature of US policy. A range of instruments was fashioned to restrict trade: bilateral voluntary export restriction agreements, orderly marketing agreements, quotas, buy-American requirements, export subsidies and discriminatory product standards. Allies and clients also practised protection, including the prosperous Asian states of Taiwan and South Korea after the Second World War, as well as the more democratic (but tightly supervised) Hong Kong and Singapore. One major pillar of the post-war order was Japan, which instituted, 'the most restrictive foreign trade and foreign-exchange control system ever devised by a major free nation'.[44] South Korea evolved first as a dictatorship under authoritarian founding fathers Syngman Rhee and Park Chung Hee, who nurtured under state protection the *chaebol* business groups, Hyundai, Daewoo and Samsung. Free markets only emerged from initially highly protected markets. The EU today insists that poor external countries drop tariffs and capital controls, even while it maintains extensive agricultural subsidies.

China occupies a central place in the debate over liberal order. Defenders of the order credit it with facilitating China's entry into capitalism, thereby driving international growth. China's model, though, is tightly controlled state capitalism. It is a notorious economic 'cheat'. Beijing maintains a non-level playing field that advantages state-owned enterprises.[45] It flouts WTO rules. It steals intellectual property and practises cybertheft. It forces foreign firms to share technology and banks to partner with local firms. China never accepted open markets, controlling investment and the movement of funds. Beijing achieved rapid industrial revolution through authoritarian measures. These included forced resettlement and urbanization schemes, population control through forced abortion and compulsory sterilization, severe working conditions, repression of civil society including trade unions, labour and human rights activists, and internet surveillance.

Foreign farmers would be baffled by the claim that the old order embodied free trade, when the USA was set on granting agricultural subsidies and other mechanisms that limited foreign governments' access to US consumers. Consider the lavish subsidies for American agriculture, both overproducing and then at times dumping produce on world markets. Efforts within Washington to liberalize American trade practices met the veto-wielding resistance of the US Committee on Foreign Investment. Euphemisms eased the path. Mercantilism was renamed 'industry policy' or 'strategic trade policy'. The post-war trading order, institutionalized first in the GATT and then in the WTO, saw a decline in tariffs that was offset by an increase in non-tariff barriers.[46]

The trading relationship between the USA and Australia offers a revealing snapshot of the economic order. The USA, the EU and other major agricultural producers like Japan practised farm protectionism to such an extent that Australia regarded it as a betrayal of wartime solidarity and sacrifices. In particular, America's Farm Bill and the EU's Common Agricultural Policy are at odds with the principles of international trade liberalism. Politically effective farm lobbies ensured that subsidies and restrictions remained strong. In 1955, the USA insisted on a 'temporary' waiver from GATT rules on import restrictions, threatening to leave if it didn't get its way. The waiver was indeed temporary, staying in force for almost forty years. The USA restricted imports of sugar, peanuts and dairy products until 1993. Affected nations created the Cairns Group of Fair Trading Nations in 1986 to advocate the liberalization of agricultural produce. Australia's foreign minister branded wheat and cattle subsidies 'the act of a hostile power'.[47] When Australian farmers advocated closing joint defence facilities, US Secretary of State George Shultz advised Australia not to link agricultural policy with defence hosting. The issue threatened to boil over when President George H. W. Bush visited a recession-blighted Australia in January 1992. Bush acknowledged that trade disputes collaterally damaged Australian farmers. Yet subsidies continued. Exercising its 'voice opportunities', Australia was met with polite silence.

In reality, there were several post-war economic orders.

Globalization on a large scale, characterized by the emergence of transnational corporations and supply chains, got underway only in the 1990s and 2000s. Mass immigration to the United States and Europe is also largely a post–Cold War phenomenon. The euro and the Eurozone date back only to 1999. Labour mobility within Europe is also a relatively recent policy. Controversial 'megaregional' trade pacts like NAFTA, the TPP and TTIP [Trans-Atlantic Trade and Investment Partnership], which go beyond old-fashioned tariff reductions to rewrite much domestic legislation, go back only to the 1990s.[48]

Earlier decades saw restrictions on the mobility of finance, with capital controls, fixed exchange rates and periodic returns to tariff barriers. The long competition with the Soviet Union moved the USA to deliberately encourage the economic growth of its Asian allies, but under the shield of a neo-mercantilist state that also brought patron and client into periodic conflict. Nostalgists wrongly historicize and seek to naturalize what is in fact a recent set of post-1989 international arrangements.

America remains a 'long-term and prolific proponent of

protectionist policies'.[49] Since the 2008 financial crisis, the country has imposed tariffs worth $39 billion, while the world's top sixty economies have adopted more than seven thousand protectionist trade measures, worth more than $400 billion. The USA and the EU both held the highest number of protectionist measures, each exercising more than one thousand, with India at a distant third at four hundred.[50] America's trade protectionism has the highest impact on other countries.

The reversion to protectionism had precedents before the global financial crisis. Some of the most strident advocates of open markets and the dismantling of trade barriers have in practice done the opposite. One was President Ronald Reagan. Reagan championed the cause of free trade as a foundation of progress and peace. As president, he increased the proportion of imports subject to restrictions by 100 per cent from 1980, as well as tightened quotas, voluntary restraint agreements, new duties and raised tariffs, and he strengthened the Export-Import Bank, in order to protect the recovery of US industries, especially the auto, computer-chip and the steel industries. Reagan justified these steps as forcing economic competitors to trade freely. President Bill Clinton also championed free trade, in words and deeds, driving through NAFTA, a free trade zone in North America, and pushed for China's admission to the WTO under 'most favoured nation' status. Yet under Clinton, rice subsidies that continued during his administration enabled US growers to dump their product onto the markets of vulnerable rural countries in Haiti, Ghana and Indonesia at depressed prices.

President George W. Bush emulated Reagan rhetorically, invoking the principles of free trade and unfettered markets. Yet in 2002 he increased steel tariffs by 30 per cent only to back down twenty months later under threat of punitive counter-tariffs by the EU. Confronted with the prospect of economic meltdown in the crisis of 2008, Bush intervened in the market with strongly protectionist measures, including bailouts of major firms, claiming: 'I have abandoned free-market principles to save the free-market system.'[51] The reintroduction of protectionist measures today, then, is not such a sudden or radical departure as is sometimes claimed. America's continual contortions on the issue reflect the inherent difficulty of liberal projects, whose architects often feel impelled to compromise with illiberal pressures. A world where even the most avowed exponents of free trade continually return to protectionism when markets exert their pressures is not the flat capitalist world we are being invited to be nostalgic for.

A Nuclear Order

The world after 1945 was also shaped by the nuclear revolution. For the first time, humanity developed a weapon that could inflict instantaneous devastation on large populations and urban centres, and could do so without first achieving military dominance over its target. Thus, the instrument was radical for its disproportionality to most strategic goals, the extreme difficulty of defending against it and its 'equalizing' capacity, whereby even a relatively weak possessor could inflict a dying sting on an adversary so severe that the damage would exceed the value of the object being fought for. Mutual deterrence became the main foundation for the avoidance of major war. Most pioneered in the USA, the weapon also became an international innovation. It spread to other major powers, often against Washington's wishes. And to its credit, the USA went to considerable lengths in collaboration with post-Soviet Russia to prevent the disastrous spread of nuclear materials, through the Nunn–Lugar Cooperative Threat Reduction Program, which dismantled WMD – weapons of mass destruction – arsenals in the former Soviet Union. Like mutual deterrence, successful arms control was a collective process. It relied for its success on pragmatic cooperation with illiberal states.

This nuclear reality made the post-war order less violent than it might have been, at least at the highest level of calculations about major war, even if nuclear weapons can also destabilize interactions at lower levels. The capacity of nuclear states to exercise deterrence via threat of punishment, holding at risk what adversaries value, was broadly restraining. To presume otherwise, that nuclear weapons were irrelevant to the absence of major war, is implausible. It would be, as Michael Quinlan writes, to hold that

Western possession of nuclear weapons could have had no impact upon the Soviet Union's assessment . . . of its options in relation to West Berlin, which it could always have overrun swiftly by non-nuclear force. It has to hold that Pakistan's possession of nuclear weapons makes no valid contribution to its sense of security in face of India's superiority at other levels of military force. It has to hold that if governments implacably opposed to Israel's existence came widely to power among its neighbours and successfully made military cause in aggression, they could and would feel confident that Israel would accept political obliteration by conventional or Chemical Weapons force rather than exercise the nuclear-weapon option . . . it has to hold that at the time of the 1990–1 Gulf War, Israel's known albeit undeclared nuclear capability not only did not play but also could not have played any part in Saddam Hussein's decision not to use Chemical Weapons against Israel as an assured means of fracturing the country's patience, and so of triggering the Israeli

95

intervention which he deeply desired to engineer in order to split the coalition against him.[52]

The arrival of nuclear weapons, their increasing range, followed by even more powerful thermonuclear ones, was a bleak new reality. It did not correspond with the values of liberalism. With their invention and the technology attached to them now permanent and ineradicable elements of the species' future, the achievement of peace and stability between major powers rested on a brutal calculus, of threatening genocide to prevent genocide. It effectively and permanently conscripted the civilian populations of those states, forcibly making them the targets of potential apocalyptic exchange. In the USA, this led to a major concentration of power in the executive branch, effectively a 'nuclear monarchy'.

To create the conditions for creative world-making, the USA first swept aside its chief Asian competitor. The same president celebrated for founding the liberal order, Harry Truman, also launched two atomic strikes on Imperial Japan in August 1945, immolating and irradiating two of its cities after a campaign of blockade, firebombing and starvation. He did so to sweep aside a competitor that had been brutally pursuing a rival vision for an Asian order of its own. Washington thereby introduced a genocidal weapon into the world. There are powerful arguments that this was the 'least bad' choice available. Tellingly, though, in panegyrics for a dying liberalism, the words 'Hiroshima' and 'Nagasaki' hardly appear. Similarly, primacists today speak of America's historical creation of a free and open Pacific and of US-led globalization as a peaceful project, but rarely mention the bloody point of origin, when Commodore William Perry forced an isolated Japan into a commercial treaty at gunpoint. Typically, orders are birthed in creative destruction, whether in the form of gunboat diplomacy or atomic terror.

Nuclear weapons and the threat of their use barely appear at all in panegyrics, except in admirable, peaceful efforts to prevent or slow their spread, such as through alliances or the Non-Proliferation Treaty (1970). But even these best case examples involve darker elements. The NPT regime is a classic instance of great power privilege in action, committing the possessor states to eventual, negotiated disarmament, while in practice Russia and the USA modernize and refresh their arsenals, reaffirming the central importance of nuclear weapons in their doctrine. Five NATO non-nuclear weapons states have also defied the cause of disarmament, volunteering to act as surrogate nuclear states by equipping their forces to deliver US nuclear weapons in wartime.

Proponents of liberal order attribute the absence of major war to American hegemony. In the avoidance of Armageddon, though, also important is the fact that enemies of the US-led order constrained the USA with the threat of annihilation, making the eruption of a third world war less likely. Since it takes at least two sides to make a war, the absence of major war was a co-creation between Washington and its nuclear-armed, totalitarian rivals. That deterrence helped constrain the USA is suggested by the fact that it went to great lengths, with mixed success, to inhibit the spread of nuclear weapons and develop counterforce capabilities to overcome the logic of mutually assured destruction, precisely because it wished *not* to be deterred.[53]

We should also be wary of triumphalist claims about the prevention of major war. The shadow of major war never went away, and indeed helped to define the period. The relationship between nuclear weapons, stability and deterrence is a complex one.[54] Threats of nuclear retaliation can both induce caution and create new sources of instability. Nuclear possession both constrains and, under some circumstances and at lower levels of conflict, emboldens. The possession of nuclear weapons may limit competition at the upper end of the violence scale, but it does not eliminate competition outright. Moreover, either side may seek bargaining advantages in manipulating the risk of escalation in games of 'chicken'. And either side may have different ideas of where the sub-nuclear threshold lies, creating the possibility of misperception and misapprehension.

If the nuclear order helped the world in the period of the *Pax Americana* avoid a major war, it was a near-run thing. There was a series of high-stakes near misses, caused by fear, misperception, false alarms or system errors.[55] In 1962, the Joint Chiefs of Staff pressed the Kennedy administration to attack Cuba, not knowing that Soviet combat forces possessed nuclear-tipped missiles and were authorized to use them, and a Soviet submarine commander who believed the war had started had to be dissuaded by fellow officers from firing a nuclear torpedo. At other moments, warning systems misidentified the moon, a flock of geese and military exercises as nuclear attacks. Between the Soviet Union and the USA, the deterrence relationship was at times unstable, with the reciprocal fear of surprise attack. If the pursuit of stable deterrence dictated that security could be achieved through mutual vulnerability, both sides at times refused to concede their own vulnerability, and competed for war-fighting advantage. A set of unstable interactions grew, through arms competitions and technological development, through a fear of having an inferior nuclear arsenal and through a fear that one's assured capacity to retaliate was threatened. To their credit, the USA and its principal opponent went to great lengths eventually to stabilize the relationship.

Thus, the boast that a liberal order prevented major war is complacent. The sources of mutual survival lay partly beyond the good deeds of a liberally minded hegemon, through a deterrence relationship that depended on others' restraining force, and organized around weapons that cannot by definition be used liberally. At times, that relationship was dangerously unstable and the threat of nuclear war came close to being a reality. Summaries of this history as 'peace and prosperity' under one power's supervision are glib, to say the least.

Spheres of Influence

According to the reigning orthodoxy, the creation of spheres of influence is antithetical to US-led world order. The clash over Ukraine in 2013–14 restaged the question. As America, its allies and Russia clashed over the status of the Ukraine, European diplomats insisted that the EU 'doesn't do geopolitics'.[56] European leaders, likewise, defined their visions of order against what they see as an atavistic form of politics. As Angela Merkel put it, 'We thought we had left all that behind us.'[57]

This is ahistorical. In the USA and the EU, the historical record shows a back-and-forth between declaratory, Wilsonian traditions of self-determination and de facto claims for their own spheres. The EU's offer to Ukraine in 2013 of a trading Association Agreement, with Washington's backing, constituted an attempt to enlarge a Euro-Atlantic sphere, both commercial and military. The Agreement contained clauses tying Ukraine to Western military and security policy, committing Ukraine to 'promote gradual convergence in the area of foreign and security policy with the aim of Ukraine's ever-deeper involvement in the European security area'. It provides for 'increasing the participation of Ukraine in EU-led civilian and military crisis management operations' and exploring the potential of military-technological cooperation.[58] Whatever the intent, Russia perceived the process as expansion against its vital interests. EU enlargement with the promise of an extended security perimeter looked to Moscow like geopolitics and an advancing sphere. This was especially so given the wider context of the Bucharest Declaration promise of eventual NATO enlargement into Ukraine and Georgia. Russian security elites feared Western expansion would dangerously convert a buffer state, and a historically vital territory, into a hostile client state, bringing potential adversaries into further proximity. In particular, Moscow feared losing its naval base in Sevastopol and its ability to project power in the Black Sea and the Mediterranean.[59] A reactive Putin improvised with subterfuge and armed proxies, and bit off the Crimea. After a US-backed protest movement – the Maidan revolution – forcibly overthrew the pro-Russian government in Kiev, Putin then supported a sustained insurgency in Ukraine against the new, Westward-leaning government. Assumptions that Russia must realize the West's benign motives, or that the EU does not 'do geopolitics', left Western officials shocked at Moscow's retaliation.

Traditionalists may resist the claim that this counts as a sphere, countering that it was merely the offer of a voluntary integration, allowing a country to enter a prosperous zone of democratic capitalism. Spheres do not have to be imposed, however. Cuba's attempt to join and enlarge the Soviet sphere, after the revolution of 1959, was encouraged but not imposed by Moscow, just as NATO was created partly by the demand of European states as an 'empire by invitation'. And although it does not always admit it, Washington itself insists on a sphere of influence. It does so in Latin America and its Western hemisphere, where it intervened militarily in 1965 in the Dominican Republic, in Grenada (1983) and Panama (1988), and in 1994–5 in Haiti. US leaders looked on sympathetically as its ally, France, repeatedly intervened in its former colonial territories in Africa. It maintains, too, a historical prohibition against outside powers interceding in its sphere. If, say, Mexico or Canada were to test this sphere by hosting Chinese or Russian military forces, or joining the Shanghai Cooperation Council, or if another great power formed alliances in the Caribbean, the USA would not react as though 'spheres of influence' were illegitimate. This is reaffirmed by the fact that hawkish primacists who exercise influence in US government explicitly insist on American exclusivity in its own hemisphere. Jealous of a Russian presence in Venezuela, National Security Advisor John Bolton affirmed that 'the Monroe Doctrine is alive and well', refusing to rule out the 'Roosevelt Corollary' of US military intervention.[60]

In the wake of 9/11, the USA effectively claimed the world as its sphere. Since terrorists could now strike from anywhere, the super-power arrogated to itself a 'hunter's licence'. This was the prerogative of pursuing, capturing or killing them, without regard for sovereignty if necessary, with 'the right to dispense with all the restraints of international law'.[61] With its self-awarded free hand abroad, the USA adopted expansive war powers, resorted to covert 'black sites', renditions of suspects without trial, and an ongoing campaign of extrajudicial assassinations, at times without the consent of host countries. After a UN special rapporteur suggested in 2013 that the Obama administration's drone bombings were possibly illegal, the White House boycotted inquiries of the UN Human Rights Council.[62] Creative legal bases for such action could be found. Pakistan, a site of frequent drone attacks, never formally consented to them and officially opposed them. It cleared airspace for drones and left them unmolested, for fear of retaliation. Washington interpreted its passivity as consent. A practice of 'coerced consent' arose, probably illegal.[63] The wording of the 9/11 Commission effectively declared that the real estate of American primacy was infinite. As globalization had shrunk the distinction between terrorism 'over there' and 'over here', 'the

American homeland is the planet'.[64] Washington could kill from the sky at its own discretion.

America's claim to an exclusive, planetary sphere reflected the imbalance of power of unipolarity. At other times, to prevent unwanted conflicts, Washington willingly entertained the proposition of mutually tolerant spheres. At the order's birth, Presidents Roosevelt and Truman in practice, and in private, in turn accepted the principle. Roosevelt's Four Powers would 'police' their respective domains. The Yalta and Potsdam summits in 1945 recognized de facto spheres while publicly denouncing the principle, just as the USA accepted the 'percentages agreement' over Eastern European states negotiated by Churchill and Stalin in Moscow in October 1944. The Red Army's presence in conquered territories made division a fact, which could only be overturned by going to war. After earlier belligerent warnings, the USA at Potsdam in July 1945 became passive in the face of Soviet broken promises about free elections in occupied Eastern Europe. By late 1945, the US government was no longer interested in the internal politics of Poland, coming to accept it 'in fact, if not in word, as an integral part of the Soviet sphere of influence'. In practice, the entire region had by December 1945 been accepted as an area where the Soviets 'would run the show'.[65] Secretary of State James Byrnes expected the Soviets to accept that Western powers would hold sway in the vital areas of Western Europe, Japan, the Mediterranean and the Middle East, in exchange for acceptance of Soviet dominance in Eastern Europe. All this was at odds with the Wilsonian tradition and American formal statements, so 'for that reason, a certain amount of discretion was always necessary'. The new president, Harry Truman, believed that a negotiated pulling apart would be necessary to avoid collision. As he conceded, and as was noted by Secretary of Defense James Forrestal, 'We shall have a Slav Europe for a long time to come.

I don't think it is so bad.'[66] This private remark was later deleted from Forrestal's published diaries.

The notion of spheres of influence was accepted by a number of presidents during the course of the Cold War. At a meeting in Paris on 4 June 1961, President John F. Kennedy expressed hope for a territorial settlement with Soviet leader Nikita Khrushchev, saying that the US government did not 'wish to act in a way that would deprive the Soviet Union of its ties to Eastern Europe', in exchange for the status quo in a divided Berlin, a statement that was then deleted from the declassified version of the document.[67] In an interview with the Soviet newspaper *Izvestia* in January 1962, Kennedy indicated that as the USA had not intervened in Hungary in the 1956 uprising, it should have a free hand in Cuba. This principle emerged from dangerous test cases, from the suppression of revolt in Hungary that the USA had initially supported in 1956, to the naval blockade of Cuba where the Soviet Union was installing medium-range ballistic missiles in 1962. From these episodes, stable mutual expectations formed. Other Cold War US presidents intervened more subversively in the Soviet orbit, only then to pull back and accept that it was more prudent if not to recognize spheres, at least to tolerate them by limiting interference. This was the case for Dwight Eisenhower after the crushing of the Hungary uprising in 1956 and Ronald Reagan during and after the Polish uprising of 1982. For much of the Cold War, Washington tacitly accepted the Soviet sphere in Eastern Europe just as the Soviets did in reverse in the Caribbean, at least to the extent of mutual restraints on excessive interference beyond the mutual propaganda war. The concept was used effectively to de-escalate tensions. The signing of the Helsinki Final Act in 1975 had mixed results, but it effectively recognized a Soviet predominance in Eastern Europe. The principle of parity guided periodic returns to détente between the superpowers.

None of this precluded proxy competition in other battlegrounds. Those in favour of the situation view the major military conflicts of the post-war period largely as sideshows, footnoted as the 'weaker, less developed and peripheral states',[68] separate acts that can be set aside from the overall story. This is a problem, because the order exerted and defined itself just as much in the shadows and at the outer edges. To preserve or advance order, the USA projected itself deliberately and forcefully into the weaker, less developed areas so as to shape the system as a whole. It is to war itself that we now turn.

Wars for Peace

Orders are warlike things. Even pacification for the common good involves much fighting. An increase in power made the USA more prone to military activity. The first two decades of the unipolar *Pax Americana* after 1989, which made up less than 10 per cent of America's history, generated 25 per cent of the nation's total time in armed conflict. That period is more bellicose by an order of magnitude than the preceding eras of bipolarity and multipolarity, in terms of frequency if not intensity.[69] Likewise, while the USA launched 46 military interventions during the Cold War, that number jumped to 188 in the 1992–2017 period. Those who defend hegemony do not deny the existence of fighting. But they do claim that their order is less lethal than the chaos they hold at bay. Defenders of the *Pax Americana* contend that their order should be judged by history's standard. The US world order is more benign than those of the Romans, Mongols, Ottomans, Europeans, Nazis, Japanese or Soviets. The issue, however, is not whether the *Pax Americana* was more liberal than its predecessors – it clearly was – but whether calling it 'liberal' adequately describes its working, and whether in fact it works. For America's busy and bellicose recent decades have not been an era of foreign policy triumph. The issue is increasingly urgent. For the republic to be secure, must it achieve unchallengeable armed supremacy and sole leadership over the earth? Liberal order visions have an uneasy relationship with war and 'hard power'. Its proponents do not deny, in fact they affirm, that the American superpower upheld peace partly through preponderance, or overwhelming military strength and its wise deployment. However, they emphasize the non-bloody uses of force and its pacifying and democratizing effects. Uses of force appear, albeit in largely clinical terms. In the foreground, American military pre-eminence deterred adversaries, reassured and united allies, dampened spirals of alarm, and prevented conflict. This makes them most at home, intellectually, in continental Europe, the strongest case study for highlighting the consensual, attractive quality of American hegemony. The actual exercise of force, the process of war and the threat of it, retreats to the background. As one account claims:

The system established after 1945 was built on US power. But it endured and, after the end of the cold war, expanded because US leadership was embedded in multilateral rules and institutions. Everyone had a stake. Washington sometimes over-reached – in Vietnam or with the invasion of Iraq. By history's standards, however, the *Pax Americana* was essentially benign, resting as much on the force of example as military might.[70]

Such rhetoric, suggesting a benign essence, brushes off disastrous and lengthy wars as episodic lapses, distances hegemony from violence and rule-breaking, deflects scrutiny and sidelines the exercise of military power that was a major aspect of world-ordering.

Some credit the USA with creating an unprecedented level of relative peace across the world. But these optimistic assessments exaggerate the decline in war. They measure the amount of war by counting the dead. As Tanisha Fazal has shown, this is misleading, as it overlooks one of the most fundamental changes in modern war, that societies are better at keeping injured combatants alive.[71] A significant shift during the life of the *Pax Americana* was the advancement of battlefield medicine, which dramatically shifted killed-to-wounded ratios. Wars that once upon a time would meet the minimum threshold for inclusion in datasets are now omitted. The difference in counting method alters the estimate of war's incidence dramatically. Exclusive focus on battle fatalities suggests a 50 per cent decrease in the incidence of armed conflict since 1946. Once non-fatal casualties are priced into the equation, that reduction falls to less than 20 per cent, a less statistically significant trend. Especially now, it is wrong to conflate war's frequency with its lethality. A narrow focus on counting the dead leads, in turn, to a neglect of the costs of war for itself, given the large number of physically and psychically wounded survivors, and the deaths that injuries can lead to, only later and far from the front.

The USA successfully reduced levels of strife in other ways, though not through mechanisms of liberal order. Consider one of the most far-reaching post-war diplomatic breakthroughs that made Asia more peaceful: the settlement between President Nixon and Chairman Mao in 1972. Mao agreed to cease sponsoring revolutions against American interests throughout the region, effectively acknowledging America's primacy in Asia and reducing threats to US interests. In return, the USA formally recognized communist China, one of the world's most internally repressive states. It agreed to the 'one China' policy, a blow to the cause of Taiwanese independence. In fact, Nixon agreed to sacrifice Taiwan later as an unimportant commitment. It abandoned

Tibet's independence movement. The rapprochement with China was set up via a secret channel to the country's leadership through an intermediary, Pakistani President Yahya Khan. In turn, Washington kept Khan's cooperative back channel open by maintaining a strict silence during the cancellation of a free election and the Bangladesh genocide of 1971, despite the pleas of the US ambassador's 'Blood Telegram', which documented the slaughter that killed hundreds of thousands and displaced millions. America purchased détente with a totalitarian regime at a heavy price.[72]

These *Realpolitik* bargains are different from the more ambitious claim, that US dominance suppressed the belligerence of others through its preponderance of power, the protection and reassurance it provided, the deterrence it exercised and the general promotion of humanitarian norms. Some of this is true for Northern zones like Europe, many of whose states under NATO's protective umbrella consciously created an anti-militarist culture. The 'peaceful' Northern states, though, enjoy peace locally while still being implicated in large-scale violence elsewhere. They export violence to the more war-torn Southern states in other ways: through a lucrative trade in arms and expertise, by supporting and arming proxies in civil wars, and through use of standoff methods such as airstrikes that transfer the burden of risk onto faraway civilian populations. Counter-arguments, that this overall reduces more than enlarges the totality of violence by strengthening client states or suppressing terrorist organizations, still involve a calculus of illiberal means for liberal ends.

Unprecedented levels of peace do not describe the experience of large parts of Africa. Even by history's bleak standards, Africa's multisided 'great war' in and through the Democratic Republic of Congo between 1998 and 2001 was an abnormal spike in concentrated violence, inflicting a total of between two and five million deaths in five years.[73] Neither can this be regarded as a separate, indigenous struggle, given Western states' involvement in the militarization of Africa, the large economy in arms transfers and military training. The US government claimed that such programmes were intended to promote order, by enhancing peacekeeping and professionalism. 'Whatever their intention', the World Policy Institute found in 2000, 'skills and equipment provided by the US have strengthened the military capabilities of combatants involved in some of Africa's most violent and intractable conflicts.'[74] Given the extent to which Western development of other countries is emphasized, it is hard to exclude these elements from the order's history.

The history of liberal order is summarized as being one of relative tranquillity and abundance. The 'world order', it is asserted, 'worked for most of the world, delivering stability, prosperity and peace. There have been violent conflicts at the peripheries, but only rarely between major powers.'[75] The map shown in Figure 2 demonstrates that the periphery was wide and bloody.[76]

The post-war order featured intense wars, especially in Asia. Including a large theatre of war spanning the 'rimland', or southern Asia, from the Middle East and Central Asia to the Manchurian Plain and Indochina, perhaps fourteen million perished in armed conflicts since 1945.[77] To treat this belt of territory, these bloodlands, as a minority and peripheral concern is not only complacent, over-privileging continental Europe and Northeast Asia; it wrongly positions those conflicts as sideshows. In fact, major powers exported money, guns and their own intrigues and firepower to the peripheries in order to shape core interests. Therefore, the deaths and maiming of millions were part of the act of ordering, intended to shape the balance of power in the world's designated 'core'.

Containment of communism, and the counter-attempt to break

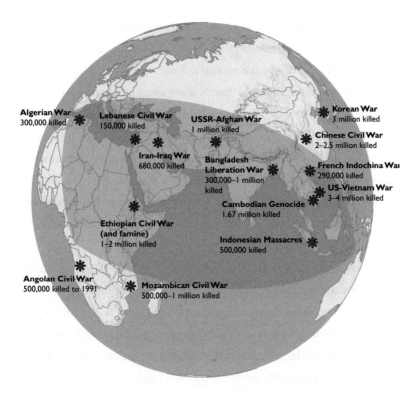

Figure 2 Superpower-fuelled conflicts of the Cold War in the Eastern hemisphere and the quadrilateral in which George Orwell predicted the war's battles would take place.

Source: Reproduced with permission from Daniel Immerwahr, with information drawn from Paul Chamberlin, *The Cold War's Killing Fields: Rethinking the Long Peace* (New York: Harper Collins, 2018); Alex de Waal and Bridget Conley-Zilkic, *Mass Atrocity Endings*, at https://sites.tufts.edu/ atrocityendings/; Bethany Lacina and Nils Petter Gleditsch, 'Monitoring Trends in Global Combat: A New Dataset of Battle Deaths', *European Journal of Population* 21:2-3 (2005), pp. 145-166.

out of the containing ring, was a brutal affair. To defend authoritarian regimes from ruthless communist adversaries, the USA waged wars that laid waste to large parts of the Korean peninsula and, later, Vietnam, Cambodia and Laos. The Korean War (1950-3) was a devastating conflict. At a conservative estimate, the US military killed one million Koreans, civilians and soldiers and 400,000 Chinese combatants.[78] For Washington, aligned with the 'volatile, autocratic' President Syngman Rhee of South Korea, at stake was America's reputation. Korea was 'a symbol [of the] strength and determination of [the] West', especially for 'countries adjacent to [the] Soviet orbit'.[79] As for Vietnam (1965–72), estimates of casualties are approximately one million communist combatants and 365,000 civilians. US firepower/punishment strategies and mass bombardment did not inflict all the casualties, of course; their opponents were also brutal and determined. But given the tonnage of ordnance dropped, and other measures such as the thirteen million gallons of Agent Orange chemical defoliant, the Americans must still have inflicted a sizeable share. That war spread also to Laos and Cambodia in bombardment to interdict reinforcements and supply, with casualties inflicted by US bombing conservatively estimated at 200,000, including 100,000 killed, while displacing approximately two million souls.

Vietnam is central to the argument. That war was one of the most significant attempts at world-ordering undertaken by an American government. The architects of the conflict sincerely believed it was a necessary act in protecting the US-led free world.[80] In the crucial 1964–5 internal debate about the escalation of US ground commitment to support the South Vietnamese regime, planners inside the Johnson administration were aware that prevailing over communist insurgents in Vietnam would be complex and difficult.[81] They believed the campaign was still worth it, to uphold many of the same imperatives espoused by believers of today's liberal order, to prevent destabilizing chain reactions from undermining the alliance and commercial system. Hostile political waves, they feared, could become tsunamis that could undermine the free world, if not as regional dominoes, then as global revolutionary waves. If the USA failed to project credible resolve to an ally on the periphery, then it would undermine the faith of allies in Europe and Asia, leading potentially to West Germany or Japan hedging or defecting to the Soviet sphere. Holding the line in Vietnam would buy time and breathing space for American allies and clients to shore up their defences. According to presidential advisor John McNaughton in a memo of 25 March 1965, US policy in Indochina was '70% – To avoid a humiliating defeat (to our reputation as a guarantor)/20% – To keep South Vietnam (and the adjacent territory) from Chinese hands/10% – To permit the people of South Vietnam to enjoy a better, freer way of life.'[82]

The doctrine of 'credibility', in which the integrity of America's alliance system rested on its international stature, defined how the domino doctrine was conceived. Similar fears animated President John Kennedy, who in November 1961 feared that negotiating over Vietnam would trigger a 'major crisis of nerve' throughout Southeast Asia. The Rusk–McNamara report of that month warned that the loss of Vietnam would 'undermine the credibility of American commitments elsewhere'. Later apologias for the Vietnam commitment, by National Security Advisors Walt Rostow and McGeorge Bundy, maintained that it prevented wider regional domino effects, buying time for Association of Southeast Asian Nations (ASEAN) states to grow their economies. In 1969, National Security Advisor Henry Kissinger reasoned that at stake in Vietnam was 'confidence in American promises. However fashionable it is to ridicule the terms "credibility" or "prestige", they are not empty phrases; other nations can gear their actions to ours only if they can count on our steadiness.'[83] The tonnage of US bombing in Vietnam was triple that of the Second World War. Concentration of such violence in one theatre, the rationale went, would limit its spread into others. They hoped illiberal means, or unremitting bombardment and secrecy, would serve ultimately liberal ends, the defeat of totalitarian communism.

The Iraq war, too, was an effort to reorder the world. Its makers aimed to spread capitalist democracy on their terms, and to demonstrate strength. In 1997, a group of hawkish intellectuals, the Project for a New American Century (PNAC), had urged the USA to 'accept responsibility for America's unique role in preserving and extending an international order',[84] and adopt 'military strength and moral clarity', urging President Bill Clinton to remove the despot Saddam Hussein from power. They got their way in 2003. A longstanding duel with a defiant regime in the Persian Gulf finally came to a head. The US-led invasion of Iraq in March 2003, its architects hoped, would not only remove a growing perceived threat, a rogue regime in Baghdad and its arsenal of dangerous weapons; it would enhance international order, in different but complementary ways.[85] The 9/11 terrorist attacks, like earlier security crises, prompted a renewed push for transformational war. If ordering involves the attempt at creation out of the wreckage of destruction, policymakers sensed such an occasion from the slaughter of civilians on American soil on 9/11. Emboldened by apparent success in Afghanistan, and on the back of a decade of successful minor wars, policymakers sensed a world-historical drama. 'Let us reorder the world', declared British Prime Minister Tony Blair in October 2001, a call that resonated in the USA. President George W. Bush identified an 'opportunity to achieve big goals', leading to 'world peace'. National Security Advisor Condoleezza Rice argued that 'this period is analogous to 1945 to 1947', an occasion to define and recast world order as the tectonic plates of world politics shifted.[86] If Afghanistan was not enough, overthrowing Saddam Hussein's regime in Baghdad was a necessary further measure, going beyond the arid hinterlands of Central Asia and driving on to the more strategically consequential, oil-rich Greater Middle East. Toppling Saddam Hussein's tyrannical Ba'ath regime would be a decisive step in regional transformation like the large-scale, mid-twentieth-century projects of transforming defeated states into beacons of liberty. As one official remarked, 'the road to the entire Middle East goes through Baghdad'.[87]

Advocates of invading Iraq conceived it as a 'world-ordering' war in two distinct respects, one romantically idealist, one a hard-nosed form of power-seeking. For hawkish liberal internationalists, it was a bid to reorder the region positively, on moral and strategic grounds: 'to liberate the Iraqi people from their dungeon' and to establish 'a beachhead of Arab democracy', for 'Iraq as a secular democracy with equal rights for all of its citizens'.[88] Toppling one rogue regime at the heart of the Middle East would begin a benign domino wave of reform. A Pentagon paper of 2003 suggested that, given Iraq's 'size, capabilities and resources', becoming a democracy would exert 'historic' impact 'in the region and the world'.[89] Paul Wolfowitz, hawkish democratic idealist, in late November 2001 oversaw the influential advisory paper 'Delta of Terrorism', the clandestine manifesto of a group of intellectuals, which anticipated a two-generation war with radical Islam, calling for regime change in Iraq to begin the transformation of the Middle East out of 'malignancy', to reverse the 'stagnation' that produced 'radicalism and breeds terrorism'.[90] For the more narrowly nationalistic, the war would send a powerful signal of American resolve to competitors and allies alike, restoring generalized deterrence after the 9/11 attacks revealed the superpower's vulnerability. A prison-yard rationale took hold, that the USA should from time to time throttle a weak country, to demonstrate its steel. This found advocates from Vice-President Dick Cheney to former foreign secretary Henry Kissinger, to columnist Thomas Friedman. The presumptions that came with power, that the

USA has a unique, hegemonic purpose to remake regions, created a dangerous confidence. 'Iraq can't resist us', one enthusiast declared.[91] And so, Baghdad fell. America's new regency in Iraq then threw up a contradiction: the liberator intended to implant market democracy but on its terms, freeing the Iraqis to conform with the occupier's preferences. This dynamic was present in the trial of the overthrown ruler, Saddam Hussein, the classic process by which the old order yields to the new. Iraqi courts prosecuted Saddam but only for historic offences in which the USA and the UK could not be implicated. A liberated order then created winners and losers, leading to conflict. The new provisional authority by fiat instituted capitalist transformation on its terms, treating the country as a laboratory for doctrinaire economics, through the privatization of public enterprises, the removal of trade barriers, the opening of Iraq's banks to foreign control and the elimination of nearly all trade barriers. Free markets and free elections to frightened locals looked like dangerously competitive, winner-takes-all affairs, and bred disorder. The American proconsul, Paul Bremer III, oversaw a destructive programme of de-Baathification and the summary mass dismissal of people from the civil service and army, which alienated and radicalized Sunni Iraqis. Yet the sacking of the old order was also the demand of Shia and Kurdish parties, wary that the foreigners could reinstall an oppressive client regime like Saddam Hussein. While Bush and his cabinet disavowed empire, growing violence demanded that US military commanders co-govern the country, with the new democracy's sovereignty circumscribed. As the undersecretary of state for political affairs assured a congressional hearing in April 2002, 'we would do our very best to consult with interim government', but 'American commanders would still have the right, and the power, and the obligation to decide on the appropriate role for their troops'.[92]

Washington imposed itself on Iraqi politics, forcing the resignation of elected Prime Minister Ibrahim al-Jaafari in May 2007, thanks to minority opposition and the disfavour of President Bush. With growing post-invasion strife in Iraq, worsening international terrorism and counterbalancing by spoilers such as Iran and Syria, and the election of anti-American candidates from Gaza to Iran, the Bush administration did not rescind but increased its declared aims – no less than the liberation of the 'Greater Middle East'. Resistance in the form of insurgency attracted counterinsurgency, with assorted illiberal practices in the form of surveillance, curfews, segregation, bribery, censorship, suppression, imprisonment and torture. Once again, contradictory drivers came together, the liberal and the imperial, the causes of liberation and domination. Once again, the results surprised the architects. The Iraq adventure turned out to be America's most disastrous war since Vietnam, an economic disaster that wasted trillions of dollars, a geopolitical disaster that bred looting, civil war, exodus, Iranian empowerment and Islamist expansion, a moral disaster of torture and abuse, and a constitutional disaster of unchecked executive power.

The history of ordering must accommodate the rougher acts done in its name, and their darker logic, rather than artificially excise them. As it evolved, the order defined itself by fighting to establish credibility and bombing to save face. Expeditions like wars in Vietnam and Iraq were intended by decision-makers to contribute to world-ordering. They were not sideshows. They consumed large amounts of time, energy, and mental and material effort in the White House, the State Department, the Department of Defense and within military commands. They were intended to have system-wide effects, to avoid dangerous humiliation, and to establish deterrence as a senior ally and security guarantor. Small wars, often at the sidelines of the orthodox story, were from the outset loaded with central significance. They drew on a similar rationale that interventionists use today, that perceived weakness in one peripheral crisis threatens to erode the global system. The USA has found other ways, and technologies, to maintain continuous military activity to tame the world back into order. Permanent war has now become almost institutionalized. In the words of US Air Force General Mike Holmes, the future is one of 'infinite war: long-time competition against peer adversaries'.[93] With the casual acceptance of the gardener, the Secretary of State for Defense describes bombing Islamists in Libya as 'mowing the lawn'.[94] Now in eighty countries and on six continents, American forces are deployed in the service of counterterrorism. Activists urge Washington to shoulder missions with objectives so ambitious and remote as to have no limit. The 'enduring defeat' of the Islamic State, members of the US Syria Study Group advise, requires the creation of 'inclusive, responsive, and legitimate governance in the areas it once controlled'.[95] Given the depth of their sectarian divides and the wider cold war between Saudi and Iranian forces, we will be waiting some time. Thus an order famously founded, in part, to end the 'scourge of war' ended up perpetuating it.

In parts of the world, such as the Afghanistan–Pakistan border, Somalia or Yemen, the liberal order is experienced as a lethal empire of drones. One pioneer of this expanded drone programme was former Director of the CIA, David Petraeus, who advocated and implemented a campaign of 'signature' drone strikes, whereby the assailant knowingly targets a group gathering – at funerals for an al Qaeda member, for instance – because of their suspicious behaviour and association, rather than through verified identification of the presence of individual persons. Such strikes, therefore, can also target non-combatants and the innocent.[96] So a senior advocate of liberal order can also advocate measures that risk 'crowd killing'. No doubt Petraeus and his peers regard themselves as guarding Americans while they sleep, and trafficking with lesser evils to keep greater ones at bay. Consider, though, the reasoning that upholding the order requires regularized assassination from a remove, almost as a routinized form of security-seeking, that seeks to transfer all risk onto foreign populations, and in ways that the USA would not tolerate from other states. If not empire, what is it? And by becoming imperial, power projection does not necessarily promote the image of a liberal West. In the words of one former US NATO ambassador, the expanded use of drones readily 'allows our opponents to cast our country as a distant, high-tech, amoral purveyor of death'.[97]

Even as they claim that the liberal order generated the 'long peace' between major powers and deserves credit for the unprecedented fall in armed conflict, many of its proponents call for more and even permanent war. There remains a powerful pathology not to let go of campaigns that were supposed to be limited in aim and duration, indeed to expand them. Even General David Petraeus, advocate of liberal order, whose signature question as commander in Iraq was 'tell me how this ends', now calls for a 'generational struggle' against Islamist militancy in the Greater Middle East.[98] That would at minimum be another thirty years of war on a similar scale. Petraeus has even called for a longer commitment on the time scale, likening it to the US–South Korea alliance, one that has lasted two generations. The difficulty with that analogy is that the US presence in Afghanistan, unlike South Korea, is forcefully resisted. Petraeus is effectively proposing a semi-permanent commitment in an ongoing war in Afghanistan that, at the time of writing, has killed 2,300 US personnel and wounded more than 20,000.

When these campaigns falter, some of those who identify with liberalism shift the blame onto the domestic audience. With the whole effort in Afghanistan under strain, pro-war visionaries turn the blame onto domestic critics. It is not the wars, but scepticism towards those wars, that allegedly marks the populace's intellectual and moral failure. Former National Security Advisor H. R. McMaster, who praised the post-war international order at the Munich conference of 2018, laments that opposition to permanent war flows not from the pursuit of unachievable goals against a determined enemy to counter inflated threats, but from defeatism at home. In Afghanistan, though, McMaster blamed fellow citizens for their defeatist storytelling. 'A young student stood up and said "all I've known my whole life is war"', McMaster said. 'Now, he's never been to war, but he's been subjected, I think, to this narrative of war-weariness.'[99] McMaster's militarism is revealed in the imputation that only those who have been to war can agonize over its costs.

Similarly, an advocate of the *Pax Americana*, academic and former National Security Council official Paul Miller, who once argued for expansive measures to spread liberal order, now believes that the culprits for failure are defeatists at home.[100] The USA must remain committed in Afghanistan 'to sustain an indefinite counterterrorism presence in South Asia to kill or capture militant leaders while avoiding a Taliban takeover in Afghanistan, nothing more'. The first objective, by being 'indefinite', lacks any limitation in time or conditions. And given the resilience and deep ethnic and political roots of the Taliban, the second one stretches at least decades into the future. It could also be self-perpetuating, given that the very force of Islamist militancy feeds on a foreign armed presence. Not only does this promise permanent war, but permanent war becomes the objective of the campaign, as well as the means. Liberal order in this context becomes upholding liberal values through continual armed pacification of the frontier, permanent war for permanent peace.

From the beginning, some have warned that US objectives in Afghanistan were hard to achieve, the costs too high and the stakes too limited. The problems of the Afghan–Pakistan theatre were wildly complex, and not even American power could extinguish them at affordable cost. The interests of the kleptocratic host government and those of the USA were misaligned. As with Vietnam, it was the attitudes of locals, the reluctance of the population to fight for a kleptocratic regime, not the political will of Americans at home, that would be decisive. External sources of support, of money and guns and sanctuary, made it hard to out-govern the insurgency. To battle the Taliban was to fight a proxy war against part of the Pakistani security state. Striking into Afghanistan might suppress terrorist capability, but at the price of energizing Islamist radicalization. In turn, it meant entanglement in a deeper geopolitical struggle across South Asia. Besides, terrorist networks could be disrupted and contained from a remove, as the USA does elsewhere, without permanent large-scale garrisons. When these warnings proved accurate, there was nothing for it but to blame those who had predicted them, and to turn the failure into a drama about American civic virtue, rather than to scrutinize the inherent problems that attended the adventure in the first place. To enable continuous war for a benign form of politics, for a world order of liberty and democratic openness, its advocates demand in effect that dissidents keep quiet about the prospects of war, the ultimate political act, so that Washington could more easily perpetuate a campaign without end. 'Ordering' the world this way, in the name of liberal values, is revealed for what it is, an illiberal and coercive act.

Looking back, the order's defenders rarely include the campaigns they supported in the indictment of what went wrong. They place the lion's share of blame for today's problems not in the misapplication of power in hubristic adventures, but in failures amongst other Americans to live up to their historic mission, whether misguided voters or policy-makers. Robert Lieber, for instance, finds that the USA's main error was 'retreat',[101] having favoured the invasion of Iraq, rebuking alternatives of containment. He forecast that toppling Saddam Hussein would deal a 'serious blow' to anti-Israel rejectionists, strengthen Arab reformers and 'send a graphic warning to the remaining states that support terrorism'. As realists warned, war made terrorism worse and empowered Iran.[102] It prompted rather than discouraged states to sponsor terrorism, like Basher Al Assad's Syria, directing jihadi militants into Iraq to conduct brutal campaigns. It brought a Palestinian state no closer. By 2004, Lieber found that debate suffered from excessive focus on the Iraq war, the same country he once claimed was critical to 'the vital interests of the United States'.

Looking away from Iraq, Lieber discovered that the main fault for the misdirection of foreign policy lies with weak executive policy, and the errors of realist intellectuals, for conducting a retreat from the *Pax Americana*. In the same year he accused Washington of 'retreat', the USA dropped 26,171 bombs on seven countries, quadrupled funding for the European Reassurance Initiative to 'reassure allies of the US commitment to their security and territorial integrity as members of the NATO Alliance', imposed sanctions on Russia, whom it had suspended from the G8, conducted the largest military exercises to date in South Korea, launched Freedom of Navigation operations to counter Beijing's expansion in the South China Sea, and maintained 30,000 troops in the Middle East. The charge that Washington is abandoning a noble internationalist past is less an observation than a political predisposition, substantively shallow yet unrelenting.

So the faith that one embodies a 'liberal order' is pernicious. It enables a country on a permanent war footing to regard itself as being essentially peaceful. In turn, this creates a warrant for constant military exertion. As Kori Schake claims, the wars democracies fight 'are about enlarging the perimeter of security and prosperity, expanding and consolidating the liberal order'.[103] We may doubt this. When classical Athens, nineteenth-century France or modern India or Israel drew their swords, they had other things on their mind than the intent to bring liberalism to others. Historically, democracies can also project force as empires. Forgetting the imperial pasts – and present – of democracies is one quirk of liberal order visions. But even if Schake is correct about a uniform set of motives, the process of war is a deeply illiberal one. The results of these armed projects to enlarge the frontier of freedom have been mixed, both abroad and at home. Confidence that one's own motives are essentially peaceful enables a belligerence that doesn't know itself.

Distrusting the Order

Supporters of the liberal order present it as universally beneficial. It offers, supposedly, a harmony of interests, where what is good for America is good for the world. E. H. Carr critiqued this fallacy, as a 'moral device invoked, in perfect sincerity, by privileged groups in order to justify and maintain their dominant position'.[104] Even if it were true, it is hard for a hegemon to persuade rivals that its intentions are benign. And even if it were possible to do so, it would be hard to reassure them that those intentions would remain benign. In other words, the proposition of harmony under US leadership underestimates the potency of anarchy. In a world without a supreme authority to keep the peace, there are powerful incentives not to take a superpower's word on trust, especially if that power continuously expands its reach and sphere, and especially if that power promotes political change in its adversaries' capital cities.

In the case of America, order-building on the hegemon's terms rests partly on the pursuit of armed supremacy, of an outsized, globe-girdling military preponderance. To rivals, this looks too much like a dangerous accumulation of power. Its demands for compliance in the realms of trade, human rights or proliferation look like a self-interested grab for power, and an attempt to subvert regional orders. Ironically, it makes America appear not as the stabilizing status quo power, but as a destabilizing revisionist. Support for democracy appears as an ideological weapon. Commitments to allies look like a calculated effort to contain adversaries. The promotion of democracy and the pursuit of hegemony are too coiled to distinguish. What hegemons regard as eternal, transcendent moral values, justice and law, look to adversaries like interests dressed up in a convenient language of virtue and imbued with moral universalism, to license the dominant power to make, remake and impose its own order at will. It is difficult to make rivals accept one's good intentions. This is one reason for the intensifying security competitions between the US and Eurasian heavyweights.

The behaviour of both China and Russia is not reducible simply to a reaction to American overreach. Both jealously pursue dominance in their backyards. Both are consolidating repressive states of surveillance and terror. Both are guilty of intransigence and thuggery. Both only began their current campaigns to counterbalance American power when they believed they had grown wealthy and powerful enough, China in its economic transformation and Russia in the temporary oil price surge. There is, though, also a strongly reactive element to their external behaviour. Both see themselves not as tearing up the order wholesale, but as asserting some of the order's foundational, Westphalian principles against American revisionism. Those include the primacy of states and the principle of non-interference in domestic affairs, even if they care more for the application of those principles to themselves. The upending of those principles, they believe, is directed at them, as an effort to change their political systems.[105] Such fears are conditioned by memories of external powers preying upon and humiliating them. This helps explain why intensive diplomatic attempts by Washington, in the form of a 'dialogue' or 'reset', or outreach via 'digital diplomacy', to communicate benign intent have not prevented relations from deteriorating.

The USA has consistently pursued primacy in Asia, to be the region's unrivalled hegemon, even as Americans debate what mix of tactics is optimal. For Beijing, the USA has always been seen as seeking dominance.[106] While the Chinese state was (until recently) cautious in its public pronouncements, its perceptions can be divined from unofficial but tolerated internal writings, which for decades have referred to the USA as the 'strong enemy'. This did not drive China immediately to begin overt counterbalancing acts while it was relatively weak. It chose instead to 'hide and bide' until its exponential economic growth enabled it to become a competitor. But at no point did Beijing regard American behaviour as part of a benign project to promote the harmony of interests. According to an army textbook of 2006, America 'ignores the rules of international relations . . . using gunboat diplomacy and relying on its own military power to serve as the world policeman, making up all kinds of rationales and excuses to push forward its hegemonic power politics all over the world'. Memories of the century of humiliation at the hands of external imperial powers provide good fodder for national propaganda, yet also feed real fears. Once the world became unipolar and the USA, unfettered by strong peer competitors, undertook military campaigns from the Balkans to the Middle East to Africa, China watched with increasing alarm.

Washington has repeatedly assured China of its peaceful intentions for a mutually prosperous regional order. This has not stopped China from paying attention to America's actions and capabilities. Between 1950 and 1972, China was always mindful of US hostility, when Washington was pressing allies to withhold diplomatic recognition, making nuclear threats, imposing a trade embargo, and building up allies in Taiwan and Japan. Even the 1972 settlement, the Shanghai Communiqué, resembled self-interested power maximization, to strengthen anti-Soviet containment and reap the benefits of closer economic ties. In the unipolar world, China again grew concerned at the USA's display of cutting-edge military technology from Gulf War One to Kosovo, its development of a nuclear defence shield, its willingness to over-throw regimes without a UNSC mandate. The bombing of the Chinese embassy in Belgrade in 1999, accidental or not, was perceived as a deliberate signal.

Today, pessimists are predominant amongst Chinese security elites.[107] The USA is deployed around China's coastal periphery with an array of alliances and defence relationships with its Indo-Pacific neighbours. The 'Asia Pivot' resembles encroachment and semi-encirclement. Freedom-of-Navigation Operations resemble anti-Chinese containment. The Chinese regard the USA as a revisionist actor 'that tries to reshape the global environment even further in its favour. They see evidence of this reality everywhere: in the expansion of NATO; the US interventions in Panama, Haiti, Bosnia, and Kosovo; the Gulf War; the war in Afghanistan; and the invasion of Iraq.' America's sponsorship of 'colour' revolutions in Ukraine, Georgia and Kyrgyzstan convinced the Chinese Director of the Foreign Affairs Division in 2005 that the US wanted to 'spread democracy further and turn the whole globe blue'.

Russia, too, distrusts American claims to benign order-building.[108]

The Russian view is probably partly driven by revanchist imperial power ambitions, to rebuild its domination of the 'near abroad'. Russia also sees itself as defensively fending off the expansion of the Euro-Atlantic world into its orbit. It places itself in a state of mobilization, enhancing its readiness to respond to emergencies in an 'arc of crisis' around its borders. Moscow fears that Washington sponsors subversion and colour revolutions along its frontiers and within its capital. Washington has inadvertently encouraged this perception. By militarily positioning itself within striking distance of Russia through a semi-encircling presence, expanding alliances and reviving the pursuit of an antiballistic missile shield, and by establishing a reputation as sponsor of political subversion, Washington looks not like the architect of a mutually beneficial order, but like an overbearing interloper. The war in Iraq that Russia opposed, in particular, persuaded Moscow that the USA was an agent of disorder, needing to be checked. At a joint news conference in July 2006, as Iraq imploded, between President George W. Bush and President Vladimir Putin, Bush spoke of his desire 'to promote institutional change in parts of the world like Iraq, where there's a free press and free religion', hoping that 'Russia would do the same thing'. What looked like liberation to some, looked like chaos to others, as Putin's tart response underlined: 'We certainly would not want to have the same kind of democracy as they have in Iraq.'[109] The toppling of Gaddafi's regime in Libya, after Russia had gone along by abstaining from a resolution that only permitted no-fly zones, then torpedoed any rebuilding of relations.

Before it publicly acknowledged an era of great power competition, Washington's intent was emphatically not to stir up a spiral of conflict with Russia. The competition arose inadvertently. The puzzle for America's Russian experts is that each administration has come into office with a stated commitment to improving relations with its former Cold War adversary, and each has failed in remarkably similar ways. The Bill Clinton years ended with a near-catastrophic standoff over Kosovo, the George W. Bush years with the Russian bombing of Georgia and the Obama years with the Russian annexation of Crimea and the hacking operation to influence the American election.[110]

Russia reacted to US actions, and in a spirit of growing distrust. Before successive rounds of NATO enlargement, the USA made informal promises about refraining from eastward expansion as the Soviet Union collapsed, to persuade it to support German reunification and withdraw, 'while keeping open the possibility of expansion and seeking to maximize US power in post–Cold War Europe'.[111] The USA later breached that agreement. If expansion, in George Kennan's words, excited Russia's 'nationalistic, anti-Western and militaristic tendencies', then both humiliation and distrust increased hostility. Vladimir Putin carped, to public acclaim, that America treated Russia as a 'defeated vassal', not a partner. US decision-makers did not think of themselves as predators suppressing a potential adversary, but as emancipators, extending their order to stabilize a continent while retaining the capacity to contain Russia if needed. A National Security Council assessment indicated in October 1994 that the rationale was primarily 'to project stability eastward', while keeping 'insurance policy/strategic hedge rationale (i.e., neo-containment of Russia) in the background only'.[112] And yet, if the USA wanted harmonious stability, it was strictly on its own terms, effectively asking Russia to trust its intentions despite the growth of its capabilities and despite allegedly breaking its word.

That context made it hard for Michael McFaul, outspoken defender of liberal order, and former Ambassador to Moscow, to cultivate good relations with Russia while encouraging liberal protesters. McFaul's interactions with Russia restage the dilemmas of liberal ordering. In 1996, the Clinton administration interfered in the Russian election to support an embattled and corrupt candidate, Boris Yeltsin, as he ran a campaign of sabotage, misinformation and obstruction against a popular communist opponent. Washington arranged a large IMF loan and proffered expertise to the Yeltsin campaign. Clinton acknowledged privately that Yeltsin was Washington's preferred client because he did want they wanted. 'We keep telling ol' Boris, "OK, now, here's what you've got to do next – here's some more shit for your face".'[113] Its unpalatable choice lay between non-interference in a fair election that would likely elevate a hostile figure, or interference to shore up that client. Yeltsin's success damaged the integrity of the newborn Russian democracy and prepared the ground for Putinism. Despite nodding to this dilemma, that democracy-promotion by foreign powers for historical reasons might look like subversion, Ambassador McFaul courted human rights activists, hosting them at Spaso House in Moscow. This encouraged the perception in Putin's circle that, as a democracy enthusiast, he was fomenting revolution.[114] The regime unleashed a campaign of intimidation against him and his family. McFaul left after two years, and conceded that while he did not go to Moscow to instigate revolution, other administrations had upended regimes from Iran to Serbia, giving Putin's paranoia 'some empirical basis'. A revealing concession.

3

Rough Beast:
How the Order Made Trump

More than any other emerging political force, President Donald Trump drives fears about the end of the liberal order. After all, Trump was the 'wrecking ball' candidate who came to power denouncing the status quo and the Washington priesthood that cherished it. He vowed to 'drain the swamp' of corruption and diminish the foreign policy establishment. He assailed the policies they had championed, pledged to wind down the long failing wars, terminate free-riding alliances and raise up walls – a vast border fortification to curb illegal immigration and tariff walls to reindustrialize the declining American heartland. Both the Donald himself and his political opponents regard him as the order's nemesis. At the same time, Trump's adversaries often shift the blame. The forty-fifth president, they say, is fundamentally a domestic miscreant. They argue that his electoral success was mainly born of parochial forces and circumstances that have little to do with the post-war order. Therefore, the coming of the 'ginger demagogue' does not reflect the order's fallibilities, but shows the dark turn things take when America abandons the order's principles. Therefore, the main task is not to investigate, but to affirm the order, to execrate populism and to exhort Americans to repudiate Trump and the regressive forces he represents.

In their postmortems, when it comes to explaining Trump, the order's admirers often separate the domestic from the international, seeking to minimize blame on established foreign policy or the need to revise it. The order itself, allegedly, is at fault mainly on managerial, implementational or technocratic grounds, for not being executed efficiently or not selling itself properly and making people realize it was good. Straining to exonerate the order, they credit the USA with shaping an 'interdependent global system', only to claim:

> The many problems the Trump administration seeks to remedy are least of all caused by global forces and most of all self-inflicted by domestic politics. The financial crisis had few international sources; inequality is deeply related to tax and fiscal policy in the US and also technological change; the Iraq war was one of choice.[1]

Even accounts of liberal order that stress the environment and climate crisis and the need to lower humanity's carbon footprint speak of these issues as though the order and its intense economic activity are hardly implicated in them. Speaking recently before the conclave of the Council on Foreign Relations, the Council of Councils, the Lowy Institute's Michael Fullilove praised the post-war American order for delivering 'prosperity' and peace, called on Washington to restore it, rather than revise it, while urging its stakeholders to sign the Paris climate accord given that a million species are at risk of extinction.[2] Only the liberal order, it seems, provides the antidote to crises that arose on its own watch.

The attraction of such 'alibis' is clear. Given that Trump's presidency – as well as wider problems – was born mainly of contingent forces and a toxic ideology at odds with the order, so the argument goes, to ascribe his rise to the order itself is to blame it unfairly. Trump's ascent is not a commentary on the soundness of the order. Major shocks somehow arose from outside the system, coming from Americans' loss of faith or nerve, or from the failure to sell the order to those whose labour, taxes and blood maintain it, or from malign populists, whose emergence proponents of the order struggle to explain. Political centrists with an eye to democratic battles are drawn to this stance, for it promises to narrow the discussion to external forces – Trump and the populists – rather than to any deeper failure. Like Romans blaming Christians for the collapse of their Western empire, this deflects attention from profound miscalculations and systemic problems.

I argue otherwise. Subjectively, Trump may cast himself, and be cast, as the old order's nemesis and a sharp break with history. Objectively, he represents less an aberration than a culmination of the order and its pathologies, contradictions and excesses. This is so in two respects. First, it is hard to understand his success as separate from the backdrop of permanent war and an increasingly dysfunctional political economy. For Trump was made possible by what he inherited from Obama, and the things Obama could not undo. Obama was also responsible for the perpetuation of military adventurism and the erosion of congressional oversight. Obama, like Trump, criticized the 'free-riding' of allies. A combination of militarism and oligarchy, a super-wealthy class that detaches itself from the commons, had led to the longer-term corrosion of public life both before and during Obama's presidency. Second, Trump, as an oligarchic militarist himself, reflects the morbid symptoms of the order's troubles, doing more to entrench than to transcend the problem.

That is not to say that Trump is a simple continuation from Obama, remembered as a defeated exponent of liberal internationalism. He is not. By an order of magnitude, he is more authoritarian, corrupt, bigoted, mendacious and erratic than his predecessors, and whipped up the 'paranoid style' of American politics with a reckless abandon like no other president has in our time. It is to say that while Trump and Obama both consciously promised and intended different things, they exercise power only within the constraints of a wider orthodoxy and a way of thinking, an American 'muscle memory' towards questions of security and political economy, a way of doing things in the world from which even strong-willed presidents struggle to escape. We can only understand Trump, and wage productive resistance against Trumpism, by recognizing him not as an abrupt interruption or anomalous 'one-off', but as the product of long built-up forces in which the order is implicated. Trump's presidency horrifies, but not, at root, because it threatens an abrupt departure from the established order. Instead, it exposes the order's contradictions in full glare. Time will tell whether he proves to be the order's gravedigger. As is already apparent, he is also its child.

Alibis and Causes

The argument that the established order is largely innocent in terms of contributing to Trump's rise offers a useful alibi. As some argue, Trump's surprising ascent was really a quirky accident, an unfortunate convergence of circumstances. But for bad luck, avoidable errors and events in the presidential campaign of November 2016 – the FBI 'Comey' intervention, the missteps of an inept Clinton campaign, and the marginal difference of fewer than 80,000 voters in three swing states[3] – Trump would not even be president. Record lows in presidential approval ratings, the Democratic Party's subsequent gains in the 2018 congressional mid-term elections and an attempt at impeachment suggest that the Trump phenomenon could be brittle and fleeting, an aberrant moment. To these cheering considerations, it can be added that Trump's rise had little to do with foreign policy. It was not an indictment of America's exercise of power or its commercial and military dispensation abroad. Those who elected Trump were aggrieved by other polarizing questions, like immigration, identity or deindustrialization, and were mostly not registering a protest against traditional US hegemonic leadership abroad. As evidence for this, Trump has increased America's military footprint, yet his approval ratings among Republican voters are stable. Moving onto the front foot, it is not only those who criticize post-war grand strategy and the security establishment who are wrong; intellectuals who blame the recent political revolt on the security bureaucracy and the consensus, they argue, sound like Trump himself, and are unwittingly furthering his agenda.

This response is symptomatic of the order's way of assimilating negative information. Confronted with resistance, it attributes adverse change to bad attitudes and defeatism rather than the force of changing material conditions. Hence the occasional recourse to loyalty tests against critics. It emphasizes poor management of the order, never the order itself, as well as unwise fatigue with the burdens of hegemony, the enervating effects of success and wealth, the slackening of political will. The order as a transcendent commitment remains essentially unimpeachable.

To be sure, no single variable created Trump. The 2016 presidential election was not simply a referendum on American primacy in the world. The suggestion, though, that Trump was made possible by indigenous forces unrelated to the order is eccentric. Direct evidence suggests otherwise. Voters may not have elected Trump primarily because of his stances on alliances or nuclear proliferation. They did, however, respond to his assaults on free trade, failed wars and the destructive workings of global capital. Registered Trump voters ranked foreign policy high on their priorities, suggesting his broader message resonated, of putting America first and ending other countries' free-riding at its expense, and that a self-serving establishment had failed to secure US interests abroad.[4]

Walling off these issues as 'domestic', and treating political economy or failed wars as somehow separate from the international order, relies on artificial distinctions. The US-led order involved policy decisions that had both external and domestic dimensions in their design and impact. Climate crisis did not arise separately. It is the corollary of the vast economic growth and prosperity that liberal order enthusiasts invite us to celebrate. It is also linked to the security order. After all, the Pentagon is a large emitter of greenhouse gases, more so than Portugal, Sweden or Denmark.[5] This is not an argument for dismantling the modern economy or scrapping all military power. Rather, it is to highlight the 'have it both ways' convenience offered by liberal order visions. The balance sheet is a poor metaphor for the problem. Increased power and wealth, even foreign policy triumphs, usually are tied to dark acts, compromises or settlements. Any responsible statecraft must take into account such trade-offs.

Likewise, if there is a crisis of capitalism, it is surely connected also to international finance. And post-war international finance in its various waves was structured and organized primarily by the USA along with its European allies. Western capitalist states and global banks headquartered in Europe were central actors in the global financial crisis, whose driving forces included transnational economic doctrines and foreign investors, an interlocking matrix of corporate balance sheets bank-to-bank, with the liberal eurozone also heavily implicated.[6] Likewise, it is misleading to claim that the Iraq war, and the War on Terror, had nothing to do causally with America's pursuit of unipolar dominance and its concern for international order, the pursuit of hegemony and the reordering of the Gulf. Indeed, war and inequality were linked. The era of institutionalized war, with military activity of varying intensity across eighty countries, has also exacerbated inequality and social strain.[7] The military adventures since 2001 were 'credit card' wars, financed by borrowing rather than by taxes, and fought by a volunteer military. This financing helped to secure political acquiescence by shifting immediate burdens away from most citizens.[8] Consequences for the population still flowed. Wealthy people and institutions were able to enrich themselves by purchasing bonds, while everyone else had to take on the fiscal burden of repaying the (increasingly unmanageable) debt. Indirect taxes also are regressive, as increased sales, value-added, excise and customs taxes fall more on low- and middle-income households, for whom spending is a larger share of disposable income. And after the discovery of the Panama Papers, with their revelations of systematic tax evasion by transnational elites, it is odd to assert that inequality at home is unrelated to public and private decisions about international political economy and US-dominated international financial institutions.

So there is no relief to be had in insulating the foreign from the domestic. If there is a crisis in the order, it is related to an interaction between failures at home and away, between domestic strife and polarization on the one hand, and international disorder on the other, each reinforcing the other in a downward spiral. Obsessed with 'greatness' and with dismantling Obama's legacy in the form of the Joint Comprehensive Plan of Action (JCPOA) nuclear agreement with Iran, Trump's inner circle of belligerent advisors deliberately precipitated a crisis with Iran. This pattern is recognizable in the long and tragic arc of classical realism. As Thucydides related, destructive political struggle and the loosening of restraint in Athens set the scene for the disastrous Sicilian expedition.

Attempts to protect the reputation of the liberal order by exception-
alizing and parochializing Trump reflect a have-it-both-ways quality in
that worldview. On the one hand, traditionalists present the American
order as world-historical in its significance and reach, transforming
the human condition and deserving the credit for every benign, major
development. On the other, when things go wrong, they insulate the
same order from responsibility, finding that the same pervasive project
was innocent, its power circumscribed after all, and unrelated to mis-
developments even though they had their epicentre in Washington.
More subtle versions of the argument do not attempt such a domestic/
foreign cleavage, instead arguing that the order is fraying because
American leaders lacked sufficient political will to uphold and defend
it. If there is increased turbulence from Ukraine to the Persian Gulf
to the South China Sea, and if this helped generate domestic revolt,
it is largely due to an insufficiency of belief. But this deflection is also
suspect, for it makes the order unfalsifiable and therefore surreally
abstract, like the twentieth-century communist ideal. Never discred-
ited, it can only be misapplied, its essence beyond question. Orders
that depend on such sophistries have not fared well, historically.

It is not possible to separate Trump from the order that preceded
him, because it is not possible to divorce the rise of Trump from the
legacy of Obama, or to reduce the problem to one of poor salesman-
ship.[9] President Obama is indelibly linked to pre-Trump order, both
its activity and its rhetoric. Obama himself explicitly identifies with the
liberal order ideal. Despite his signature campaign theme of change,
he ended up articulating the case for conserving and fine-tuning a
traditional centrist inheritance and its precepts. As Aziz Rana puts it,
as president, 'Obama marshalled his personal story and oratorical gifts
to defend hollow tenets: the righteousness of American primacy, the
legitimacy of global market liberalism, the need for incremental reform,

the danger of large-scale structural overhaul'.[10] This left fundamental problems barely addressed, a working poor suffering stagnating conditions in America's interior alongside a prospering coastal oligarchy, a failing but growing militarism, and a fragmentation of the country into warring tribal factions. Obama was neither oblivious to these problems nor passive in tackling them. The approach he and his advisors took, though, was by means of technocrats, optimistically believing they could make an essentially decent order work better, which is a characteristic attitude of the order itself.

But wasn't Trump really a one-off accident? Even if, on a minimal rewrite of history, he had lost rather than won with knife-edge majorities in three states, the fact remains that he would still have won the nomination of a major political party with more than fourteen million votes and in the face of vocal denunciation by 'never-Trumpers', party elders and grandees. He would still have attracted more than sixty million American votes in the presidential election. He would have done so against a candidate with a billion-dollar war-chest, the largest in American history, who also had endorsements from the vast majority of the national media. To paraphrase Montesquieu, if in these conditions Trump's election relied on an accident, there must have been a general reason why the status quo was so fragile that an accident led to its fall. To show that Trump's election relied on contingencies, or the distortions of the electoral college, is not to disprove what is apparent on many measures, that a deeper, convulsive political crisis is under way. Comparative studies suggest that general alienation has led to a broad dealignment of voters from party affiliations in their older ideological settings, and they are increasingly receptive to populist appeals.[11] There remains a structure of discontent in Western democratic politics, a Trumpism that will outlive Trump. What are its sources?

Trump as Caesarist

In a direct sense, war and its ripples made President Trump. His rise is partly to do with America's two decades of war, and the interrelationship between war and the body politic. Consider a simple point. America's war in the Middle East played a non-trivial role in winning the presidency for this authoritarian demagogue. As a recent study found,

> [There is] a significant and meaningful relationship between a community's rate of military sacrifice and its support for Trump . . . [I]f three states key to Trump's victory – Pennsylvania, Michigan, and Wisconsin – had suffered even a modestly lower casualty rate, all three could have flipped from red to blue and sent Hillary Clinton to the White House.[12]

To be sure, countries can fall prey to demagogic rogues without fighting continuous wars. In the same sense, people can get lung cancer without smoking twenty cigarettes a day. To stick with that metaphor, military expeditions to fix broken states became a bad habit, with consequences that went to the heart of the body politic.

There is something more complex happening here than an outright rejection of war. Grievance against military casualties and their unfair burdens, which helped give rise to Trump, represents something more conflicted than anti-war rebellion. Trump in his mode of rule is best recognized not with the hackneyed terms 'isolationist' or 'anti-war', but as a Caesarist. A Caesarist is a darkly charismatic and militarist ruler with mass appeal. He mobilizes the masses and aims to challenge their remote and malign oppressors, while setting up an authoritarian regime in practice. The ruler's disproportionate tilt to martial power and corrupt indulgence undermines the republic.[13] Democratic life is hollowed out, as elitism manipulates populism. The Caesar comparison is imperfect, to be sure. Trump did not come to power from a familial tradition of high office. He never exercised military command abroad. And the American courts, Congress and civil society resist his decrees more readily than the late Roman republic could constrain its warlords. But the Caesarist model captures this president's aspirations and his pattern of behaviour.

Like the liberal order itself, Trump has a complex and at times inchoate relationship with war.[14] He came to power repudiating futile, open-ended conflicts and has since declared that America should avoid endless war and railed against the waste of blood and treasure in the Middle East for bad allies who exploited America's goodwill. He also declares himself the 'most militaristic person you will ever meet'.[15] Yet by the end of his first term, Trump had ended no wars, and there were more troops, not fewer, in Africa, the Middle East, and Europe. Even the small garrison he drew down in Syria was redeployed to Iraq. Trump opposes not militarism but unsuccessful militarism, and exhibits a cultish attachment to hard power. He promises an unabashed American dominance without failed campaigns, declaring 'I'm really good at war. I love war in a certain way. But only when we win.'[16] This suggests a desire to select only winnable wars with achievable and limited goals, yet this sits oddly with the Trump administration's dalliance with the possibilities of overthrowing hostile regimes. It also encourages a bad long-term development, making the foreign policy process increasingly praetorian. While critical of their predisposition to permanent military operations, Trump still appoints to his cabinet stridently hawkish advisors, such as Mike Pompeo and John Bolton, as well as serving and former officers ('my generals') to senior roles in the White House, the National Security Council and the Pentagon;

ROUGH BEAST: HOW THE ORDER MADE TRUMP

he even delegates unilateral authority to the Department of Defense to set troop levels in Afghanistan and give commanders more authority to order drone strikes. He denounces imperial overstretch, while exacerbating its fiscal imbalance, weakening the State Department and the sinews of diplomacy, handing office increasingly to military appointees. He has increased America's footprint, especially in the Greater Middle East, raising civilian and military personnel there by 33 per cent,[17] and Pentagon contractors by 15 per cent to 53,062;[18] he escalated a confrontation with Iran, reinforced ties with Saudi Arabia and the Gulf monarchies, and bombed Syria twice to punish the use of chemical weapons. Over the course of both the Obama and the Trump presidencies, between 2013 and 2017, arms sales to the region rose by 108 per cent.[19] Trump and his most belligerent advisors sabre rattle and threaten designated rogue states – Venezuela, Cuba, Iran and North Korea – with punishment and, in the case of the last two, annihilation. The president has even spoken of bombing Afghanistan until it no longer exists.

Trump is drawn above all not to force itself, but to the show of force linked to his person, to Napoleonic majesty and public spectacle, coveting, for example, the military parades at the Bastille Day procession in France.[20] On 4 July, Washington, DC, founded to be the capital of a republic, now plays host to a gaudy taxpayer-funded and militarized spectacle, a commemoration with a display of tanks and flyovers for fighter jets, celebrating as focal point the commander-in-chief. Normally commemorating its armed forces at other times, Trump moved this partisan and militarized spectacle to the centre of the day on which it celebrates its birth as a polity. Unlike other capitals, Washington's streets cannot bear the load of tanks, physically or ideologically.

The mix of imperial grandiosity, militarism and a failure to take war seriously results in a set of contradictions that were part of American statecraft before the arrival of Trump. So the same president who threatens annihilation and speaks of the evil determination of his opponents also craves historic, highly choreographed peace summits with these enemies, believing that shows of American power can quickly bring implacable foes to heel. He abandons arms control treaties and pursues nuclear supremacy over the same authoritarian rivals he openly admires, constantly seeking out grand moments of entente and the kudos of talks with Kim Jong Un, Vladimir Putin, Xi Jinping or Ayatollah Khamenei. He hopes that a mixture of uncompromising 'maximum pressure' coercion along with magnanimous, unconditional public outreach will make them negotiate pliantly. Alliances too attract contradictory behaviour. Trump abuses and bullies NATO allies as obsolete free-riders, demands tribute, then reluctantly reinforces them and demands their support against adversaries. Like earlier presidents, Trump apparently wants allies to be compliant followers who obey US demands, while at the same time increasing their defence spending significantly, without grappling with the obvious tensions therein. Like earlier presidents, Trump demands hegemony and its prerogatives, but, when it comes to satellite states, resents paying the bill.

Trump's incoherence around war is greater than most previous presidents. This is a matter of temperature, though, not of substance. His attitudes to force in general are a parody of pre-existing trends in public life. Trump seems to feel the exhilaration of projecting violence more than most presidents. In other ways, he accentuates an older set of patterns. There is a determination to project strength and instil awe, with a narrowly militarized statecraft stressing the extraordinary dangerousness of this exceptional moment, but along with a concern to limit liability. Trump supports torture and openly enthuses over the bombings he authorizes. Yet he expresses shock at adversaries when they forcibly retaliate. Iran is not a state with legitimate security interests but a monster driven by 'bloodlust'. 'When committed by terrorists, criminals, or protesters, violence is horrific, and its perpetrators are subhuman. ("Animals" is a favourite Trump word.) But when committed by Trump's side, violence is righteous and heroic, evidence of a functioning moral order.'[21] Who will say that this mentality is unique to Trump?

To say Trump is a militarist is not to say he is consistently enthusiastic for war. Rather, craving the grandiosity of imperial power, he is a militarist who at the same time fails to take war, or the possibility of war, seriously. Against weak adversaries that lack the capacity for major retaliation, he enlarges and intensifies war-making with little internal scrutiny. He has dramatically increased the volume of airstrikes in Afghanistan, against Islamists in Somalia, against the Islamic State in Iraq and Syria, as well as increasing assistance to Saudi Arabia's catastrophic onslaught in Yemen. He has expanded the repertoire of remote control, night-and-day killing that he inherited from Obama and makes its details more secret, readily and routinely against distant targets while suppressing information about civilian losses, presenting combat as antiseptic to the home front.[22] It is a different story with stronger opponents. Against adversaries who can attack US interests instantly, Trump ramps up crises only to recoil in the hour of decision. Having ratcheted up international confrontations with threats, strengthened sanctions and incitements to revolution, as with Iran in the summer of 2019, he is then notably reluctant to pull the trigger, backing away from further escalation or from ordering airstrikes where adversaries' capacity to retaliate is too daunting. This enthusiasm to go to the brink, only to shrink back, bespeaks an ultimately shallow attitude to war and the projection of power, unwilling to contemplate its gravest consequences in advance. It reflects a pathology of the national security state, many of whose officials and supporters do not want a state of 'war', exactly, but insist on openly threatening it regularly, regularly using military force without declaring a formal state of hostilities, to tame the world into order. And if the general trend since the War on Terror has been both to emphasize the exceptional yet un-ending moment of crisis, while urging people to maintain a normal daily existence, Trump reinforces this with the modality of television melodrama, reducing American citizens to passive consumer-spectators, whose applause he craves. This reluctance to allow middling adversaries to walk the talk could also have escalatory effects over time, adding pressure to make good on threats 'next time'.

Important here is the difference between the president and the presidency. Trump cannot be understood as a single individual exercising power, but as part of a system that at once endows him with concentrated powers, yet that also constrains his choices, which both encourages his taste for militarist swagger while resisting his instincts to disavow military adventures. Like earlier presidents – Clinton, Bush II and Obama – Trump vowed fundamental change to US grand strategy, only to be readily constrained in doing so by his appointees, the expert officials and hawkish primacists who protect it.[23] Trump's predecessor in the White House said so explicitly, warning of both longer-term developments that he could not overcome, the emergence of an insulated oligarchy and a bellicose 'Washington playbook'.[24]

If militarism is the excessive veneration of state military power, a veneration that leans towards undemocratic and absolutist politics, twenty-first-century American militarism predated Trump, along with a general coarsening of the public sphere.[25] This is an American militarism, distinct from the classical archetype of the garrison state with its mass conscription, enforced billeting and crushing wartime taxes. The militarism of Trump's America is less severe and is constitutionally informal (Congress has not declared war since 1942). Still, it is a set of attitudes and behaviours that are not symptoms of a healthy constitutional republic. Before Trump, the War on Terror had already imported the techniques of organized violence from abroad, heightening domestic surveillance and militarizing policing.[26] It had already militarized the enforcement of US borders in ways that went beyond strict invigilation into draconian severity, herding immigrants into squalid detention camps. Whether or not we accept the 'double government' hypothesis, long before Trump a permanent security bureaucracy, seasoned people who manage intelligence, military and law enforcement agencies, operated increasingly without constitutional restraints to constrain busy and distracted policymakers.[27] A more diffuse militarism too seeped into the broader culture. A general 'warspeak' entered everyday political language and public discourse, undermining proportionality, worsening polarization and even desensitizing citizens to political violence.[28] Civic rituals, too, reflect the political and cultural shift. Even the National Football League is militarized, with taxpayer-funded 'paid patriotism' displays at preambles to games, denounced as wasteful and confected gimmicks in a report co-headed by the hawkish Senator John McCain.[29] The linkage of national football with rally-around-the-flag exhibitions of martial pageantry predated, and paved the way for, Trump's denunciation of football players who showed dissent by taking a knee during the anthem.

Here is a political correctness but with a hyper-nationalist twist. It narrates national life in a drama of wartime emergency and tribal rallying against foreign demons and domestic fifth columnist traitors. Lest this seem novel, recall the Republican Party convention of 2004 in Madison Square Garden, which chronologically falls within the alleged seventy-year life span of the 'liberal order' and when Trump was a registered Democrat:

> In the construct of recent history promoted by the White House, and by speaker after speaker and video after video at Madison Square Garden, America's great wound [the 9/11 attacks] was featured as a sort of national treasure – the ultimate and all-justifying source of legitimacy of the Bush Presidency. So the constant invocations of mass death and devastation were proffered to the conventioneers and their television audience not only as a bad thing but also, perversely, as something to cherish, even to celebrate, as a source of unity and purpose . . . So it went: blood and fire and God and country and 'Amazing Grace'. It was a proper war party at the Garden, charged with the language of Christian martyrology.[30]

If anything, Trump breathed fresh life into this political legacy and ramped it up, affirming a chauvinism that had always been latent within the conceit of a War on Terror and which earlier presidents had tried to resist. As well as embracing its xenophobic elements, Trump extended the War on Terror to even more adversaries, including Iran, finding the long war's instruments usefully to hand, including the highly permissive Authorization for Use of Military Force of September 2001.[31] Neither has this contagion spared the other major political party. Anxious in an age of terror not to be outflanked on the question, many Democratic candidates for office feel pressure to burnish their national security credentials, stressing their desire to maintain armed supremacy, only more efficiently.

In terms of instrumental and constitutional power, Trump's brand of militarism heightens one pre-existing tendency, the institutionalization of permanent war and expanding military activity through ever greater presidential executive prerogative. As one instance of this shift, Trump sold arms to Saudi Arabia without congressional approval. Again, this is possible partly because of what Trump inherited. Previous administrations ignored strictures of the Missile Technology Control Regime to allow allies like South Korea and Saudi Arabia to extend the range of their ballistic missiles while imposing sanctions on Iran for its missile tests.[32] Consequential foreign policy decisions could thus be taken out of the hands of Congress. It could also have far-reaching domestic consequences. The Patriot Act wrought an era of secret sites, extraordinary rendition and torture, extrajudicial assassinations on an industrial scale, and involvement in the aggression of client states. The apparatus of unaccountable, secretive powers stretched also to 'national security letters', instruments of state power whereby the federal authorities can audit and investigate an individual while prohibiting them from seeking counsel or informing anyone. Like Bush II, Obama increased the practice of bypassing legislature and circumventing the War Powers Act with *ultra vires* directives. Expanding presidential privileges in wartime was hardly new – Lincoln introduced detention without trial. Only now the 'war' is permanent. In turn, this results in concentrations of power at odds with the founding principles of the constitution. It damages the constitutional authority of Congress, which has helped marginalize itself in foreign policymaking and in checking the exertions of the executive branch. The clause of the Constitution regarded by James Madison as paramount, vesting war powers in Congress, became a de facto nullity, and partly through the acquiescence of Congress itself.[33] As a distant and imperfect but still useful historical warning about the linkage between imperial expansion and the erosion of republican norms, the Roman republic's degeneration is a marker here. In the words of Andrew Sullivan:

The strain of managing a huge empire did indeed weaken Rome's democratic institutions – just as our empire has weakened ours, giving the president extraordinary powers (including the ability to end all life as we know it on the planet), a vast surveillance apparatus, emergency powers beyond anything imagined before, and a withered Congress. If you wanted a direct parallel with, say, Iraq, you could even point to the endless fight the Romans had with Jugurtha, a warlord in North Africa, in the second century BCE, a man who innovated an insurgency it took Rome a very long time to defeat.[34]

Even when Congress in the summer of 2019 debated an amendment to prohibit funding for an unauthorized war with Iran, to reassert its authority over presidential whim, both the Pentagon and some congressional members denounced their institution for affirming its principles and checking executive action. Militarism above all is a conception of the relationship between the citizen and the state. In this case, it proposes the inversion if not of civilian control, certainly of congressional oversight. Republican Senator Tom Cotton, for instance, charged that 'Democrats are trying to tie the hands of the Commander-in-Chief and our troops as they face down Iran. They want Congress to debate how to respond while American forces are at risk.'[35] Militarism rarely articulates itself so concisely. To optimize the safety and success of the armed forces and give their commander a free hand, Cotton demanded that Congress should obey. Again, this was not a sudden, Trump-era irruption, but the culmination of a politics of national security and its loyalty tests, and what came with it: a shift towards an imperial presidency and the erosion of the constitutional balance that observers had long warned against. Far from a discrete area of policy, this goes to the heart of the nation's civic life.

ROUGH BEAST: HOW THE ORDER MADE TRUMP

For war, the decision to kill and be killed on the polity's behalf, is the ultimate political act.

The Political Economy of Trump

In the field of economics, as with that of security, Trump is the product of a defective order that he vowed to dismantle but instead reinforces. Styling himself as the opponent of plutocratic privilege, in a campaign that trafficked also on anti-Semitic images and innuendo, Trump played to popular outrage about the inequities of international capital and unfettered globalization, promising the rebirth of communities shattered in its wake, and a new dawn of reindustrialization. In office, he quickly proved to be the friend of Wall Street and Goldman Sachs, staffing his administration with some of their veterans. He stripped away regulations and enacted tax cuts for high earners and corporations.

The alienation that propelled Trump to office is not reducible to material grievance. Economic grievance with a certain form of conspicuous equality is core to the revolt. As two advocates of liberal order admit, against the standard sweeping claim that the order generated unprecedented 'prosperity', the order as it evolved over the past few decades is 'rigged' in favour of an overclass, and against the working class and the poor.[36] At the very moment when defenders of the order congratulate it for delivering sustained economic growth and making life longer, richer and better for the multitudes, we are witnessing the long-term consequences of a settlement that creates great aggregate wealth but is making material life in fundamental ways worse, and stirring voters towards retribution.

What some recall as a post-war order is in fact a more recent post-Cold War economic dispensation, a drive towards globalization on American terms. The political economy that has prevailed for three decades has been wrongly historicized, when the arrangements that people accepted and expected in earlier decades were markedly different. Rather than an unbroken economic continuum from the moment of creation, the political economy of American power in fact took a fundamental new turn in the era of unipolarity. A commitment to unrestricted capital flows and the flow of labour was a break from earlier decades. And with that experiment came an economic order that was celebrated for its creative dynamism – and even its permanence – by its champions, but which also turned out to be an increasingly and dangerously inegalitarian form of capitalism. A drive towards an open, borderless and cosmopolitan globe became the alibi for companies to press for tax cuts, deregulation, monopoly power and corporate welfare, and the latitude to outsource and offshore industries and jobs. And it served as a pretext for a culture of unrestrained acquisitiveness, celebrating self-gratification and self-enrichment, to both secret hoarding as revealed by the Panama Papers documents, and open displays of opulence. Paradoxically, the state whose frontiers the neoliberal ideology looked to roll back also became instrumental in creating, enforcing and protecting the new economic order. State law-making power remained fundamental to the working of the system, and the deregulation of US campaign finance resulted in secret funding and compromising lobbying, a pattern of rent-seeking behaviour that Russ Feingold, former Democratic senator from Wisconsin, called an 'opaque system of legalized bribery and legalized extortion'.[37] Financial institutions fell prey to systemic corruption, from investment banks to ratings agencies, bringing on a general crisis while its main offenders went largely unpunished. As the college admissions scandal revealed, even universities became susceptible to dynastic privilege, accepting bribes and tolerating fraud from alumni families. In Transparency International's index of corruption among countries, the USA has fallen out of the top twenty least corrupt and is a 'country to watch'.[38] This hardly makes it a pariah relative to worse cases elsewhere. But the exemplary light on the hill has dimmed.

What were the results of these interlocking developments? The economy increasingly both financialized and deindustrialized; indeed, it became an oligopoly rather than a dynamic capitalist market. This had dangerous consequences. As large corporations raked in fortunes, working-class wages stagnated. Coastal cities hosted large, oligarchic concentrations of wealth linked to technology, financial services, media and lobbying, while a growing mass of working poor had to make do with decaying public infrastructure. A sense of basic injustice spread. An order that allows criminal banking executives to go unpunished or alleged torturers to go unprosecuted while there is also mass incarceration for lesser felonies becomes hard to defend. There were also international injuries. Although the USA would probably endure as a major power, American democracy was hollowing out as it became a 'sick man' with the international reputation of a ruling class that could be bought, the legitimacy of its institutions frayed, the sense of shared civic purpose weakened.[39]

Trump's mode of rule underscored and strengthened these tendencies. He denounced corrupt plutocrats and Wall Street privilege after a career of fraud and tax evasion,[40] lavished blandishments on the super-rich, and shifted the centre of policymaking away from the White House and into his private palaces, through dynastic appointments and abuse of public funds entangling state affairs in his family business. He condemned iniquitous foreign influence and threatens to purge the beltway of insiders, while opening Washington further to international lobbying, even giving diplomatic posts to donors.

One of the strongest arguments for Trumpian economic dis-continuity relates to tariffs. Yet to the extent that Trump shocked tradition by reintroducing the tariff as an instrument of economics and foreign policy, he accentuated in unusually stark ways a trend notice-able since 2008, the return of mercantilism and trade barriers as part of a return to geopolitical competition, one in which the USA preached free trade while practising protection. Five months before Trump was elected, both the WTO and the Global Trade Alert monitors warned of a return of trade barriers and a stockpiling of trade-restrictive prac-tices by G20 economies. Since the 2008 financial crisis, the USA has imposed tariffs worth $39 billion, while the world's top sixty economies have adopted more than seven thousand protectionist trade measures worth more than $400 billion. The USA and the EU both accounted for the highest number of protectionist measures, each exercising more than one thousand, with India a distant third at four hundred.[41] Even the TPP is exclusionary, and Hillary Clinton announced during her campaign that she was going to abandon it.

The difference, this time, was again partly rhetorical. Trump preached differently. 'America First' entailed unabashed, zero-sum competition and an aggressive pushback against disadvantageous trade imbalances and surpluses. Another difference was a willing-ness to go all in for competition, confident that his unique bargaining acumen would prevail. Trump had been banging that drum publicly for decades, and the propitious political-economic moment had at last arrived. He even welcomed the prospect of trade wars. While the prudence of this approach is open to doubt, given the propensity of uninhibited trade wars to inflict damage on the very vulnerable work-ing communities Trump claims to assist, it can also be recognized as a typically Trumpian phenomenon, where he accentuates a longer-term structural shift. In an ever more competitive, multipolar world, the shift was already towards a world of increasing protectionism, and given the important development of China's rise, to a world in which exports imperil under-protected industries. Indeed, China's refusal to liberalize its governance as it got richer is one of the greatest disappointments for liberal internationalists. Outgoing president Bill Clinton had prophesied in 2000 that admitting China to normalized trade status would bring about a benign convergence:

> We want a prosperous China open to American exports; whose people have access to ideas and information; and that upholds the rule of law at home and plays by global rules of the road on everything from nuclear non-proliferation to human rights to trade. . . . It will open a growing market to American workers, farmers, and businesses. And more than any other step we can take right now, it will encourage China to choose reform, open-ness, and integration with the world.[42]

These were also the hopes of politicians across partisan lines.[43] But it is far from what happened. Not only did economic participation in international markets fail to liberalize China politically; it also failed to make it economically liberal. If the People's Republic was growing prodigiously, it was on the back of systematic cheating that most great powers practised as they rose – currency manipulation, copyright and patent violations, industrial espionage, and the dumping of subsidized products. None of this is to deny that a future president could tilt back towards genuine reductions in trade barriers. The winds, though, are blowing strongly against it. This has powerful material causes.

What is the right response to China's trade mercantilism and global trade disparities? As we have seen, the USA has practised protec-tionism particularly towards agriculture throughout the lifespan of the alleged liberal order. It is its manufacturing base that has been decimated. A number of interests have benefited from the shift to the offshoring of industry, corporations, investors, retailers and indeed consumers – but the price has been the desolation of once stable working communities. To reassert the nostrums of liberal economics in the pursuit of cheap imports, under a borderless global labour market, is a weak response. The most prudent trade policy in an age of mercantilism may not be a full-blown trade war. But it would require an element of protective state intervention, if not in the form of tariffs, then in the form of subsidies, favourable credit policies, tax incentives or local content requirements. And it would need to strike a balance, seeking an acceptable level of mercantilism with a touch of the Hamiltonian tradition of nurturing infant industries, in the spirit of arms control preserving high-value indigenous industries while moderating international rivalries.[44] Intellectually, designing a prudent industry policy would require jettisoning the conceit that an era of borderless free trade once reigned.

Before the Fall

The celebrated political realist, the late Robert Gilpin, argued that a certain kind of intellectual corruption attends decline of great powers and orders, a corruption that is both symptom and catalyst:

[The] generation in the minds of a dominant people of the belief that the world they (or, rather, their forbears) created is the right, natural and God-given state of affairs. To such a people the idea the world of their rule and privilege could be otherwise becomes inconceivable. The goodness and benefits of the status quo, as they know it, are so obvious that all reasonable men will assent to its worth and preservation. With such a state of mind, a people neither concedes to the just demands of rising challengers nor makes the necessary sacrifices to defend its threatened world.[45]

This is not an exact description of the present. Proponents of the liberal order are, after all, full of worry about the demise of their world in this twilight moment. They remain impressed, however, by its goodness and benefits, and can only explain the revolts under way as a loss of faith by an America that has failed to live up to its own promise. They certainly do demand sacrifices, to the point where hegemony becomes more the end than the means. That rising challengers might have 'just demands' is hardly entertained. Gilpin's further warning was more exactly prophetic: that the process of disequilibrium and decline would result in an 'increasingly severe political conflict' over the allocation of wealth among guns, butter and investment, moving from a 'benign politics of growth' into a 'virulent politics of distribution'. At the time of writing, the USA's debt has exceeded the size of its economy, yet defence spending has soared and deficits have reached record levels. Nevertheless, the USA continues to insist on engaging in combat with all comers, declaring open competition against rivals in Europe, Asia, the Middle East and Latin America. Another government shutdown threatened the capital. Amidst this material strain, there was authoritarian swagger to spare. A president with openly absolutist tendencies boasted that, against ruthless domestic opponents, he had the support of 'tough' military, police and bikers who would rally to his side in ways that were 'very, very bad'. Against media criticism, he pined for a time when presidents with a strong economy were 'immune from criticism'. Challenged in the courts, he remarked: 'I have to get rid of judges.' He even flirted with the constitutional possibilities of extending presidential pardon to himself.

This was where the republic had come, once founded by the

even flirted with the constitutional possibilities of extending presidential pardon to himself.

This was where the republic had come, once founded by the overthrow of an abusive monarch. As the anxious and the gloomy had warned so often, the effort to enlarge benign order on ambitious terms abroad, and the creation of the apparatus to do so, threatened liberty and good order at home. In this respect, if not in others, the USA proved unexceptional.

4

A Machiavellian Moment: Roads Ahead

American order did not, and cannot, function as domestic liberal preferences writ large. This is partly because its behaviour abroad reflects the constraints and pressures that come with power-seeking. Washington got a taste of this problem in July 2010, when the Obama administration competed against Beijing for the favour of Indonesia, a semi-authoritarian Asian power that is getting larger and richer. After an internal debate, Washington lifted a longstanding ban on Kopassus, an Indonesian special forces unit with a long record of atrocities in East Timor, Aceh and Papua. It did so after the Indonesian government hinted it might cancel the president's visit to Jakarta and explore military ties with China unless the ban was lifted.[1] In order to balance against one authoritarian state, it might be necessary to tolerate the illiberality of another. These are the grim choices of international life. If such a dilemma imposed itself when America's relative power over China's was greater, it will increasingly feature in an era of increasing competition.

We have been delivered into a new world. It is a world of power shifts, political revolts and multipolar competition, in which homilies about global leadership will prove a poor intellectual resource. The world unfolding now is one of competitive multipolarity, when powers compete for influence and standing under the shadow of war, a world defined by issues that states are willing to bleed for. The pursuit of international dominance in the belief that liberal values exempt American power from the tragic limits that afflicted previous hegemons has made policymakers insensitive to the limits of power, neglectful of the problems of security dilemma, presumptuous about how others see the assertion of power and heedless of how ordering abroad can inflict disorder at home. The USA ought to approach the unfolding disorder as a 'Machiavellian moment'. In such a moment, anticipated in medieval debates, a republic must reckon with the survival of its institutions and civic virtues in an increasingly hostile world. It should do so by abandoning the core historical claim of liberal order, which the USA itself secured by domesticating the world to its liberal values under its hegemony, as well as the idea that the USA or any one power can dominate the globe. As we have seen, post-war American statecraft worked differently. Even while Washington tried to reshape the world, the international system and its inherent dilemmas also imposed themselves upon the superpower. America's 'ordering' activity was in fundamental ways illiberal, whether in its actions or in its results. Revisiting that past is needed. A richer historical consciousness can widen our sense of possible options. By confronting the historical reality that ordering is a rough and compromised process full of betrayals, and that attempts to expand liberalism have had tragic results, the USA can better husband its power and temper its ambitions. It can return to its original purpose, to secure its interests as a constitutional republic in a plural world. In this chapter, I will assess where the USA fundamentally 'is'. I will then show that the mytho-history of liberal order, which recognizes danger predominantly in the retreat from global domination, will not help understand how to make the USA more secure in an increasingly multipolar world. Lastly, I offer an alternative road ahead. Without offering an exhaustive programme of policies, I identify a number of steps Washington could take, to secure itself better.

A Republic in Danger

The foundational purpose of American statecraft is to 'preserve the US as a free nation with our fundamental institutions and values intact'.[2] That means shaping an international environment that is conducive to a way of life. If so, as things stand, the United States is imperilled. As the last chapter demonstrated, the rise of Donald Trump was symptomatic of a deeper crisis in the country, as disorder at home and abroad feed off one another to fray the cohesion and even the legitimacy of its ideals, its institutions and the state. Rather than a mere course correction, to return to the default settings of the pre-Trump era, the country should realize that it has reached a Machiavellian moment. Such a moment is a more profound point of reckoning, where a republic originally concerned for virtue could unravel, threatened by hostile forces (and in his time, the threat of invasion) from without, corruption and disorder within, and the intrusion of chaotic time – what Robert Kagan rightly called the 'Return of History' – into what it once thought was a stable permanence.[3] In that instance, a clash between universal morality and a morality of *virtu* opens up, as public necessity requires 'actions that private ethics and religious values might condemn as unjust and immoral'.[4]

Few debates are genuinely new. The debate over liberal order restages in secular language older debates about the possibility of moral and Christian order in the public sphere. Central was the tradition of the Florentine diplomat and political thinker Niccolò Machiavelli (1469–1527) and reactions to him.[5] To Machiavelli, politics was about the gaining and holding of power. The irresponsible misuse of power had led to chaos and invasion. Machiavelli counselled that the prudent prince cannot bring private morality into the public sphere, because most men 'are not good'. Instead, the prudent exercise of power on behalf of the ruled should be guided by an alternative moral standard, the reason of state. The securing of the republic, especially when threatened, requires dirty hands. In such a world, virtue meant the capacity to behave 'usefully', in the form of bloody ruthlessness or cold restraint as circumstances dictate. Christian charity, suited for private life, could be a dangerous indulgence for the state. Timid passivity could jeopardize the common good. Equally, gratuitous violence could trigger dangerous reactions or threaten the republic's soul. In the mind of the prince, Christian sentiment must yield to a different steely morality of *virtu*, guided by public necessity. The cut-throat world Machiavelli inhabited, of competing Italian city-states, lent the question high stakes. Crucially, beyond mere survival was concern for the health and freedom of the republic. Indeed, the order of the domestic realm and the potential menace of external forces were interlinked: that cities had become faction-ridden had led to their fall. The state could only learn how to survive these dangers by studying how states actually live – the real – not by dreaming up the ideal, 'republics and kingdoms that bear no resemblance to experience and never existed in reality'.[6]

Against Machiavelli's brutally direct arguments for a separate morality ran a counterblast of Christian universalism, variously driven by 'false nostalgia for a world at peace within one empire', a utopian search for a universal monarchy as 'saviour of mankind', or a 'spiritually motivated attempt to take the world back into the temporal control of the universal church'. Whether by means of the Inquisition, or the prohibition of his books, or subtler efforts at dilution, there was a concerted effort to repudiate Machiavelli and keep alive the promise of a transcendent order that harmonized private and public morality.

Like the medieval papacy and moral critics ever since, liberal order visions resist Machiavelli's public–private dualism. Against the notion of a dualistic international order, they look to the possibility of an order domesticated by a guiding leader. They insist that American-designed order is born of a moral statecraft that infuses benign, altruistic liberal values into the international system. In the Wilsonian tradition, America did, and can, remake the world with the clean hands of institutions, alliances, free trade and far-sighted leadership, constraining itself like no former hegemon. As President Woodrow Wilson exhorted the Senate in his Address of 1917, the USA should fight for a transcendent order, a 'just and secure peace', 'not a balance of power, but a community of power'.[7]

As with Machiavelli and the papacy, so too with arguments about America acting abroad. The pursuit of such a transformed world, a 'peace without victory', required actual victory and a violent rebalancing of power, achieved partly via illiberal and coercive means at home, culminating in a punitive settlement at Versailles that he strongly defended.[8] Wilsonianism is a conflicted thing – some emphasize President Woodrow Wilson's historic stress on international law and institutions, others the need to spread democratic freedom at the point of a bayonet if necessary.[9] Rather than reconciling this, we should recognize it as the core problem of liberal order. As one historian notes, such contrasts reflect the 'fundamental paradox of Wilson's security strategy – the paradox of practising power politics to end power politics'.[10] Liberalism as an engine of American statecraft is jealous, intolerant and messianic. Applied unchecked, from Wilson to the Bush Doctrine, it leads to its own illiberal opposite.[11] The practitioners of rough geopolitics often believed they were serving the ultimate cause of forging a liberal peace under American oversight, but that, to do so, they had to accommodate illiberal allies and pitilessly destroy liberalism's enemies. In this way, a superpower presuming to create a liberal order permits itself to employ unsentimental methods.

In thinking about liberal order, two decades of unipolar hegemony in this century suggest that the Machiavellian insight holds. The world cannot be domesticated, but instead imposes its constraints on powers that would presume to transform it. The greater the exertion to domesticate the world into liberal values, the more the effort depletes power and strains liberalism at home.

With this recurring debate in mind, consider a brief audit of where the USA 'is', after two decades of ambitious exertion in this century and the sustained attempt at 'global leadership'. Looking back, it must reflect on disappointment.[12] Despite a declared aim to destroy threats, it has failed on most fronts, either failing to extinguish them or leaving greater ones in place. It failed to prevent North Korea from acquiring deliverable nuclear weapons, and then failed to disarm it. It failed to persuade Russia to submit to the US-led order or to abandon its empire-building in Ukraine or Georgia, or its international campaign of political subversion. It failed to persuade China to submit to the US-led order in Asia, where China now bids aggressively for hegemony. Its forces are deadlocked against the Taliban in Afghanistan, which is still a kleptocratic state despite years of nation-building. It has not eliminated terrorism. Militant jihadism proliferates. It has failed to broker an Israel–Palestine settlement. It failed to guide the Arab Spring revolutions towards a stable, democratic Middle East. Bashar al Assad and his Alawite regime still rule Syria. Libya after its liberation is politically shattered and economically much poorer. Iraq is more an Iranian client than an American one, and Operation Iraqi Freedom unleashed sectarian conflict which spawned the Islamic

State. America is engaged in escalating confrontations with the ruling regimes in Iran and Venezuela. Despite maximum pressure and threats of annihilation, it has failed to dissuade Iran from conducting missile tests or expanding its influence in the Middle East. The attempt to create an unchallengeable balance of power in its favour has failed to dissuade challenge or permanently transform the world away from competitive power politics. At home, economic policies did not lead to sustained and stable growth, but to the global financial crisis and the Great Recession.

It is sobering to consider that America suffered these failures when its power was at its post-war apex. Even when the USA enjoyed a relative power unprecedented in history, it could still be effectively fought to a stalemate or defeat, as in Korea, Vietnam or Iraq. And increasingly, the international environment is making it harder for the USA – or any state – to impose itself as a hegemon. As its relative power and economic strength wanes, the weight of its commitments is increasing. The concept of single global leadership looks back to a different time, when the distribution of power was far more lopsided in Washington's favour. Underpinning these arguments, there is a distinctively American theme, that of the 'sleeping giant'. That is, the assumption that despite recent strains, the USA has not tapped its full potential power. Maintaining global order is a task that can only be assumed by an exceptionally powerful state. Primacists assume that, since primacy in the world is eminently affordable, if only Washington could recover its will and cohesion, it could readily regenerate itself and its ordering capacity. This sense of great latency derives from the scale of American capabilities but also its peculiar historical pathway to hegemony.[13] The USA rose to power relatively inexpensively compared to other great powers. Americans typically remember the Pearl Harbor attack of December 1941 awakening a sleeping giant that only then realized its capacity. As Daniel Yergin noted, 'American leaders – moved by a traditional missionary impulse, convinced of their global responsibility, full of the self-confidence that comes of success, fundamentally unhurt by war in a wounded world – eagerly reached for their mandate of heaven.'[14] Few periods in history had seen such a sudden power shift on so large a scale. As rivals destroyed themselves and allies exhausted themselves, the USA emerged from the war holding most of the cards.[15] Stimulated by industrial and military mobilization, America experienced unprecedented industrial expansion. Its GDP doubled. Its industrial base was unmolested by bombardment and blockade, it reached the highest per capita productivity in the world. It had the highest standard of living, domination of the world's gold reserves and the Bretton Woods economic system. It exerted great influence through the dollar as reserve currency, and became the largest creditor and exporter. Its capacity to project power with long-range bombers and carrier task forces was unparalleled. It had an atomic monopoly. There was worldwide demand for its loans, arms, expertise and patronage. The manner of this ascent, and the centrality of the mid-twentieth-century moment in the consciousness of policymakers, encourages a long-term way of thinking about American primacy. It predisposes its admirers to assume that the main problems faced by the order are not systemic but intellectual or ideational.

This attitude loses sight of the significant change in material conditions. Consider the economic foundations that are the fundamental basis for power. As a general observation, wealth is shifting from West to East. Across different measures of relative size, there is a pattern of contraction. In 1960, the USA produced 40 per cent of global GDP, measured in terms of Purchasing Power Parity. By 2017, that had fallen to 15 per cent.[16] The IMF estimates it will fall to 14.2 per cent by 2022.[17] The USA is no longer the largest trading nation. This shift has consequences. It does not mean that America is finished as a great power. It still has the largest share of global GDP in terms of market exchange rates, and the dollar is still the reserve currency. It remains militarily the most powerful state, with the greatest reach and striking power, and a large nuclear arsenal. It is demographically more cohesive than its competitors. Neither does it mean the trendline is irreversible. A Chinese contraction, an Indian meltdown, another Asian financial crisis, European stagnation: all are possible, and the USA could recover some ground as it did in the Reagan era. It does mean that we are witnessing the decline of unipolarity, America's capacity to dominate the international system. The distribution of material strength has passed an inflection point, making it unlikely that it will ever predominate as it did in 1960. As difficult as China's and India's internal problems are, for instance, they are unlikely to return to their weaker, more agrarian pasts. As a more multipolar world emerges and the pecking order is more unsettled, America's diplomatic position has been gradually weakening. Its allies are now in many instances hedging their bets and proving reluctant to align themselves unambiguously. India triangulates with China; Turkey purchases air defence weapon systems from Russia; and, against American urgings, allies like Australia and Britain join the Asian Infrastructure and Investment Bank (AIIB), and others like New Zealand join China's Belt and Road Initiative.

A shift in strategic conditions is also reducing America's edge. None of its rivals are likely to supplant the USA as an equivalent superpower. Rather, the world for a number of reasons is now no one's to conquer. It is harder to dominate militarily than it was in the unusual – and brief – post-war period. Outright conquest and expansion are difficult, because the diffusion of military technologies is defence-dominant in its overall effect, making the world larger strategically.[18] Especially significant is the coming of anti-access/area denial (A2/AD) systems, a panoply of sensors, missiles, air defences and electronic instruments that can destroy or disable surface ships, bases, satellites, logistical hubs and ground forces. In Asia, the focus of wealth, growth and great power rivalries, we have entered a period of sea denial rather than sea control, where conquest across water, when resisted, is increasingly difficult. The coming of anti-ship weaponry that can be based on land – with information technology and long-range precision munitions such as the anti-ship missile – makes it easier to find and sink ships, even without a blue water navy, than to command the maritime commons. The rapid spread of technology in an accelerated international marketplace makes it harder for any one state to exert an overwhelming preponderance of power for long. In the aggregate, while the USA is militarily stronger than its rivals in Europe and Asia, those rivals now possess enough capability to raise costs significantly, enough to make their regions the contested ones. This is a double-edged problem, for the same forces that now make it harder for the USA to project power affordably can also be the basis for preserving a workable balance against rising challengers.

Just as international conditions make unrivalled hegemony a thing of the past, the United States faces the mounting problem of 'insolvency'.[19] This is a dangerous state in which a country's commitments, power and political will are unbalanced, or misaligned. Overextension abroad, exhaustion and fiscal strain at home, and political disorder all feed off one another in a downward spiral, cumulatively threatening the survival of the republic.[20] It has too many commitments, for resources that are increasingly scarce, in an environment that is more resistant to it. It cannot proceed on its present course without the imbalance of means and ends getting worse.

As it is currently organized, US grand strategy gives Washington a proclivity to continuous wars that it pays for through deficits.

Ballooning deficits have created a debt level larger than the US economy. America's deficit has grown to $895 billion a year, as tax cuts, interest on debt, defence build-ups and rising domestic costs outstrip revenue gains from economic growth. The Congressional Budget Office (CBO) warns that 'the prospect of large and growing debt poses substantial risks for the nation'.[21] According to it, federal debt will reach 150 per cent of GDP by 2047, with the share of GDP devoted to interest repayments doubling from 1.6 to 3.1 per cent, becoming the third largest programme behind Social Security and Medicare.[22] Unfunded liabilities and the fiscal imbalance are likely to worsen with an ageing population. The Trump administration has not reversed this imbalance, but aggravated it with tax cuts as well as a renewed deficit-financed military build-up. Heavy fiscal burdens beyond a certain proportion of debt-to-GDP tend to choke economic growth, by crowding out private investment and raising interest rates.[23] A growing debt load directly impedes the country's ability to sustain its way of life alongside its extensive international commitments. The CBO describes the scenarios that rising deficits could lead to: 'Higher interest rates would increase concerns over repayment, which would continue to raise interest rates even further. Even in the absence of a full-blown crisis, such risks would lead to higher rates and borrowing costs for the US government and private sector.' It would also likely result in a political crisis. Confronted with foreign investors' doubts about the USA's capacity to repay its debts and hold down inflation, or even doubts over the dollar as reserve currency, Washington would be pressured to cut expenditure, reduce entitlements, and raise taxes and interest rates.[24] That would induce a political fight over resources, and a collision between defence and welfare expenditure, that would exceed the polarizations of recent time. The current fiscal imbalance also leaves open the possibility of another financial crisis, but without the reserves this time to combat it. Of course, some argue that deficits don't currently matter much, that the USA as a wealthy, creditworthy country enjoys exceptional trust in international investment markets that will not take fright, and can sustain its deficit-financed model. While that could be true, the hazards of running that experiment and being wrong are unacceptable, as the last global financial crisis demonstrated. As Deborah Lucas argues:

> The laws of gravity have not been repealed. Debt, whether issued by households or by governments, is an obligation that will almost certainly crowd out the capacity to pay for pressing future spending needs. The unprecedented levels of peacetime debt accumulation in the developed world, and the cost of caring for an aging population, are on a collision course ... the growing social discontent is nothing compared to the consequences of running down future fiscal capacity to dangerously low levels.[25]

Regarding America's own military casualties, primacists might claim that the casualties of these campaigns are affordable. Max Boot infers that permanent frontier war is well within America's means, given that fatalities in Afghanistan hardly rise above the loss rate of normal training accidents.[26] That disregards the increasing burden of survivors' mental and physical wounds, the costs of non-fatal casualties in disability benefits, through-life care, and loss of income to families, with the costs of care likely to climax decades into the future. Military suicides average twenty per day, higher than the rate of the general population.[27] That these wars are tormenting minds is evident in the appeal to veterans' audiences of classical Greek tragedies about the moral injuries of war, like Sophocles' *Ajax*, about a returning Greek warrior driven to suicidal rage by the Trojan War.[28]

Then there is domestic division. Americans disagree profoundly over their country's international posture. Public attitudes to foreign policy are a mixed picture. Out-and-out isolationist sentiment has dwindled, and the majority still wants the USA to remain sole military superpower and favours the continuation of treaty-based alliances. At the same time, the majority also believes that America 'does too much in helping solve world problems', and prefers a 'shared' than a 'sole' leadership role.[29] Political elites predominantly prefer a single leadership role, are oriented to continuous military activity, and assert American indispensability in solving world problems.

Looking ahead, America's outlook abroad is one of continuous war, and possibilities of war that come hard on the heels of appeals to order. Washington now openly declares an era of great power competition.[30] There is an ominous fatalism in the air. In May 2019, Vice-President Mike Pence told graduating students at West Point that it was a 'virtual certainty' that they would all see combat, naming multiple opponents in multiple theatres, including nuclear-armed ones: against 'radical Islamic terrorists in Afghanistan and Iraq', on the Korean Peninsula and in the Indo-Pacific, 'where North Korea continues to threaten the peace, and an increasingly militarized China challenges our presence in the region', in Europe against an 'aggressive Russia', and even 'in this hemisphere'.[31] Pence too has invoked 'rules-based order'.[32] A state of continuous alarm persists. The Trump administration both depletes its State Department and steps up defence investments to keep America's edge over opponents, raising defence spending by 9.3 per cent, while introducing tax cuts for wealthy classes, creating a combined shortfall in the budget that may outstrip even the fiscal benefits of economic growth. Despite – or because of – America's attempt to double down on primacy, America's allies are hedging their bets, for instance through their participation in the Asia Infrastructure Bank,

China's Belt and Road Initiative, their opposition to Washington's abrogation of the JCPOA nuclear agreement and its new sanctions against Iran, all against Washington's urging.[33] Emerging powers, such as India, and established allies like Turkey also hedge, sharing intelligence with Washington while buying S-400 missiles from Russia and muting criticism of Beijing.[34]

One signature of a state's relative decline is the interaction of war and debt, especially if it is regular war and unsustainable debt.[35] America's defence expenditure and its war-making are expensive in economic and human terms. The Costs of War project at Brown University estimates that the combined costs of the post-9/11 campaigns reached \$5.9 trillion.[36] The orthodox view is that America's defence burdens, at a ratio of 3.6 per cent of GDP, are affordable, and indeed lower than their Cold War highs. This is misleading, however. First, real annual spending on national security as a whole approximates \$1.25 trillion,[37] if beyond the increased defence budget we factor in spending on contractors, the 'war budget' of current operations, the nuclear budget, intelligence, homeland security, the veterans affairs budget, military aid programmes, and the share of all this in interest repayments, and bureaucratic waste. The true call of overall national security investment on GDP is closer to 6.5 per cent.

Second, the historical era of higher defence budgets should not be taken as a precedent for sustaining record defence spending now, as the burden was not easily affordable for Cold War America. At its postwar height from the Korean War/Eisenhower to the Vietnam/Johnson era build-ups, it ranged from 14 per cent in 1953 to 10 per cent in 1968. These investments came with a grave 'guns versus butter' opportunity cost. As Eisenhower warned, it represented a serious diversion of material and human capacity from the poor, hanging humanity 'from a cross of iron'.[38] In those decades, the allocation of scarce resources to arms left one-fifth of the population in poverty, from rural agrarian and mountain coal workers to the African Americans and Hispanics who emigrated to the northern industrial cities living in penury and squalor, which left a bitter legacy that later erupted in racial violence and urban riots, with inner-city neighbourhoods being destroyed. If the internal state of the country is a guide to the affordability of the pursuit of global domination, then Cold War precedents, if nothing else, serve as a warning. Moreover, large deficit-financed military build-ups after external shocks – in the 1960s, 1980s and after 2001– were not part of a stable state of prosperity. Rather, by enlarging budget and current account deficits and leading to unsustainable credit booms and banking crises, they helped to feed a destructive 'boom/bust' dynamic in the business cycle.[39]

Third, another revealing measure of the defence expenditure burden is how much state capacity it consumes, at a time of pressing domestic need. Military spending is primarily a form of consumption. While defence spending can stimulate growth, it is relatively unproductive of wealth compared to other kinds of investment.[40] Current defence spending represents roughly one-quarter of all federal government outlays. It also represents the lion's share of annual discretionary spending (for the financial year 2019, $1.45 trillion). By financial years 2017 and 2018, defence spending had risen to 53 per cent, and the Trump budget will take the proportion to 65 per cent by 2023.[41] Security spending amounts to 'more than the combined total outlays from 2001 to 2016 for the federal departments of education, energy, labor, interior, and transportation, and the National Science Foundation, National Institutes of Health, and the Environmental Protection Agency'.[42] As a result, the country's public infrastructure deteriorates. The American Society of Civil Engineers reports crumbling roads, rusting bridges, decaying railroads and transit systems.

Whether measured in social cohesion or the tangible and visible signs of decay, efforts to expand liberal hegemony abroad are eroding civil society, and democracy, in America. What is to be done?

Paths to Security

For believers in liberal order, there is one supreme historical lesson. It is this: that the surest pathway to security is American leadership of a particularly ambitious kind. Conversely, the main pathway to peril is retreat, a turning inwards from the pursuit of unrivalled dominance. The problems of inaction predominate, the problems of action almost disappear. In the words of Joseph Nye, the memory of the twentieth century is the folly of the USA as a 'great power holding itself aloof from an increasingly turbulent world'.[43] Granted, traditionalists acknowledge that there are multiple pathways to disaster. But their 'primal scene' is the prospect of a post-American world in which the superpower abdicates its responsibilities, leaving unacceptable chaos in its wake. The world, in this view, is a fragile and interconnected ecosystem. An American departure, pullback or even scale-down anywhere threatens to cause a chain reaction of insecurity everywhere. This worldview shares the logic of NSC 68, the seminal Cold War strategic planning document. According to that blueprint, the interlinked world required not just a positional grand strategy to counter specific enemies, but a systemic milieu-oriented strategy to maintain general order. In the words of the NSC 68 report:

> In a shrinking world, which now faces the threat of atomic warfare, it is not an adequate objective merely to seek to check the Kremlin design, for the absence of order among nations is

becoming less and less tolerable. This fact imposes on us, in our own interests, the responsibility of world leadership.[44]

And because it associates the preservation of order with forward-leaning primacy, when things go wrong, especially when aggressive forces attack, the default explanation is that there was not enough American power or resolve present.

Primacists have a sense of the 'tragic'.[45] For them, the tragedy is that a successful superpower can forget the fragility of life, the possibility of chaotic breakdown and the need to confront unpleasant truths square in the face. It grows weary of its responsibilities and seeks to retire, forgetting its own indispensability in terms of maintaining the order, which then implodes. Informed by this logic, proponents of liberal order assume that the USA is obliged morally and strategically to maintain the pursuit of armed supremacy across the globe.

This account of order rests on a certain reading of history, and two regnant historical analogies that warn against the twin errors of isolationism and appeasement. The first is the Wilsonian precedent of the post-First World War period, when American policymakers repudiated international commitments such as alliances or the League of Nations. The second is the Munich analogy, whereby wishful statesmen attempted to appease the unappeasable Nazi Germany. Taken together, these twin errors allowed a super-threat to grow, one that could have been eliminated earlier. That miscalculation, committed by established powers that were unwilling to confront harsh realities, led to a worse war, genocide and catastrophe. Implicit in this analogical reasoning is an optimistic counterfactual claim of missed opportunities. In other words, it presumes that statesmen could have acted earlier and decisively, perhaps with anticipatory war, to destroy potential threats at source. Munich in particular functions as the master-analogy and universal template. It turns a particular, atypical historical episode, in which a fanatically, risk-prone militarist regime took command of a powerful host state, into a cosmic event with general applicability. As former Secretary of State Madeleine Albright repeatedly remarked, 'My mindset is Munich.'[46] Political analyst Bill Kristol was even more impressed by the salience of the precedent, invoking Churchill and Munich sixty-one times in public since 1997 to comprehend foreign policy problems.[47]

The Munich mindset has multiple defects.[48] First, it offers a simplistic account of the dilemmas that confronted policymakers, too readily assuming that anticipatory military action would have worked. Contrary to myths that isolationism led to the Pearl Harbor attack, America was not dormant before 7 December 1941. As well as arming, funding and supplying Britain and creating garrisons and bases across the Atlantic, Washington was already involved in an escalating conflict with Japan over its rapacious occupation of China. From July 1941, its embargo on raw materials and oil, and asset freeze, placed a stranglehold on Japan. This presented Tokyo with the choice between abdicating its imperial ambitions and challenging American power, which it did. America's war originated not primarily in a failure of appeasement in Europe, but in a failure of coercion and deterrence in the Pacific. Would an American alliance with France and/or Britain, and perhaps with American troops in Europe, have deterred Hitler's aggression? That is possible, and to the extent that the policies that were undertaken failed to prevent war, such an attempt is preferable. We cannot be confident in the judgement, however. Such an Anglo-French-American alignment would probably not have been enough to arrest the deeply rooted forces for conflict in inter-war Europe. It probably would not have restrained France's fiercely independent and belligerent attitude to Germany, or reassured a Stalin fearful of Western capitalist predation. Nor would it have reduced the Nazi regime's appetite for a racial war in the East. And nor would it remove German leaders' own pessimistic and preventive calculation that a dangerous Soviet threat was rising, given that its ideological adversary and geopolitical competitor to its east with three times its population and forty times its land mass was undertaking an accelerated industrial revolution. Germany also had a vote in the matter. The 'earlier deterrence' model assumes that Germany would have resigned itself to being restrained, as the USA ferried military forces over to the European continent. The same regime in Berlin that they rightly viewed as pathologically aggressive, they assume, would then cooperatively have agreed to be deterred from its deeply held, ideological commitment to expansion. That a build-up in Europe could have brought about a spiral, rather than a stand-down, leading to a German temptation towards preventive strikes, is hardly considered.

As for Britain, there were compelling strategic reasons to postpone a clash with Nazi Germany. Prime Minster Neville Chamberlain and others were hardly blameless in their suppression of dissent and innocent appraisals of the Führer. But every option seemed murky. Emerging from the Great Depression and in a world of many totalitarian potential threats, Britain was dealing with a weak hand of economic vulnerability, multiple commitments and scarce resources. It was trying to protect far-flung imperial interests in East Asia, the Mediterranean and in continental Europe with stretched navies and allies of whom they were wary. At home, its population constrained any belligerence. Having been branded a warmonger in 1935, when he was Chancellor of the Exchequer, for beginning rearmament, Chamberlain, by then the prime minister, was by 1940 denounced for his capitulations. As it was, Britain rearmed more slowly than it might have, for fear of causing economic dislocation. Time was a vital commodity. The country needed time to develop its air defence system of extended radar and effective fighter planes, which turned out to be critical to staying on the chessboard. Could a grand Anglo-French-Soviet coalition have done the job? Perhaps, but alliance blocs had seemed suspect ever since the July Crisis in 1914 that led to the start of the First World War. States were coy about chain-ganging themselves to the conflicts of distrusted others. Stalin's purging of his officer corps did little to build faith in his ability to checkmate Hitler on the eastern flank. And as the subsequent war underlined, cooperating with the Soviet Union to destroy the Nazi threat would involve appeasement of Stalin's territorial demands in Eastern Europe.

Neither is it clear that a preventive war in 1936 would have been a prudent alternative. As British decision-makers feared, along with even the most hard-line advocates of rebalancing like Winston Churchill, attacking Germany over the Rhineland remilitarization crisis of 1936 could have made the threat, and the underlying problem, even worse. The early action counterfactual proposes that a limited war would somehow have reversed the direction of a regime whose leader had desired major war ever since coming to power in 1933. It may have strengthened rather than weakened the Nazi regime domestically, and, like the earlier French occupation of the Ruhr in 1923, may not instil a lesson of punishment and deterrence. It could well instead have inflamed grievances, increased Germany's revisionist hyper-nationalism and growing public sympathy for the Reich, 'feeding Hitler's characterisation of Germany as besieged by hostile forces conspiring to keep it weak and suppressed'.[49] Contrary to his retrospective claims, even Winston Churchill in 1936 did not advocate preventive war, but diplomacy, rearmament and collective security guarantees under the League of Nations, to protect the balance of power, a position shared by the government. Pre-empting rather than responding to Hitler would have meant initiating war without domestic consent or international support. Neither was the later Czechoslovakia crisis an auspicious opportunity to attack. War in 1938 would have sacrificed the participation of empire states like Australia, Canada and South Africa, which were not prepared to bleed for Czechoslovakia. And anticipatory war would probably have been denied the economic and material support of the USA that would prove so critical. Given these uncertainties and dilemmas, while appeasement did not prevent war, it bought Britain valuable time. In the battle of ideas and legitimacy, it left the burden of aggression on Germany. The suggestion that, instead, a limited war could have eliminated such an intense force for nationalist belligerence as Nazism is fanciful.

The analogy is also dangerous because it over-privileges one pathway to insecurity. There are multiple pathways through which a hegemonic power can fall into disaster. It is true that 'under-balancing' and restraint can allow dangerous threats to grow. Overbalancing – arming rapidly and on a large scale, forming more alliances, or making threats of preventive war – can also lead to disaster, as in the case of the *Kaiserreich* and a militarized Europe in 1914. In fact, of the major wars in history, a more prevalent pattern is not the Munich model of appeasing dangerous aggressors and under-reaction to a growing threat, but of established powers seeking to arrest their own decline by suppressing a rising challenger.[50] States can also bring themselves down in the long run by saddling themselves with unaffordable debt and multiple, exhausting wars, as in the case of Philip II of Spain or the Polish-Lithuanian Commonwealth. Hegemons can fall precipitously when they fail to anticipate changes in the balance of power, fail to diagnose its roots and so fail to adjust.[51] History suggests strategies that bring a state's power and commitments into balance and that

175

can successfully prevent overstretch, insolvency or exhaustion.[52] As Michael O'Hanlon argues:

[C]ompetitive great powers can produce cycles of insecurity, rivalry and provocation that lead to a war no one would have wanted. That kind of danger, in today's world, is at least as real as the fear that an insatiable aggressor nation could keep expanding its appetite and ambitions the way that Nazi Germany or Tojo Japan did in the 1930s and 1940s. In other words, mutual overreaction to small crises can produce war just as easily as weakness and deterrence failure can.[53]

In 1936, having gone through the ordeal of the First World War, as a consensus shifted towards rearmament, British policymakers still worried that both pathways were possible.

The historian Margaret MacMillan has reasserted the Wilson and Munich analogies, only to demonstrate their limits as a guide. In her account, the tragic pattern of history points in one direction, the folly of retreat or inaction:

[T]he calamity of World War II owed as much to the failure of the democracies' leaders in the interwar decades to deal with rule-breaking dictators such as Mussolini, Hitler, and the Japanese militarists. One wonders how history might have unfolded if London and Washington, instead of turning away, had built a transatlantic alliance with a strong security commitment to France and pushed back against Adolf Hitler's first aggressive moves while there was still time to stop him. . . . Today's world is not wholly comparable to the worlds that emerged from the rubble of the two world wars. Yet as the United States once again turns inward and tends only to its immediate interests, it risks ignoring or underestimating the rise of populist dictators and aggressive powers until the hour is dangerously late. President Vladimir Putin of Russia has already violated international rules and norms, most notably in Crimea, and others – such as President Recep Tayyip Erdoğan of Turkey or Chinese President Xi Jinping – seem willing to do the same. And as Washington and other democratic powers abdicate their responsibility for the world, smaller powers may abandon their hopes for a peaceful international order and instead submit to the bullies in their neighbourhoods. A hundred years on, 1919 and the years that followed still stand as a sombre warning.[54]

This is an ill-considered indictment. Today's world is not 'wholly comparable', yet that insight does not preclude MacMillan from making sweeping and flawed comparisons. She overlooks the US attempt to 'deal with' Imperial Japan, a confrontation that led to genocidal war in Asia. She presumably calls for brinksmanship or preventive war against Germany and Italy in the 1930s, as evidently she regards the rearmament that happened as insufficient, on the assumption that the 'aggressive' 'rule-breaking dictator' could be easily stopped. MacMillan's assertion that the US-led West is passive today is simply wrong. It overlooks the Trump administration's intensification of US primacy, such as its dangerous brinksmanship abroad in the Gulf. She then demands, without spelling it out, simultaneous competition with China, Russia and Turkey, showing a cavalier disregard for the limits of power and the necessity of trade-offs.

With regard to Russia, against Macmillan's claim that America is supine in the face of Putin's aggression, the USA under two presidents has imposed increased sanctions, expelled scores of diplomats, increased NATO deployments and provided non-lethal, then lethal, equipment to Ukraine. While Trump may be instinctively conciliatory towards the Putin regime, the USA's posture towards Russia is increasingly hostile.[55] Trump's advisors, the security bureaucracy and Congress have ensured a hard line on the basis that Russia is an aggressive revisionist power, bent on dominating its near abroad and shattering Western alliances. Trump has appointed hawkish American primacists and Putin critics to Russia-related official posts. He has expanded sanctions, including an extended list of targets under the Magnitsky Act. The Justice Department has forced the television channel Russia Today to register as a foreign agent. Trump has expelled Russian diplomats and he has armed Ukraine, Romania and Poland. The USA has reinforced NATO's enhanced forward presence in Poland and the Baltic states with increased troop numbers and more exercises, and has presided over the expansion of NATO into Montenegro and Macedonia, against Russian efforts to keep its clients in the Balkans and resist EU-NATO enlargement, while courting Ukraine and Georgia as future alliance members. The USA also acquires low-yield nuclear weapons with the explicit rationale of creating competition against Moscow, to remain 'top of the pack' among nuclear powers. It abrogated the Intermediate Nuclear Forces Treaty, partly on the basis that Russia has been in violation of it for some time, and partly to free its hand in order to compete with China. Trump twice authorized airstrikes against Syria, Russia's Middle Eastern client state, against Putin's protests. He loosened the rules of engagement in Syria, struck Russian troops and mercenaries there, and bragged about it. So far, the USA refuses to recognize Crimea as part of Russia. The net effect in Moscow is to create the impression that détente with Trump's America is impossible.

If such measures are not enough, MacMillan and other traditionalists should specify what more confrontational steps the USA should take. Such policy details go missing. Inattention to the fact of US coercive measures, and to the problem that there are multiple pathways to danger, serves MacMillan's general and suspect point, that early and militarized confrontation works, that restraint fails, that the only danger worth worrying about is turning inwards, not belligerence. It reflects a worldview that can only comprehend disappointment as the result of isolation. The application of this reductionist mentality, the incautious use of the Munich analogy and the desire to play Winston Churchill, has a dismal record. It trapped decision-makers into thinking and acting with imprudent belligerence, and intellectually informed the disastrous expeditions into Korea beyond the 38th parallel in 1950, Suez in 1956, the Bay of Pigs in 1961, Vietnam in 1966 and Iraq in 2003.[56] We should expect that persisting with the same mythology about the past will produce similar results in the future. Let us consider alternatives.

What Is to Be Done?

As a language of power, paeans to liberal order frame the discussion in narrow terms as a choice between the *Pax Americana* in updated or adjusted form, versus a replay of the disastrous inter-war period. This is a false choice. The order's visionaries assume that their order is largely innocent of its own problems, or that it contains the source of its own remedies, and that the solution is more and better-applied American power. They scold Americans for their insularity and neglect of international duties, summoning them back to greatness. Their outlook is born of long success, an assumption of latent American power, and a mytho-historical memory rooted in the Wilson and Munich moments. They believe America must promote democratic capitalism abroad in order to secure it at home. The upshot is that America's only prudent path is to maintain its leadership, its alliance and its commercial system, and assert its armed supremacy against its three main competitors, China, Russia and Iran, in the hope that they will one day become supplicants in an American-led order. The results of this wishful thinking were not encouraging when American power was at its height. Now that the margin of its relative power is narrowing, the supplication of rivals under American primacy is less and less likely. What, therefore, should the USA do instead?

Some critics conclude that America would be better off pulling back from some or all of the theatres traditionally valued for their power potential (Northeast Asia, Western Europe and the Middle East), and focusing instead on the critical region of Asia or coming home altogether.[57] America can better secure itself, some argue, by bidding farewell to geopolitics, and relying on the dynamics of balancing, nuclear deterrence and distance to shield itself from threats.[58] Key US allies in these regions, such as Japan, Germany, Britain, France and South Korea, are wealthy, militarily proficient and technologically advanced, with two also already possessing their own nuclear arsenals. A post-American Asia or Europe would pose little threat, because local states would balance against rather than bandwagon with the rising power and because nuclear deterrence would make expansion unlikely in the first place, and America would remain secure with its ocean moats, formidable material capability and its own nuclear deterrent. If balancing is the default condition of international relations, then, left to their own devices, America's potential adversaries in Eurasia will have their hands full dealing with one another. Geographical proximity to one another, nationalism and the insecurities of an anarchic world would drive them into ceaseless balancing and counterbalancing, checking one another's capacity to project power beyond their hemispheres/theatres. The heartland mostly checks itself. Progressive versions of this argument call for America to dismantle its empire and renounce geopolitical competition, renew nation-building at home and address common international problems like climate change.[59]

Before offering an alternative to 'coming home', we need a coherent account of American security. What are Americans supposed to protect, and how? The referent object – the thing supposed to be shielded – is not mere biological survival, or the mere maximization of power. Rather, it is the institutions and liberties of the republic. And in the weightiest American traditions of security thought, the gravest threat is not that of being annihilated by an external power, but of self-defeat. As Abraham Lincoln prophesied in his Lyceum speech of 1838, 'If destruction be our lot' it would not come at the hands of a 'transatlantic military giant'. Rather, 'we must ourselves be its author and its finisher'.[60]

Rather, two alternative insidious threats can destroy the republic's character. First, a concentration of threatening power abroad could force America to become an illiberal garrison state. A hostile hegemony in Eurasia would be dangerous not primarily because it could lead to a direct assault on the USA. Rather, it would endanger the nation's *republican* political life, by frightening it to turn itself into Sparta on a large scale. While America would remain a difficult target for conquest or strangulation and could well physically survive such a state of permanent emergency, it would be tempted to militarize and regiment its society, thereby weakening civil society, wasting resources and empowering the state and a military elite to such an extent that it would suffocate its constitutional liberties. Second, the excessive pursuit of power abroad also could destroy the republic, by turning it into a militarized, overextended empire in a permanent state of alarm. Both scenarios have driven the agonies of US debate about world affairs, especially after America became a 'national security state' during and after the Second World War.[61]

The task for US statecraft is to steer away from both perils: the scenario of leaving behind a vacuum where hostile imbalances form, and the scenario of militarized overreach that two decades of the War on Terror have partly realized. To preserve its way of life, the USA still has a strong interest in helping prevent one hostile power from acquiring hegemony over Europe or Asia. To this end, the USA does not have to choose between dominating the world and coming home. Neither can it abandon geopolitics outright, as the international system condemns its inhabitants to competing for security as well as cooperating. America should give up the pursuit of global dominance, which has proven to be more the problem than the remedy. It should cease trying to expand democratic capitalism and regime change abroad, a project that inadvertently breeds violent blowback, and undermines the republic at home. Attempting to hold on to hegemony globally and suppressing rivals in every major theatre will exhaust the USA, while incentivizing its rivals to cooperate. Equally, America should retain a hand in Europe and Asia, a hand that it uses to maintain a favourable balance of power, without inadvertently creating monsters to destroy. It can negotiate a new multipolarity, safe enough for its institutions to thrive.

America pulling back to its own hemisphere could lead to a China-dominated Asia, or worse: the formation of a combined Eurasian adversary. China or Russia are not currently true peers of American power. They do possess enough latent potential and/or extant capability to threaten America's core security interest. While Russia carries far less weight economically than China, a Moscow–Beijing axis remains a possibility in the right conditions. That may not be a probable outcome, but it is possible enough to hedge against. Sometimes empires and agglomerations of power are formed, rather than the more competitive dynamics that often accompany power transitions.[62] Even if a reversion to balancing is probable, just how confident can we be that, without US presence, the world reverts to it, that rival hegemonies do not form and that nuclear and conventional deterrence would prevail? It is a question of knowledge and risk. And at its best, the tradition of realism stresses the uncertainty of things. Part of realism's critique of the War on Terror and adventures in nation-building – alliance expansion – is that Washington has presumed, time and again, to know more than it does or can. Bandwagoning is less prevalent than balancing, historically, but not unknown. And while the logic of nuclear deterrence is powerful, we cannot know how likely it is to hold. Would it be wisest to 'bet the farm' on balancing and deterrence?

Consider a different prudential calculation, that retaining some forward presence is an extra layer of protection against the possibility of hostile rival hegemons even taking place, by keeping a balancing mechanism abroad. The 'threat picture' here is not that one foreign power would 'run the table' by sheer conquest. Rather, in the absence of a rival pole of power, smaller states, if not well coordinated or if offered the right mix of carrots/sticks, just might bandwagon, submitting themselves to the new hegemon's authority. China's exponential growth, if it continued, could prove attractive enough to bring Asian states under its sway. Indeed, we are already seeing much hedging behaviour by US allies in the region. Certainly, a state/bloc that obtained regional hegemony over Asia could become a peer. A hostile/ rival Asia organized in such fashion would likely frighten Americans. That in itself could create dangerous competition and confrontation, and the internal weakening of the republic. While such an outcome may not presently be likely, there are regional actors with both reason to find it tempting and sufficient capability to at least contemplate region-wide coercion in pursuit of dominance.[63]

Of course, remaining present abroad and attempting to hold on to pre-eminence carries its own obvious security risks. As things stand, and with the default setting of Washington as forward-leaning domination, it is the second scenario that is currently the most likely. With escalating rivalries under way against two Eurasian heavyweights, Russia and China, and potential confrontations with two designated proliferation 'rogues' in Iran and North Korea, the USA is in danger of being locked into combat, or collision course, with four adversaries simultaneously.

To correct this dangerous direction of travel, Washington should take three, interlinked, grand strategic steps: to contain a rising China, to divide China and Russia, and to reduce its footprint in the Middle East. Readers will likely disagree with some or all of these recommendations. If so, a general observation should hold: that, as in the past, successful statecraft will require Washington to make bargains with illiberal forces, and to compromise with liberal principles. To navigate ahead, Washington will need clear eyes about the nature of its choices. To contain China and reach an entente with Russia for the greater good, to limit its commitments in line with its power, the USA and its allies will have to flout rules, bend principles, betray populations and make dark bargains. That is true of every geopolitical competition in history. Repeating ahistorical mantras won't make that ugly fact go away, and could hinder the effort to deal with it.

China, Russia and America are already in a security competition. The question is how to create a balance of power in Eurasia by keeping it divided. Designing an intelligent containment strategy against China's expansion will be a difficult task, a 'goldilocks' problem of creating enough counterpower to limit Beijing's capacity to dominate its region, without repeating the hubristic measures that made America's last Cold War so dangerous and damaging. Judging from public pronouncements and observations from government advisors, China's aspirations are dominance in the Asia-Pacific and the restoration of its historic role as the Middle Kingdom, predominant in eastern Eurasia with the United States side-lined.[64] Across multiple dimensions, China asserts itself aggressively, seizing disputed territories in the South China Sea, infiltrating the domestic politics of America's democratic allies as far away as Australia, openly threatening Taiwan with reunification by force and attempting to bring states into its orbit via the Belt and Road initiative of infrastructure development.

For its part, Russia places itself in a state of mobilization, enhancing its readiness to respond to emergencies in an arc of crisis around its borders.[65] Whether it is primarily driven by revanchist imperial power ambitions, to rebuild its domination of the 'near abroad', or is defensively fending off the expansion of the Euro-Atlantic world into its orbit, it accepts security competition with the USA as a fact of life. Moscow fears that the superpower sponsors subversion and 'colour' revolutions along its frontiers and within its capital. Ominously, Moscow regards major war as possible, even likely.

Recognizing that any opportunity for a grand bargain with rivals has passed, seasoned policy hands have urged Washington to contain this or that revisionist power, whether China or Russia, or coerce rogue states to denuclearize.[66] Any of these efforts may be justifiable. But they cannot be sustained all at once. Washington should decide which adversaries it most wishes to suppress or resist, and in rank order. It should then try to reduce the number of adversaries by limiting the terms of competition, and, if possible, create the conditions in which those adversaries compete with (or distance themselves from) one another. To divide adversaries would break from recent policy but not be a radical departure, historically. In the mid-twentieth century, the USA help defeat the Axis powers by allying with the totalitarian Soviet Union. It prevailed in the Cold War by actively dividing the Soviet Union against China. It defeated Al Qaeda in Iraq by realigning with former Sunni insurgents.

There is little sign of active splitting currently, however. Rather, the USA is encouraging the perception of a common enemy. By militarily positioning itself within striking distance through a semi-encircling presence, expanding alliances and entertaining further expansion, by establishing a reputation as sponsor of colour revolutions, and as an overthrower of regimes, Washington helps draw China and Russia closer together into a balancing coalition. A nascent Russia–China alliance, or at least convergence, is suggested by Russia's own inter-agency enquiry into the possibility,[67] the frequency of Putin–Xi contact, deliberate tightening of economic interaction and overt displays and declarations of close military ties through joint exercises and arms sales.[68] A combined Eurasian competitor may be emerging.

It does not have to be this way. The USA has a geopolitical advantage, that it is based far away. Most powers, most of the time, are more concerned by the potential threat of other nearby land powers than of distant sea powers.[69] Based in the Western Hemisphere, the USA has less of a compelling security interest in adversaries' backyards than they themselves, and it can choose to adopt a more distant pose. Russia and China, by contrast, are neighbours, so cannot withdraw; both are primarily continental land-based military powers, and historically such proximity can exacerbate rivalries and mutual fears. Sino-Russian antagonism is not a natural condition. Only under the right conditions can these rivalries again grow. This is not a plea for a trilateral realignment whereby one state agrees to be the USA's 'geopolitical hammer' and teams up with America to contain the other.

Rather, it is to suggest that more American restraint in one theatre could make space for Russia–China frictions to take effect in another.

To assist a distancing between Russia and China, to concentrate effort and to stabilize the East European theatre, the USA will need to do something that liberal order orthodoxy would preclude: attempt a settlement with Russia with significant mutual concessions, including sacrificing the interests of non-NATO countries on its eastern flank, in order to ease the growing sense of mutual threat.[70] To facilitate negotiations, the USA should revive government-to-government dialogue to reach a new bargain.

On the Western side, meeting Russia halfway will involve at minimum a cancellation of the Bucharest Declaration of 2008, the pledge to enlarge NATO into Ukraine and Georgia at a future date. Incursion, or the threat of incursion, into Russia's self-declared sphere is a matter of existential importance to Moscow, far larger in importance than it is even for the most hawkish Americans. Russia has said so repeatedly, and acted on it. In reaction to the Bucharest Declaration, it struck into Georgia in the summer of 2008 by recognizing the independence of Russian exclaves in that country, bombing its coast and its capital. And in reaction to the unseating of a pro-Russian government in Kiev in 2014, Russia bit off the Crimean peninsula and sponsored an armed secessionist movement in eastern Ukraine. Since the USA cannot withdraw from NATO without risking the destruction of the alliance itself, it should visibly reaffirm its commitment to NATO countries and the Baltic States, as it is doing. It should also draw a line under further eastward expansion. Informally, the USA will have to concede that Crimea is gone and will remain in Russian hands, which American policymakers privately concede. This need not be the beginning of a juggernaut of Russian expansion. Putin's acquisition of Ukraine has come at some cost to Russia, as its investments there are expensive, so imperial prestige does not come cheap. Given the correlation of forces and the limitations on Russia's capacity to aggrandize its sphere, there is some basis for restoring stability. Washington should terminate the policy that effectively forces Ukrainians in an ethnically fractured country to choose between the Euro-Atlantic and Russia. Some argue that this should lead to a direct Russian sphere of influence, in which Ukraine and Georgia are 'Finlandized' or 'Hong Kong-ized', whereby a smaller country cedes control of its foreign policy to a more powerful neighbour in return for control over its domestic affairs.[71] If this is too much to ask, a militarily non-aligned Ukraine with greater autonomy for Donetsk and Luhansk, with Russian forces and arms removed from Ukrainian soil, would be a realistic and sustainable objective. More broadly, the USA should end its campaign of encouraging democratic regime change in Moscow, a commitment that makes it harder to credibly insist on an end to foreign electoral interference, and one that America has no trouble keeping with more authoritarian states like Saudi Arabia. Washington as the main security provider should also demand that Baltic governments more consistently respect ethnic Russians, both a real issue and a potential pretext for Russian aggression. On the Russian side, it will involve at minimum the end of sabotage operations, election interference and targeted assassinations against and within Western democracies. It will require a mutual commitment to cyber restraint. It will involve renewed negotiations over the bilateral nuclear strategic balance.

There is no guarantee that Russia would be willing to cooperate. But it is worth a try. Russia's long-term stagnation, and the strain it is already suffering in waging competition, means that it may be open to a new and less expensive relationship. US-led sanctions have inflicted attrition and significant damage to Russia's economy, adding to the incentives for concessions on non-core issues. Without such a possibility, to avert its long decline it may turn to a new strategic partner in Beijing. In fact, it already is. While Russia is not strong enough to bid for hegemony in Europe, it is strong enough to add significant capability to geopolitical competition. On multiple fronts, it has the capacity to divert China's attention, to enlarge or reduce its overall position – through arms sales to China, their common border, or Russia's UNSC veto.

Unlike Russia, China on its current trajectory is large, wealthy and determined enough to directly challenge America's pre-eminence. If it cannot do so globally, certainly it can and is doing so in Asia. And Asia is the central theatre of power politics in the twenty-first century. China is now unmistakably challenging American primacy in its own large neighbourhood in the 'Indo-Pacific' region. But America is pushing back. If there was once an opportunity for the two Asian heavyweights to negotiate a settlement in which they would share power, that moment has probably passed.[72] The People's Republic may not pose a global ideological challenge in the way that Soviet communism did. Neither does it match America's aggregate power as yet. It may, however, have an imbalance of resolve in its favour. By being located in Asia where the contest is, and with its history, it cares more, and is willing to run greater risks, than the USA, given its higher stakes in the region. Its autocratic system also enjoys rapid economic growth, something that confers legitimacy amongst its own vast population for the time being, and to purchase military capabilities that make it a difficult target. Should both countries ever go to the mat, although the USA would be most likely to prevail, China could now inflict grievous costs. The danger is not primarily that China will attempt a direct assault on America. Rather, it is that a gradual shift in the balance of power could lead to bandwagoning by other states. It could also lead to a dangerous *fait accompli* moment, where China seizes territory and places the burden of response on America, giving it the choice of dangerous military escalation or humiliating backdown. America's choice, therefore, is whether to withdraw and abandon the field to Asian states to cooperate or compete as they choose, trusting in America's other strengths for its security. Alternatively, it is to stay in Asia and apply an intelligent containment strategy.

What would an intelligent containment strategy against China look like? The USA and its allies are already taking prudent steps in some policy areas, to prevent hostile control of critical national infrastructure by screening the investments of state-owned enterprises from hostile powers, and reviewing digital defences and countermeasures against cyber infiltration by hostile actors.[73] Washington can also capitalize on a general shift in the military offence–defence balance, to make it difficult for China to impose itself on other countries. Fortunately, the very forces that are reducing America's military edge also make it difficult for adversaries to expand in the face of determined resistance. It can equip Asian states with the means to impose heavy costs on an aggressor in order to blunt attacks.[74] This is important with regard to direct clashes, to deter attack. It is important also as a way of deterring *fait accompli* aggression, whereby China would launch focused attacks on a limited scale below the threshold of American retaliation, picking off US allies or initiating crises for stakes that are limited, forcing a climb-down. Placing small units as 'tripwire' forces, making it harder for China to attack smaller allies without attacking US forces, would help dissuade *fait accompli* measures, with further layers of more protected forces placed within range to reinforce. And reinforcing the A2/AD capabilities of Asian states is also important as a means to maintain a rough balance, making states secure enough not to give up and 'bandwagon' in the face of a preponderant Beijing. This would include arming Taiwan enough to make it a 'porcupine', a target that can inflict heavy losses on an amphibious invader. Of course, these efforts can only work with allied cooperation. US protective measures would help shape allies' choices: resisting the rise of hegemon in their backyard would make more sense if a larger and more powerful state would help them do so.

As part of tending to the strategic balance in Asia and checking China's adventurism without the process escalating out of control, the USA will need to cooperate with other balancing actors that are not permanent allies. This will include emerging middle powers like Malaysia and Indonesia, and major tier two powers like India. As with separating China from Russia, this will make it necessary to strike illiberal bargains. To get its way and to cultivate the support of other rising states in containing China, the USA will probably have to sacrifice the interests of others: for example, to limit or mute criticisms of India's human rights violations in Kashmir, or Indonesia's repression of groups within its own archipelago. To keep competition with China stable enough, with scope for bargaining once the outer limits of expansion are clear, the USA should disavow the cause of regime change within Beijing. To prevent North Korea's nuclear arsenal and missile programme from becoming a flashpoint for catastrophic war, Washington will have to learn to live with Pyongyang's bomb as a political reality, by abandoning the failed effort to coerce disarmament or bring about internal collapse, and instead attempting to build a stable deterrence relationship. And given the economic interdependence between China and America, part of the price of containment will be a reduction in economic growth. Limiting the access of Chinese state-owned companies and Chinese investment in areas critical to security capability, like public infrastructure, will be necessary.

An intelligent containment strategy will consciously differ from the excessive aspects of its Cold War precedent. It would conscientiously attempt to sustain a balance, doing enough to check China's expansion without turning the competition into a generalized struggle without geopolitical limit. Avoiding minor, open-ended brushfire wars would be an important – and difficult – part of prudent containment. Brushfire wars are conflicts that seem to begin as minor engagements but are accompanied by extravagant and growing ambitions, without time limitations or well-defined goals. Such wars normally involve either overthrowing an embattled oppressive government or creating and supporting a corrupt and weak regime. Alternatively, they begin as efforts to curtail a humanitarian disaster or stabilize a war zone, only to inflict unanticipated costs. And they typically endure to the point where an additional 'great power' obsession takes hold, namely the feared loss of credibility. These minor conflicts can, and often do, turn out to be expensive in blood and treasure, compared to what decision-makers expected, and 'there is always the chance that the great power could miscalculate and find itself embroiled in a protracted and bloody stalemate'.[75]

In a security competition, it is tempting to view all conflicts as interlinked, to obsess over saving face and waging wars to establish credibility. Powers are well advised to avoid becoming involved in continuous wars that lack specific, achievable political goals, especially those designed to exterminate '-isms' that lack geographical boundary. Likewise, as far as possible, Washington should resist the temptation to shape the overall balance of power through the theatre of war to display strength to a global audience. Such struggles are likely to be internationalized and therefore longer and bloodier, as other powers intervene to bleed their competitor.[76] Indeed, to get caught in a grinding minor war presents opportunities to one's rivals to inflict attrition from a distance. Recall French support for American revolutionaries against the British Empire; British support for Yugoslav, Greek and

Albanian insurgents against Nazi occupation during the Second World War; Soviet assistance to Viet Cong insurgents against the USA; and US sponsorship of the international mujahideen against the Soviet Union in Afghanistan. Brushfire wars are also likely to involve client regimes whose interests do not harmoniously align with those of their patron, and recent history is a reminder of the 'misalignment' problem.[77] If anything, getting embroiled in a drawn-out campaign against weaker but determined opponents, where an imbalance of will favours them, is more likely to drain precious resources and divert diplomatic energies, exhibit fatigue rather than strength, exacerbate domestic division and reveal the limits of one's power. Indeed, a war to uphold 'dominoes' can trigger a political crisis in the heart of the metropole, jeopardizing in turn the domestic consensus needed to sustain competition abroad in the first place.[78]

In Washington, it is contentious to suggest that the USA should divide Russia and China, and accommodate one while resisting the other. The bipartisan consensus amongst security experts is to assume that only a state of supremacy over all rivals will suffice, and to assume that the problem lies in the insufficiency of *means* or the inefficiency of its application of power, and to call for the allocation of more resources and their smarter use in order to sustain US dominance. That the pursuit of dominance could be the source of the problem is scarcely considered. The 2018 National Defense Strategy Commission report, for instance, assumes dominance to be America's obvious national interest. It complains that as rivals challenge American power, US military superiority and its capacity to wage concurrent wars have been eroded, because of reduced defence expenditure, and advises that the government spend more while cutting entitlements.[79]

Even the USA cannot prudently take on every adversary on multiple fronts. The costs of military campaigns against these adversaries in their backyards, whether the Baltic States or Taiwan, would outstrip the losses that the US military has sustained in decades. To risk escalation on multiple such fronts would court several dangers. It would overstretch the country. If in such conditions, current and lavish expenditure is not enough to buy enough security or military preponderance – and it may not be – then the failure lies not in an inability to spend even more. Neither does it lie in the lack of success in sacrificing the quality of civic life at home to service predominance abroad according to an increasingly unachievable 'two war standard'. It lies, rather, in the pursuit of hegemony itself, and the failure to balance commitments and power.

To attempt to suppress every adversary simultaneously would drive enemies to operate together, creating hostile coalitions. It also may not succeed. Counter-proliferation in North Korea is difficult enough, but the task becomes more difficult still if China refuses to cooperate over enforcing sanctions. Concurrent competitions would also split American resources, attention and time. By exacerbating the strain on scarce resources between defence, consumption and investment, it would raise the polarizing question of what preponderance is for, undermining the domestic consensus needed to support it. At the same time, reduced investment in infrastructure and education would damage the economic foundations for conducting competition abroad in the first place. Altogether, indiscriminate competition would risk creating the thing most feared in traditional US grand strategy – a hostile Eurasian alliance leading to continuous mobilization against hostile coalitions, turning the republic into an illiberal garrison state. If the USA's prospects as a great power face a problem, it is not the size of the defence budget, or the material weight of resources at America's disposal, or popular reluctance to exercise leadership. Rather, the problem lies in the size of the policy that those capabilities must serve.

To make the problem smaller, Washington should take steps to make the pool of adversaries smaller.

As well as dividing Russia and China, the USA should limit its liability in the Middle East. Those who advocate greater restraint towards that unrewarding region vary in the extent to which America should draw down. Some advocate a withdrawal offshore, to remain within striking distance and act as balancer of last resort. Others advocate a light footprint onshore. Still others, including the author, advocate a wholesale withdrawal from the region except for a minimal diplomatic presence. All agree that current commitments in the region impose too much cost and risk for not enough reward, that the region is declining in its international salience, and that an on-the-ground presence of garrisons, bases and ceaseless military activity does not reliably increase US security, and in many ways undermines it. The experience of permanent war for two decades has been an education in the limits of power, and a caution against reflexive interventionism. As Janan Ganesh argues:

> [T]here is a record from which to draw some empirical judgement. The US, it is not 'too soon to tell', lacks the resources, knowledge or domestic public backing to direct the destinies of nations in other hemispheres with minimal democratic pedigree. That there will never be a good time to leave is not a reason to stay.[80]

The United States cannot afford, and does not need, to transform recalcitrant Middle Eastern societies, pursuing either regime change or 'eliminationist vision of counter-terrorism'.[81] Except in atypical circumstances, occupying countries does not stabilize them affordably or end conflict, but catalyses further conflict.

Return to modest, conventional counterterrorism – ending the War on Terror – is needed, delegating the task to coordinated and patient international police work, with fewer and more discriminate acts of force. The case for withdrawing outright from a theatre of declining importance is compelling. If that is too much to ask in today's Washington, at the least the USA could initiate a 'blank sheet' policy with its regional allies. Beginning on the assumption that it may leave, the USA could ask its allies to outline how they will start the relationship afresh, and how they will do things differently. An 'agonizing reappraisal' is due.

Along with these large geopolitical moves, the USA should take other steps at home to strengthen its own governance, social cohesion and capacity for sound statecraft. These would include a reassertion of the role of Congress in foreign policy, and a return to proper congressional review over war-making decisions, as a check on an overmighty executive. It would also include ending the deficit financing of military campaigns, returning wars to citizen accountability. It would require a fiscal correction, along the lines of the Simpson/Bowles deficit reduction report of 2010, which outlined six reforms to reduce the federal deficit by $3.8 trillion. In short, in forging a new grand strategy, it should rebuild a coalition at home by consulting more, by saving more and borrowing and spending less, by restoring its negotiating power, to make its arms less central to its statecraft.

The Big Story

The measures outlined here would carry public opinion in its broad outlines. Against the polarization of our time, most people prefer a political, economic and diplomatic settlement somewhere in the middle. They would prefer to restore constitutional government at home while limiting the enthusiasm for liberal crusading adventures in regime change. They have no desire for escalating trade wars, but also believe the brute force of international markets should be tamed, with a mixed economy offering some protective intervention at home, and with trade agreements that include greater protections for labour. They value some alliances in principle, and some power projection abroad, but would like Washington to revise some commitments and some alliances, to stop expanding them, and to shift some burdens onto rich allies. They support a robust defence force, and also support raising the threshold for military action. On the question of homeland security, they would like to go beyond the reductionist debate over walls versus bridges, to balance humane generosity with secure borders. And they doubt whether the core interests, or values, of freedom-loving nations really are served by embroilment with Saudi Arabia and its bloc of Gulf monarchies. They sense that America should try to find an alternative path in its dealings with rivals, other than either pulling back or escalating rivalry without limit. And they accept that the USA ought to continue to be a major shaper of our world, but that solo leadership or primacy is no longer possible in a more contested planet where wealth and power have shifted.

However, it is not the broad populace that is most continuously engaged in making foreign policy. For the USA to revise its role prudently, it would require that the foreign policy establishment be receptive to them, and for the ideas to gain enough legitimacy. For a reassessment to be realistic, the country must be able to consider retrenchment, burden-shifting, the accommodation of (and triangulation between) potential rivals, and the limitation of commitments. To do this, decision-makers can draw on an American tradition of prudential, realist thinking about aligning resources and goals. As Samuel

P. Huntington summarized it, to address the gap between ambitions and capabilities, states can

> [attempt] to redefine their interests and so reduce their commitments to a level which they can sustain with their existing capabilities; to reduce the threats to their interests through diplomacy; to enhance the contribution of allies to the protection of their interests; to increase their own resources, usually meaning larger military forces and military budgets; to substitute cheaper forms of power for more expensive ones, thus using the same resources to produce more power; to devise more effective strategies for the use of their capabilities, thereby securing also greater output in terms of power for the same input in terms of resources.[82]

Primacists often treat any pullback, of any scale, as the prelude to a global retrenchment. They did so, too, after the withdrawal from Vietnam. Defeat in Vietnam, though, did not persuade Moscow that the USA would abandon Western Europe, any more than the Soviet Union's bleeding in Afghanistan meant the Warsaw Pact was a paper tiger. Prudent retreats can be the prelude for successful rebalancing. The history of Sino-US relations suggests so. Recall that after withdrawing from its domino war in Vietnam, the USA made a grand bargain with Mao's China that strengthened its position as the dominant state in Asia and put an end to Chinese-backed revolution in the region.

If Washington is held to a fictitious and demanding historical standard, considering any retrenchment will be impossible. If liberal order visions prevail, it will be deemed immoral even to consider an alternative of restraint. A pernicious by-product of such nostalgia is its reductionism, asserting a false choice between primacy, or global leadership, on the one hand, and inward-looking isolation on the other.

If Washington could look past cumulative and long-held assumptions, it could take the necessary measures to restore its solvency. To realign its power, commitments and public opinion, Washington could end its wasteful programme of permanent war in the Greater Middle East and lighten its footprint in that region; it could reduce its deficits through prudent retrenchments, cuts and burden shifts; divide adversaries (like Russia, Iran and China) rather than driving them together; manage threats by accommodating some and containing others; rebuild its diplomatic capability; promote republican democracy by exemplifying it rather than spreading it; and restore deterrence as the core of American security. The USA can do this. Only it is unlikely to, enough and in time. The habits of hegemony, a muscle memory acquired over decades of growing power, are hard to shake off. The foreign policy establishment is already resisting a shift in US grand strategy, and is doing so effectively. As much as allies, onlookers and American critics can urge a managed and graceful decline from its brief unipolar moment, it is hard for such a power in such a place to decline gracefully. It is hard, therefore, to be optimistic.

Afterword: Before Our Eyes

The world emerging before our eyes is one of increasing power struggle. It is likely, then, to increase the dilemmas of ordering. It will confront the USA with ever more agonizing choices that betray values or even partners or allies. In navigating that world, fictions about a rules-based liberal order, or the image of the USA as the natural occupant of a single global 'throne', are of limited value. Such strategic visions have proved to be disappointing before. They helped put the USA in its current position. Clinging to this same mythology will produce the same results, reinforcing America's state of overstretch, polarization and exhaustion.

There is one more argument to deal with. It is usually made not in writing but in person as a last-ditch objection. 'Of course', people say, 'you are right. All this "rules-based" order is a charade. It is a darker story.' No sooner does the edifice crumble than it is rebuilt. *'But we need our myths.'* Of course, they say, there was a history of hierarchy, hypocrisy and violence. We need, though, an America that goes abroad to lead, to solve problems. Or, as one Deputy Defense Secretary put it, 'There is just too much to do in the world, and we need clever ideas on how to be everywhere.'[1] Too much truth-telling about the past, people argue, will damage America's sense of mission. America, for all its blemishes, has a liberal conscience, or so the logic goes, one that gives hope to the world. If we snuff that out with critical scrutiny, what is there left? How, it is asked, will we impel young people to go out in the world to do good, without benign stories? Isn't it counterproductive to gaze too long at this dark sun?

There is an irony here. The complaint that we should avert our eyes and tell stories in order to re-enchant the world, hardly pausing to wonder what it leaves out, comes from the same worldview that presents itself as the force of reason, expertise and enlightenment, against post-truth barbarism. And myths simply retold, without rude interruption, will not serve us well. It hasn't done so historically. The view of the world as a problem to be solved by enthusiasm has not produced uniformly excellent results. The wages of utopianism in the twentieth century were the concentration camp and the gulag. Powered by uplifting myths – the revolutionary proletariat, the chosen race, manifest destiny – our species has practised barbarism almost without limit, or unleashed chaos by accident. Many problems of international relations cannot be solved, only lived with. Solutions, the pursuit of decisive resolutions, themselves often generate further problems. There are parts of the world still recovering from the deadliness of great powers' good intentions, the benevolent military campaigns, the incitements to revolt, the structural adjustment programmes. In our time, some of its best efforts have made a refugee crisis and metastasizing transnational jihadism worse.

The very attitude, that we should tell stories to incite people to 'be everywhere', to go into the trenches to do good in a spirit of youthful altruism, 'like swimmers into cleanness leaping',[2] is part of the problem. Left unchecked and uninterrogated, the suggestion of liberal order leads to mischief. It offers the bewitching notion of 'who we are', the claim that consensual internationalism defined the order, while somehow its darker aspects were aberrations that don't reflect its essence, an attitude that encourages complacency, carelessness or worse. After decades of paeans to 'global leadership', it is surely time for something else, a little clear-eyed sobriety.

The task of scholars, if not to eradicate myths, is to help civilize the impulse, to caution against the notion of a pure essence, to keep a sense of humane irony alive. Only by confronting the darkness of history can we turn attention to the real choices decision-makers now face, and their possible consequences. Other powers tell misleading and dangerous stories about themselves. China, for instance, claims that it has no history of empire or aggression, a claim that in itself becomes a warrant for atrocities. If the West isn't willing to confront its own past, why should it?

At the core of liberal order storytelling is an anxiety about American uniqueness. A most unsettling historical truth, one that lurks in the shadow of the panegyrics, is the suggestion that the USA is not exempt from historical patterns of rise and fall. It is a constitutional republic but also an empire, of sorts, and it too could destroy its republic through its empire. Other powers, too, have been beset by the issue of how a republic can secure itself in a hostile world. It will be recalled that Rome, a state more or less in permanent war year-on-year, destroyed its own republic. Ever greater concentrations of wealth and ever more military campaigns led to the unravelling of constitutional constraints, and to warlords who, in partisan days, set themselves up as the people's tribunes against the wicked elites, turned their armies on the state. America is not Rome, of course, and has no recent equivalent of war or mobilization on a Roman scale. But the republic has taken on the normalization of war, undeclared and almost routine, for two decades. It is now gripped by destructive partisanship, and ruled by a corrupt potentate with a penchant for martial display, whose personal court debauches the public sphere, heightening the spiral of domestic strife and international crisis. Violent ordering leaves its mark.

These are all ancient questions, and the most acute classical witnesses are still our best source of inspiration. Tacitus, born in the provinces and close to power, empathized with the 'barbarians', those on the receiving end who had to taste the realities of empire. He also feared what empire fuelled at home, the rising corruption, deference to the armed forces, the love of triumphal monuments, the absolutist terror of the autocrats. His purpose was not to reject the exercise of power abroad. A Roman senator who had served at the front, he regarded the empire as more than just one large act of nihilism. If his reproach had a purpose, it was more exact. It was to puncture the sweet words and affectations that blinded and deceived. He sought to retell brutal acts of power unsparingly. In the rhetorical schools it was known as *sub oculus subiectio*, or 'putting it before their eyes'.[3] To see the choices before us, and what they cost, we should open our eyes.

Notes

Introduction: Nostalgia in an End Time

1 Richard Ned Lebow, *The Rise and Fall of Political Orders* (Cambridge: Cambridge University Press, 2018), pp. 7–8.

2 Tacitus, *On the Life and Character of Julius Agricola* (AD 98).

3 Robert Gilpin, *War and Change in World Politics* (Cambridge: Cambridge University Press, 1981), p. 24.

4 'Remarks by President Donald Tusk before the G7 Summit in Charlevoix, Canada', at https://www.consilium.europa.eu/en/press/press-releases/2018/06/08/remarks-by-president-donald-tusk-before-the-g7-summit-in-charlevoix-canada/.

5 Hedley Bull, *The Anarchical Society: A Study of Order in World Politics* (London: Macmillan, 1977), p. 209.

6 Cited in Phillips Payson O'Brien, *British and American Naval Power: Politics and Policy, 1900–1936* (Westport, CT: Praeger, 1998), p. 117.

7 Warren Zimmerman, *First Great Triumph* (New York: Farrar, Straus and Giroux, 2002), p. 476.

8 UN Special Rapporteur on Unilateral Coercive Measures, 'Sanctions on Iran and Cuba Need Phasing Out, Says Expert', 29 July 2015, at https://news.un.org/en/audio/2015/07/602872. I am grateful to Nicholas Mulder on this point.

9 Stephen Kotkin, 'Why Realism Explains the World', *Foreign Affairs* 97:4 (2018), pp. 10–15: p. 10.

10 Michael Burke, 'Biden: "The America I See Does Not Wish

to Turn Our Back on the World"', *The Hill*, 17 February 2019.

11 'Democrats and Foreign Policy: There's Something Happening Here', *The Economist*, 4 May 2019.

12 Julio Rosas, 'Joe Biden Says He Wants to Make America Straight Again', *Washington Examiner*, 25 April 2019.

13 Anne Applebaum, 'Is This the End of the West as We Know It?' *Washington Post*, 4 March 2016; Patrick M. Stewart, 'Trump and World Order: The Return of Self-Help', *Foreign Affairs* 96:2 (March/April 2017), pp. 52–57; James Kirchick, *The End of Europe: Dictators, Demagogues, and the Coming Dark Age* (New Haven, CT: Yale University Press, 2017).

14 'Is the Liberal Order in Peril?' *Foreign Affairs* (online), n.d., at https://www.foreignaffairs.com/ask-the-experts/liberal-order-peril.

15 Statement of Former Swedish Prime Minister Carl Bilt, promoting the Declaration of Principles for Freedom, Prosperity and Peace, at https://www.atlanticcouncil.org/programs/brent-scowcroft-center/fsr-initiative/declaration-of-principles.

16 Klaus Schwab, 'Globalisation 4.0: The Davos 2019 Manifesto', at https://www.rappler.com/thought-leaders/220862-davos-2019-manifesto-globalization; Adam Tooze, 'Framing Crashed', at https://adamtooze.com/2019/02/09/framing-crashed-10-a-new-bretton-woods-and-the-problem-of-economic-order-also-a-reply-to-adler-and-varoufakis/.

17 Susan B. Glasser, 'John McCain's Funeral Was the Biggest Resistance Gathering Yet', *New Yorker*, 1 September 2018; Ishaan Tharoor, 'Trump, McCain and the Waning of the Liberal Order', *Washington Post*, 27 August 2018.

18 Charles A. Kupchan, 'Unpacking Hegemony: The Social Foundations of Hierarchical Order', in G. John Ikenberry, *Power, Order and Change in World Politics* (Cambridge: Cambridge University Press, 2014), pp. 19–61: pp. 25–27.

19 Patrick O'Brien, 'The Pax Britannica and American Hegemony: Precedent, Antecedent or Just Another History?', in Patrick

O'Brien and Armand Clesse, eds., *Two Hegemonies: Britain 1846–1914 and the United States 1941–2001* (Aldershot: Ashgate, 2002), pp. 3–64: pp. 3–4.

20 Robert Kagan, *The Jungle Grows Back: America and Our Imperilled World* (New York: Knopf Doubleday Publishing Group, 2018).

21 'Why We Should Preserve International Institutions and Order', *New York Times*, 23 July 2018.

22 'Petition: Preserving Alliances', July 2018, at https://docs.google.com/forms/d/e/1FAIpQLSesHdZWxpp13plS4nkLOSMHv4Dg1jaksBrCC6kWv6OfVAmO5g/viewform.

23 Foreign Affairs Select Committee, *China and the Rules-Based International System: Sixteenth Report of Session 2017–19* HC 612, 4 April 2019.

24 Adam Garfinkle, 'Parsing the Liberal International Order', *The American Interest*, 27 October 2017.

25 Centre for American Progress, 'America Adrift: How the US Foreign Policy Debate Misses What Voters Really Want', 5 May 2019, at https://www.americanprogress.org/issues/security/reports/2019/05/05/469218/america-adrift/; Ruth Igielnik and Kim Parker, 'Majorities of US Veterans, Public Say the Wars in Iraq and Afghanistan Were Not Worth Fighting', *Pew Research Center*, 10 July 2019, at https://www.pewresearch.org/fact-tank/2019/07/10/majorities-of-u-s-veterans-public-say-the-wars-in-iraq-and-afghanistan-were-not-worth-fighting/.

26 Damir Murasic, 'Making up Monsters to Destroy: The Illiberal Challenge', *The American Interest* 14:5 (2019).

27 Perry Anderson, *The H-Word: The Peripeteia of Hegemony* (London: Verso, 2017), pp. 1–4.

28 Joseph Nye, Condoleezza Rice, Nicholas Burns, Leah Bitounis and Jonathon Price, *The World Turned Upside Down: Maintaining American Leadership in a Dangerous Age* (Aspen, CO: Aspen Institute, 2017); Kurt Campbell, Eric Edelman, Michèle Flournoy, et al., *Extending American Power: Strategies to Expand US Engagement in a Competitive World Order* (Washington, DC: Centre for a New American Security, May 2016).

29 Kenneth P. Vogel, 'Concerned by Trump, Some Republicans Quietly Align with Democrats', *New York Times*, 24 May 2018; see also the American Enterprise Institute and the Centre for American Progress, 'Partnership in Peril: The Populist Assault on the Transatlantic Community', at https://www.americanpro gress.org/issues/security/reports/2018/07/31/454248/partnersh ip-in-peril/.

30 Stephen Wertheim, 'Return of the Neocons', *New York Review of Books*, 2 January 2019.

31 Julian Borger, 'Trump is Building a New Liberal Order, says Pompeo', *Guardian*, 4 December 2018; Jeffrey Goldberg, 'A Senior White House Official Defines the Trump Doctrine: We're America, Bitch', *The Atlantic*, 11 June 2018.

32 G. John Ikenberry, *After Victory: Institutions, Strategic Restraint, and the Rebuilding of Order After Major Wars* (Princeton, NJ: Princeton University Press, 2001); 'The Plot Against American Foreign Policy: Can the Liberal Order Survive?' *Foreign Affairs* 96:3 (2017), pp. 2–9; (with Daniel Deudney), 'The Nature and Sources of Liberal International Order', *Review of International Studies* 25 (1999), pp. 179–196; James Goldgeier, 'The Misunderstood Roots of Liberal Order, And Why They Matter Again', *Washington Quarterly* 41:3 (2018), pp. 7–20; Ivo H. Daalder and James M. Lindsay, *Empty Throne: America's Abdication of Global Leadership* (New York: Public Affairs, 2019); Richard N. Haass, 'Liberal World Order: R.I.P.', *Project Syndicate*, 21 March 2018; Robin Niblett, 'Liberalism in Retreat: The Demise of a Dream', *Foreign Affairs* 96:1 (2017), pp. 17–24; Kori Schake, *America vs The West: Can the Liberal World Order Be Preserved* (Penguin: Lowy Institute Paper, 2019); Eliot A. Cohen, *The Big Stick: The Limits of Soft Power and the Necessity of Military Force* (New York: Basic Books, 2016); Paul D. Miller, *American Power and Liberal Order: A Conservative Internationalist Grand Strategy* (Washington, DC: Georgetown University Press, 2016); Hal Brands, *American Grand Strategy in the Age of Trump* (Washington, DC: Brookings Institution, 2017); 'America's Global Order Is Worth Fighting For; The Longest

Period of Great-Power Peace in Modern History Is Not a "Myth"',
Bloomberg, 14 August, 2018; David H. Petraeus, 'America Must
Stand Tall', *Politico*, 7 February 2017; Joseph S. Nye Jr, 'The
Rise and Fall of American Hegemony from Wilson to Trump',
International Affairs 95:1 (2019), pp. 63–80; Robert Kagan, 'The
Twilight of the Liberal World Order', in Michael O'Hanlon, ed.,
Big Ideas for America (Washington, DC: Brookings Institution,
2017), pp. 267–75; Edward Luce, 'The New World Disorder',
Financial Times, 24 June 2017; Bonnie S. Glaser and Gregory
Poling, 'Vanishing Borders in the South China Sea', *Foreign Affairs*
97:3 (2018); Daniel Drezner, 'Who Is to Blame for the State of the
Rules-Based International Order?' *Washington Post*, 5 June 2018;
Gideon Rose, 'What Obama Gets Right: Keep Calm and Carry
the Liberal Order On', *Foreign Affairs* 94:5 (2015), pp. 2–12; Marc
Champion, 'International (Dis)Order', *Bloomberg*, 26 September
2018; Hans W. Maull, 'The Once and Future Liberal Order',
Survival 61:2 (2019), pp. 7–32; Michael Fullilove, 'The Fading of
an Aging World Order', *Financial Times*, 23 October 2015. A more
agnostic account is Rebecca Lissner and Mira Rapp-Hooper, 'The
Liberal Order is More Than a Myth: But It Must Adapt to the New
Balance of Power', *Foreign Affairs* 97:4 (2018).

33 G. John Ikenberry, 'The End of Liberal Order?' *International
    Affairs* 94:1 (2018), pp. 7–23: p. 9.

34 Robert Jervis, 'International Primacy: Is the Game Worth the
    Candle?' *International Security* 17:4 (1993), pp. 52–67: pp. 52–3.

35 Charles L. Glaser, 'A Flawed Framework: Why the Liberal
    International Order Framework is Misguided', *International
    Security* 43:4 (2019), pp. 51–87; John Mearsheimer, 'Bound to
    Fail: The Rise and Fall of the Liberal World Order', *International
    Security* 43:4 (2019), pp. 7–50; Adam Tooze, 'Everything You Know
    About Global Order Is Wrong', *Foreign Policy*, 30 January, 2019;
    George Friedman, 'The Myth of the Liberal International Order; It's
    Dangerous to Pine for a Time That Never Really Was', *Geopolitical
    Futures*, 19 September 2018; Paul Staniland, 'Misreading the
    "Liberal Order": Why We Need New Thinking in American Foreign

Policy', *Lawfare*, 29 July 2018; Graham Allison, 'The Truth About the Liberal Order: Why It Didn't Make the Modern World', *Foreign Affairs* 97:4 (2018), pp. 124–133; Amitav Acharya, *The End of American World Order* (Cambridge: Polity, 2014); Stephen M. Walt, 'Why I Didn't Sign Up to Defend the International Order', *Foreign Policy*, 1 August 2018; Jeanne Morefield, 'Trump's Foreign Policy Isn't the Problem', *Boston Review*, 8 January 2019; Stephen Wertheim, 'Paeans to the Postwar Order Won't Save Us', *War on the Rocks*, 6 August 2018; John Mueller, 'An American Global Order? Has the US Been Necessary?', ISSS–IS Annual Conference, November 2018; Christopher Fettweis, 'Unipolarity, Hegemony and the New Peace', *Security Studies* 26:3 (2017), pp. 423–451; Patrick Porter, *A World Imagined: Nostalgia and Liberal Order*, CATO Policy Analysis Number 843 (Washington, DC: CATO Institute, June, 2018); Naazneen Barma, Ely Ratner and Steven Weber, 'The Mythical Liberal Order', *The National Interest* 124 (2013), pp. 56–67; Andrew Bacevich, 'The Global Order Myth', *The American Conservative*, 15 June 2017; Brahma Chellany, 'Mirage of a Rules-Based Order', *Japan Times*, 25 July 2016; Michael Brendan Dougherty, 'The Endless Hysteria about the Liberal World Order', *National Review*, 27 March 2018; Adrian Pabst, *Liberal World Order and Its Critics* (London: Routledge, 2018).

36 Naazneen Barma, Ely Ratner and Steven Weber, 'The Mythical Liberal Order', *The National Interest* 124 (2013), pp. 56–67.

37 John Glaser, 'The Amnesia of the US Foreign Policy Establishment', *Free Republic*, 15 March 2019; David C. Hendrikson, *Republic in Peril: American Empire and the Liberal Tradition* (Oxford: Oxford University Press, 2018), p. 168.

38 Francis Fukuyama, 'America: The Failed State', *Prospect*, January 2017.

39 Jake Sullivan, 'More, Less or Different', *Foreign Affairs* 98:1 (2018), pp. 168–175: p. 173; G. John Ikenberry and Daniel Deudney, 'Liberal World', *Foreign Affairs* 97:1 (2018), pp. 16–24: p. 17.

40 George Packer, *Our Man: Richard Holbrooke and the End of the American Century* (New York: Knopf, 2019), p. 5.

41 Michael Sherer, 'Democrats Distance Themselves from Hillary Clinton's "Backward" Claim', *Washington Post*, 13 March 2018.

42 Hillary Rodham Clinton, 'Security and Opportunity for the Twenty-First Century', *Foreign Affairs* 86:6 (2007), pp. 1–18: p. 3.

43 Marc Trachtenberg, 'Preventive War and US Foreign Policy', *Security Studies* 16:1 (2007), pp. 1–31; William Burr and Jeffrey T. Richelson, 'Whether to Strangle the Baby in the Cradle', *International Security* 25:3 (2000–1), pp. 54–99.

44 Max Boot, 'Nostalgia Isn't a Foreign Policy', *Commentary*, 11 November 2015; 'The Case for American Empire', *Weekly Standard*, 15 October 2001; 'Why Winning and Losing are Irrelevant in Syria and Afghanistan', *Washington Post*, 30 January 2019; *The Savage Wars of Peace: Small Wars and the Rise of American Power* (New York: Basic Books, 2002).

45 Blighty, 'The Vote of Shame', *The Economist*, 30 August 2013.

46 Damon Linker, 'Elliot Abrams and the Absurd Paradoxes of American Foreign Policy', *The Week*, 15 February 2019.

47 Emile Simpson, 'There's Nothing Wrong with the Liberal Order That Can't Be Fixed by What's Right With It', *Foreign Policy*, 7 August 2018.

48 G. John Ikenberry and Daniel H. Nexon, 'Hegemonic Studies 3.0: The Dynamics of Hegemonic Orders', *Security Studies* 28:3 (2019), pp. 1–27.

49 Walter A. McDougal, *Promised Land, Crusader State: The American Encounter with the World* (New York: Houghton Mifflin, 1997).

50 Daniel H. Nexon and Thomas Wright, 'What's at Stake in the American Empire Debate?' *American Political Science Review* 101:2 (May 2007), pp. 253–272: p. 266.

51 G. John Ikenberry, *Liberal Leviathan* (Princeton, NJ: Princeton University Press, 2011), p. 270.

52 G. John Ikenberry, Thomas J. Knock, Anne-Marie Slaughter and Tony Smith, *The Crisis of American Foreign Policy: Wilsonianism in the Twenty-first Century* (Princeton, NJ: Princeton University Press, 2009), p. 10.

53 Perry Anderson, *American Foreign Policy and Its Thinkers*

(London: Verso, 2013); Inderjeet Parmar, 'The US-led Liberal Order: Imperialism By Another Name?', *International* Affairs, 94:1 (2018), pp. 151–172.

54 Jeanne Morefield, *Empires without Imperialism: Anglo-American Decline and the Politics of Deflection* (New York: Oxford University Press, 2014).

Chapter 1 The Idea of Liberal Order

1 Christopher J. Fettweis, *The Pathologies of Power: Fear, Honour, Glory, and Hubris in US Foreign Policy* (Cambridge: Cambridge University Press, 2013), pp. 184–226: p. 185.

2 Ron Suskind, 'Without a Doubt', *New York Times Magazine*, 17 October 2004.

3 Peter Beinart, *The Icarus Syndrome: A History of American Hubris* (New York: Harper Collins 2010), p. 343.

4 David A. Graham, 'The Wrong Side of the Right Side of History', *The Atlantic*, 21 December 2015.

5 Ivo H. Daalder and James M. Lindsay, 'The Committee to Save the World Order' *Foreign Affairs* 97:6 (2018), pp. 72–84: p. 72.

6 Hal Brands, *American Grand Strategy and the Liberal Order: Continuity, Change and Options for the Future* (Santa Monica, CA: RAND, 2016), pp. 1, 2.

7 Jake Sullivan, 'The World after Trump: How the System Can Endure', *Foreign Affairs* 97:2 (March/April 2018), p. 10.

8 John G. Ruggie, 'International Regimes, Transactions, and Change: Embedded Liberalism in the Post-war Economic Order', *International Organization* 36, no. 2 (Spring 1982): 380.

9 G. John Ikenberry, 'Liberal Internationalism 3.0: America and the Dilemmas of Liberal World Order', *Perspectives on Politics* 7:1 (2009), pp. 71–87: p. 71; 'The Plot against American Foreign Policy: Can the Liberal Order Survive?', *Foreign Affairs* 96:3 (2017), pp. 2–9: p. 8.

10 G. John Ikenberry and Daniel Deudney, 'Liberal World', *Foreign Affairs* 97:1 (2018), pp. 16–24: p. 16.

11 Robert O. Keohane, 'Twenty Years of Institutional Liberalism', *International Relations* 26:2 (2012), pp. 125–138, p. 133.

12 Stewart Patrick, 'What, Exactly, Are the Rules?' *Washington Quarterly* 39:1 (2016), pp. 7–27: p. 9.

13 Andrew Moravcsik, 'Taking Preferences Seriously: A Liberal Theory of International Politics', *International Organisation* 51:4 (1997), pp. 513–553.

14 Joseph S. Nye Jr, 'Will the Liberal Order Survive?' *Foreign Affairs* 96:1 (2017), pp. 10–16: p. 16.

15 James Rogers (Director, Global Britain Programme, Henry Jackson Society), Written Evidence, 23 February 2018, House of Lords, Select Committee on International Relations, *UK Foreign Policy in a Shifting World*, 5th Report of Session 2017–19 (18 December 2018), HL Paper 250.

16 David Lake, 'Dominance and Subordination in World Politics', in G. John Ikenberry, ed., *Power, Order and Change in World Politics* (Cambridge: Cambridge University Press, 2014), pp. 61–83; Josef Joffe, 'Is it Really RIP for the LIO?' *The American Interest*, 6 February 2019.

17 Duncan Bell, 'What is Liberalism?' *Political Theory* 42:6 (2014), pp. 682–715: p. 703.

18 G. John Ikenberry, 'The Illusion of Geopolitics: The Enduring Power of the Liberal Order', *Foreign Affairs* 93:3 (2014), pp. 80–90.

19 'The 1992 Campaign; Excerpts from a Speech by Clinton on US Role', *New York Times*, 2 October 1992; Presidential Papers, George H. W. Bush, Address to the Nation Announcing Military Action in the Persian Gulf, 16 January 1991 (Washington, DC, 1992), p. 44; Fred Weir, 'Hillary Clinton Slams Russia Over Georgia', *Christian Science Monitor*, 6 July 2010; 'Obama and Merkel Warn of Tougher Sanctions against Russia over Ukraine', *Guardian*, 5 June 2014; Will Dunham, 'Kerry Condemns Russia's "Incredible Act of Aggression" in Ukraine', *Reuters*, 2 March 2014.

20 Gideon Rose 'What Obama Gets Right: Keep Calm and Carry the Liberal Order On', *Foreign Affairs* 94:5 (2015), pp. 2–12.

21 David E. Sanger, 'With the Generals Gone, Trump's America First Could Fully Emerge', *New York Times*, 21 December 2018.

22 Melvyn P. Leffler and Jeffrey W. Legro, eds., *To Lead the World: American Strategy After the Bush Doctrine* (New York: Oxford University Press, 2008), p. 252.

23 Paul Schroeder, cited in Walter Scheidel, 'Republics between Hegemony and Empire: How Ancient City-States Built Empires and the USA Doesn't (Anymore)', Princeton/Stanford Working Papers in Classics, February 2006, p. 4.

24 Ulrich Speck, 'The Crisis of Liberal Order', *The American Interest*, 12 September 2016.

25 G. John Ikenberry, 'Illusions of Empire: Defining the New American Order', *New York Times*, 16 March 2004.

26 Ivo H. Daalder, 'America Shrugs While Democracy Around the World Retreats', *Chicago Tribune*, 14 February 2019.

27 Cited by Amitav Acharya, *The End of American World Order* (Cambridge: Polity, 2014), p. 40.

28 Jeremy Suri, 'How Trump's Executive Orders Could Set America Back 70 Years', *The Atlantic*, 27 January 2017.

29 Editorial Board, 'Why NATO Matters', *New York Times*, 8 July 2018.

30 Cited in Jake Sherman, Anna Palmer and Daniel Lippman, 'POLITICO Playbook: GOP to the World: What Would You Like Us to Do?' *Politico*, 17 July 2018.

31 Ivo H. Daalder, Tweet, 16 February 2019, at https://twitter.com/ IvoHDaalder/status/1096708797366747136.

32 Nicholas Burns and Douglas Lute, Press Release, 'New Report Focuses on NATO at Seventy: An Alliance in Crisis', Belfer Centre for Science and International Affairs, 14 February 2019.

33 As Tony Wood argues, 'Rhetorical differences aside, successive US governments have always been clear that NATO is not a gathering of peers. Its function has been to bind European states into an international order dominated by the US – and to do it on Washington's terms. NATO communiqués talk about shared security goals, but it has always been the US that determines what

those goals are; they are only shared after the fact. From that point of view, browbeating from Washington has been a structural feature of the alliance from the outset.' 'NATO and the Myth of the Liberal International Order', *New York Review of Books*, 21 August 2018.

34 Peter Ricketts, 'What's the Secret of NATO's long life? It's Not Just a Military Pact', *Guardian*, 2 April 2019.

35 Francis J. Gavin, 'The Gold Battles Within the Cold War: American Monetary Policy and the Cold War, 1960–1963', *Diplomatic History* 26:1 (2002), pp. 61–94: pp. 90–92.

36 TV Interview for BBC, 1 September 1982, at https://www.margaretthatcher.org/document/104815.

37 Gene Gerzhoy, 'Alliance Coercion and Nuclear Restraint: How the United States Thwarted West Germany's Nuclear Ambitions', *International Security* 39:4 (2015), pp. 91–129.

38 Anne Applebaum, 'Trump Hates the International Organizations that are the Basis of US Wealth, Prosperity and Military Power', *Washington Post*, 2 July 2018.

39 'Obama's Legacy Could be a Revitalized NATO', *Washington Post*, 22 August 2014; Anne Applebaum, 'Trump Hates the International Organizations that are the Basis of US Wealth, Prosperity and Military Power', *Washington Post*, 2 July 2018.

40 Robert Kagan, 'Things Will Not be Okay', *The Washington Post*, 12 July 2018.

41 Ivo H. Daalder, 'What NATO Needs to Hear from Trump', *CNN*, 24 May 2017.

42 Ivo H. Daalder and Robert Kagan, 'The "Allies" Must Step Up', *Brookings*, Sunday 20 June 2004, at https://www.brookings.edu/opinions/the-allies-must-step-up/.

43 Kosovo Commission, *The Kosovo Report: Conflict, International Response, Lessons Learned* (Oxford: Oxford University Press, 2002), pp. 163–4.

44 Adam Garfinkle, 'Parsing the Liberal International Order', *The American Interest*, 27 October 2017.

45 I am grateful to Joshua for permission to reproduce these charts.

46 Speech, Senator John F. Kennedy, Mormon Tabernacle in Salt Lake City during the 1960 presidential campaign, at https://www.jfkli brary.org/archives/other-resources/john-f-kennedy-speeches/salt-lake-city-ut-19600923-mormon-tabernacle.

47 See Dianne Kirby, 'Divinely Sanctioned: The Anglo-American Cold War Alliance and the Defence of Western Civilization and Christianity, 1945–1948', *Journal of Contemporary History* 35:3 (2000), pp. 385–412.

48 Stephen Wertheim, 'Paeans to the Postwar Order Won't Save US', *War on the Rocks*, 6 August 2018.

49 Kurt M. Campbell, *The Pivot: The Future of American Statecraft in Asia* (New York: Twelve, 2016).

50 See, e.g., Jeanne Kirkpatrick, 'Dictatorships and Double Standards', *Commentary* 68:5 (1979), pp. 34–45.

51 Robert Dreyfuss, *Devil's Game: How the United States Helped Unleash Fundamentalist Islam* (New York: Owl Books, 2005), pp. 65–94, pp. 244–270; Max Blumenthal, *The Management of Savagery: How America's National Security State Fuelled the Rise of Al Qaeda, Isis and Donald Trump* (London: Verso, 2019), p. 3.

52 G. John Ikenberry, *Liberal Leviathan* (Princeton, NJ: Princeton University Press, 2011), p. 66; see also the caveats outlined in Ivo H. Daalder and James M. Lindsay, *Empty Throne: America's Abdication of Global Leadership* (New York: Public Affairs, 2019).

53 G. John Ikenberry, 'The Illusion of Geopolitics: The Enduring Power of the Liberal Order', *Foreign Affairs* 93:3 (2014), pp. 80–90: p. 83.

54 Joseph S. Nye Jr, 'Will the Liberal Order Survive?' *Foreign Affairs* 96:1 (2017), pp. 10–16: p. 12.

55 Robert Kagan, 'The World America Made, and Trump Wants to Unmake', *Politico*, 28 September 2018.

56 Daniel Immerwahr, *How to Hide an Empire: A History of the Greater United States* (New York: Farrar, Straus and Giroux, 2018); Peter Harris, 'Not Just a Military Base: Reframing Diego Garcia and the Chagos Islands' *African Affairs*, 110:440 (2011), pp. 491–499.

57 R. Taggart Murphy, 'With Friends Like Us', *The New Republic*, 8 June 2010.

58 Stephenie van den Berg, 'World Court: Britain Must Return Indian Ocean Islands to Mauritius', *Reuters*, 25 February 2019.

59 Cited in Stephen Grey, 'Raiders of the Night', *The Times*, 5 June 2011.

60 Max Boot, 'Why Winning and Losing Are Irrelevant in Syria and Afghanistan', *Washington Post*, 30 January 2019.

61 Paul D Miller, 'Non-Western Liberalism and the Resilience of the Liberal International Order', *Washington Quarterly* 41:2 (2018), pp. 137–153: p. 151.

62 Nuno Monteiro, review of G. John Ikenberry, ed., *Power, Order and Change in World Politics* (Cambridge: Cambridge University Press, 2014), *H-Diplo*, September 2015.

63 Michael J. Mazarr, *Measuring the Health of the Liberal International Order* (Santa Monica, CA: RAND, 2017), p. xviii.

64 G. John Ikenberry and Anne-Marie Slaughter, *Forging a World of Liberty Under Law: US National Security in the Twenty First Century*, Final Report of the Princeton Project on National Security, 27 September 2006, p. 7.

65 Robert Saunders, 'The Myth of Brexit as Imperial Nostalgia', *Prospect*, 7 January 2019.

66 Paul Kelly, 'Seduction by Trump Is a Corruption of Conservatism', *The Australian*, 11 July 2018.

67 Bret Stephens, 'Only Mass Deportation Can Save America', *New York Times*, 16 June 2017; 'America First, America Hated, America Alone', *New York Times*, 13 July 2018.

68 Madeleine Albright, *Fascism: A Warning* (New York: Harper Collins 2018); Jason Devaney, 'Bill Kristol: Replace "White Working Class" with Immigrants', *Newsmax*, 19 May 2019; Jane Coasten, 'Bill Kristol Thinks "People Are Just Too Unhappy with the Status Quo"', *Vox*, 10 January 2018.

69 'Read Hillary Clinton's "Basket of Deplorables" Remarks About Donald Trump Supporters', *Time*, 10 September 2016; 'Remarks on American Leadership', *Council on Foreign Relations*, 31

January 2013; 'Hillary Clinton Reviews Henry Kissinger's World Order', *Washington Post*, 4 September 2014.

70 Emile Simpson, 'Britain's Declaration of Independence from Reality', *Foreign Policy*, 24 June 2016.

71 Dan Roberts, 'Death of 1.5m Oldsters Could Swing Second Brexit Vote, Says Ian McEwan', *Guardian*, 17 May 2017; Ian McEwan, 'Brexit Denial: Confessions of a Passionate Remainer', 2 June 2017.

72 Michael McFaul, *From Cold War to Hot Peace: An American Ambassador in Putin's Russia* (Boston, MA: Houghton Mifflin, 2018)

73 Robin Emmott, 'Creditors, Greece Need to Talk Like Adults', *Reuters*, 18 June 2015; James Mann, 'The Adults in the Room', *New York Review of Books*, 26 October 2017; Anonymous, 'I Am Part of the Resistance Inside the Trump Administration', *New York Times*, 5 September 2018.

74 Michael C. Desch, 'America's Liberal Illiberalism: The Ideological Origins of Overreaction in US Foreign Policy', *International Security* 32:3 (Winter 2007/2008), pp. 7–43.

75 Jake Sullivan, 'Why the Liberal International Order Can Survive Trump: How the System Can Endure', *Foreign Affairs* 97:2 (2018), pp. 10-19: p. 16

76 James Goldgeier, 'The Misunderstood Roots of Liberal Order, And Why They Matter Again', *Washington Quarterly* 41:3 (2018), pp. 7-20: p. 9.

77 Richard N. Haass, 'Rebooting American Foreign Policy', *Foreign Affairs* 96:4 (2017), pp. 2-9: p. 9; Emile Simpson, 'There's Nothing Wrong with the Liberal Order that Can't Be Fixed by What's Right With It', *Foreign Policy*, 7 August 2018.

78 Josh Rogin, 'How Russia is Corrupting the Liberal World Order', *Washington Post*, 31 January 2019; Carol Morello, 'Middle East Peace Conference Opens with Warnings that All Problems Originate in Iran', *Washington Post*, 14 February 2019.

79 Doug Stokes, 'Trump, American Hegemony and the Future of the Liberal International Order', *International Affairs* 94:1 (January 2018), pp. 133-150.

80 For an exception, see Jeff D. Colgan and Robert O. Keohane, 'The Liberal Order Is Rigged', *Foreign Affairs* 96:3 (May/June 2017), pp. 36–44.
81 Stephen Kinzer, *True Flag: Theodore Roosevelt, Mark Twain and the Birth of American Empire* (New York: Griffin, 2018).
82 Richard N. Haass, 'Imperial America', Paper at the Atlanta Conference, 11 November 2000, at https://monthlyreview.org/wp-content/uploads/2003/05/Imperial_America_Richard_N_Haass.pdf.
83 Bill Kristol, 'Fox News Sunday', *Fox News Network*, 27 April 2003.
84 Ken Silverstein, 'How to Make Millions by Selling War', *Vice*, 17 December 2015.
85 Bruce Jackson, 'A Conservative Case for German Leadership in Europe', *The American Interest*, 13 February 2019.
86 Ivo H. Daalder and James M. Lindsay, 'American Empire: Not "If" but "What Kind"', *New York Times*, May 2003. All quotes in this paragraph are from this article; my italics.
87 Paul K. MacDonald, 'Those Who Forget Historiography Are Doomed to Republish It: Empire, Imperialism and Contemporary Debates about American Power', *Review of International Studies* 35 (2009), pp. 45–67.
88 Jonah Goldberg, *Suicide of the West: How the Rebirth of Tribalism, Populism, Nationalism and Identity Politics is Destroying American Democracy* (New York: Crown Forum, 2018); 'A Continent Bleeds', *National Review*, 3 May 2000; 'Goldberg's Africa Invasion', *National Review*, 10 May 2000; 'Baghdad Delenda Est', *National Review*, 18 April 2002.
89 Robert Cooper, 'The New Liberal Imperialism', *Guardian*, 7 April 2002; Robert Cooper, *The Breaking of Nations: Order and Chaos in the Twenty-First Century* (New York: Atlantic Books, 2004), pp. 61–2.
90 Michael Ignatieff, 'The American Empire: The Burden', *New York Times*, 5 January 2003.
91 Jane Mayer, 'Outsourcing Torture', *New Yorker*, 14 February 2005, pp. 106–123.

92 G. John Ikenberry, 'The End of Liberal International Order?' *International Affairs* 94:1 (2018), pp. 7–23: p. 1.

93 Ronald Syme, *The Roman Revolution* (Oxford: Oxford University Press, 1939), pp. 322–323

94 Zbigniew Brzezinski, *The Grand Chessboard: American Primacy and its Geostrategic Imperatives* (New York: Basic Books, 1997), p. 40.

95 Max Boot, 'The Case for American Empire', *Weekly Standard*, 15 October 2001; 'Imperialism!' *Weekly Standard*, 6 May 2003.

96 Interview, *CBS News*, 20 October 2011.

97 Patrick Goodenough, 'Clinton: US Intervention in Libya was Smart Power at its Best', *CNS News*, 14 October 2015; Gareth Evans, 'The Responsibility to Protect After Libya and Syria', 20 July 2012, at http://www.responsibilitytoprotect.org/index.php/component/content/article/35-r2pcs-topics/4283-gareth-evans-speech-the-rtop-after-libya-and-syria; Ivo H. Daalder and James G. Stavridis, 'NATO's Victory in Libya: The Right Way to Run an Intervention' *Foreign Affairs* 91:2 (2012), pp. 2–7.

98 Jeanne Morefield, 'Business as Usual: Donald Trump and American Empire', *The Disorder of Things*, 15 December 2016.

Chapter 2 Darkness Visible: World-Ordering in Practice

1 Tony Blair, Letter to George W. Bush, 12 September 2001, at https://webarchive.nationalarchives.gov.uk/20171123123634/ http://www.iraqinquiry.org.uk/media/243716/2001-09-12-note-blair-to-bush-note-for-the-president.pdf.

2 Schlesinger to McGeorge Bundy, 27 May 1961, cited in John Lewis Gaddis, *Strategies of Containment* (Oxford: Oxford University Press, 2005 [1982]), p. 208.

3 Paul Staniland, 'Misreading the 'Liberal Order': Why We Need New Thinking in American Foreign Policy', *Lawfare*, 29 July 2018.

4 Hans J. Morgenthau, 'The Evil of Politics and the Politics of Evil', *Ethics* 56:1 (1945), pp. 1–18, p. 18.

5 Peter Baker, *Days of Fire: Bush and Cheney in the White House* (New York: Anchor Books, 2013), pp. 375; 'As Democracy Push Falters, Bush Feels Like a "Dissident"', *Washington Post*, 20 August 2007.

6 Henry Farrell and Martha Finnemore, 'The End of Hypocrisy: American Foreign Policy in the Age of Leaks', *Foreign Affairs* 92:6 (2013), pp. 22–26.

7 Mark Tran, 'France and Germany Evade Deficit Fines', *Guardian*, 25 November 2003.

8 Secretary of State Madeleine Albright, Interview on NBC-TV *The Today Show*, 19 February 1998, at https://1997-2001.state.gov/statements/1998/980219a.html.

9 Michael Spagat, 'Truth and Death in Iraq Under Sanctions', *Significance* 7:3 (2010), pp. 116–120.

10 Richard N. Haass, Tweet, 14 July 2018, at https://twitter.com/richardhaass/status/1018245342989516805?lang=en; tweet, 8 September 2018, at https://twitter.com/richardhaass/status/1038420381856612352?lang=en.

11 Stephen Schlesinger, *Act of Creation: The Founding of the United Nations* (Boulder, CO: Westview, 2003), p. 331.

12 'Barack Obama Makes Last Phone Call to Angela Merkel', *Politico*, 20 January 2017; 'How NSA Spied on Merkel Cell Phone from Berlin Embassy', *Der Spiegel*, October 2013; Ewan MacAskill, 'Germany Drops Inquiry Into Claims NSA Tapped Angela Merkel's Phone', *Guardian*, 12 June 2015.

13 Dov Levin, Partisan Electoral Intervention by Great Powers dataset (PEIG), at http://journals.sagepub.com/doi/abs/10.1177/0738894216661190; Lindsey A. O'Rourke, *Covert Regime Change: America's Secret Cold War* (Ithaca, NY: Cornell University Press, 2018).

14 Teresa Young Reeves, 'A Global Court? US Objections to the International Criminal Court and Obstacles to Ratification', *Human Rights Brief* 8:1 (2000), p. 30.

15 Linda Pearson, 'US War Crimes Immunity and the International Criminal Court', *Verso*, 13 September 2018.

16 'Ambassador's Call on Prime Minister', 2 June 2006, Telegram, at https://wikileaks.org/plusd/cables/06MASERU261_a.html.

17 Blake Welton, 'David Cameron: Don't Leave Syria Decision to UN', *Liverpool Echo*, 6 September 2013.

18 Stephen Biddle, 'Assessing the Case for Striking Syria', Before the Committee on Homeland Security, 10 September 2013.

19 Jim Michaels, 'Defence Chief Blasts Russia's Aggressive Actions and "Saber Rattling"', *USA Today*, 3 May 2016.

20 Ashton B. Carter and William J. Perry, 'If Necessary, Strike and Destroy', *Washington Post*, 22 June 2006.

21 G. John Ikenberry and Anne-Marie Slaughter, *Forging a World of Liberty Under Law: US National Security in the Twenty First Century* Final Report of the Princeton Project on National Security, 27 September 2006.

22 Anne-Marie Slaughter, 'Good Reasons for Going Around the UN', *New York Times*, 18 March 2003.

23 Randall L. Schweller, 'The Problem of International Order Revisited', *International Security* 26:1 (2001), pp. 161–186: p. 179.

24 Jack L. Goldsmith and Eric A. Posner, *The Limits of International Law* (Oxford: Oxford University Press, 2005), pp. 3–23, 45–83, 135–167.

25 Zaya Yeebo, in 'Is Africa on Trial?' *Global Policy Forum*, 27 March 2019, at https://www.globalpolicy.org/international-justice/the-international-criminal-court/general-documents-analysis-and-a rticles-on-the-icc/51455-is-afriica-on-trial.html.

26 Roman Rollnick, 'World Court Has Prestige but Little Power', *UPI Archives*, 12 May 1984.

27 Stewart Patrick, 'What, Exactly, Are the Rules?' *Washington Quarterly* 39:1 (2016), pp. 7–27: p. 13.

28 G. John Ikenberry, 'American Leadership May Be in Crisis, but the World Order Is Not', *Washington Post*, 27 January 2016.

29 Michael J. Mazarr, Astrid Stuth Cevallos, Miranda Priebe, et al., *Measuring the Health of the Liberal International Order* (Santa Monica, CA: RAND, 2017), pp. 32–33.

30 Butch Bracknell, 'There is a Rules-Based Order. It's Just Not Omnipotent', *The National Interest*, 1 September 2016.

31 Stephen Wertheim, 'Instrumental Internationalism: The American Origins of the United Nations, 1940-3', *Journal of Contemporary History* 55:2 (April 2019), pp. 265–283: p. 279.

32 Warren F. Kimball, *The Juggler: Franklin Roosevelt as Wartime Statesman* (Princeton, NJ: Princeton University Press, 1991), p. 191.

33 Cordell Hull, *The Memoirs of Cordell Hull*, vol.1 (New York: Macmillan, 1948), pp. 731–732.

34 Cited in Robert Skidelsky, *John Maynard Keynes: Fighting for Freedom, 1937-1946* (New York: Viking, 2000), p. 127.

35 Clark Clifford to President Truman, 24 September 1946. Clark Clifford Papers, Harry S. Truman Library, cited in Thomas H. Etzold and John Lewis Gaddis, *Containment: Documents on American Policy and Strategy 1945-1950* (New York: Columbia University Press, 1978), pp. 69, 66, 67.

36 Linda Hunt, 'US Coverup of Nazi Scientists', *Bulletin of the Atomic Scientists* 41:4 (1985), pp. 16–24.

37 Herbert P. Bix, *Hirohito and the Making of Modern Japan* (New York: Perennial, 2000), pp. 533–581.

38 Stephen Cohen, *Failed Crusade: America and the Tragedy of Post-Communist Russia* (New York: Norton, 2000), p. 15.

39 'Eastern Europe's Economies', *The Economist*, 13 January 1990.

40 Lawrence R. Klein and Marshall Pomer, 'Mass Privatisation and the Post-Communist Mortality Crisis: A Cross-National Analysis', *The Lancet* 373:9661 (January 2009), pp. 399–407.

41 Joseph E. Stiglitz, *Globalization and Its Discontents* (New York: Penguin, 2002), pp. 144–145.

42 'Mass Murder and the Market', *The Economist*, 22 January 2009.

43 Ha-Joon Chang, *Bad Samaritans: The Myth of Free Trade and the Secret History of Capitalism* (New York: Random House, 2008).

44 Leon Hollerman, 'International Economic Controls in Occupied Japan', *Journal of Asian Studies* 38 (1979), p. 719.

45 United States Trade Representative, *2017 Report to Congress on China's WTO Compliance* (January 2018), pp. 9–24.

46 Edward D. Mansfield and Marc L. Bush, 'The Political Economy of Non-tariff Barriers: A Cross-National Analysis', in Jeffrey A. Frieden and David A. Lake, eds., *International Political Economy: Perspectives on Global Power and Wealth* (Boston: MA: St. Martin's, 2000), pp. 353–365.

47 Michael Wines, 'Bush, in Australia, Under Fire on Trade', *New York Times*, 177 January 1992.

48 Michael Lind, 'There's No Such Thing as "the" Liberal World Order', *The National Interest*, 5 September 2017.

49 Gowling WLG, *Global Protectionism: Are You Leaving Yourself Open?* (2017), p. 6. at https://gowlingwlg.com/en/ insights-resources/topics/global-protectionism/overview.

50 Marc Jones, 'World Has Racked Up 7,000 Protectionist Measures Since Crisis: Study', *Reuters UK*, 15 November 2017.

51 'Bush Says Sacrificed Free-Market Principles to Save Economy', *CNN*, 17 December, 2008.

52 Michael Quinlan, *Thinking About Nuclear Weapons: Principles, Problems, Prospects* (Oxford: Oxford University Press, 2009), p. 29.

53 Francis J. Gavin, 'Strategies of Inhibition: US Grand Strategy, the Nuclear Revolution, and Nonproliferation', *International Security* 40:1 (2015), pp. 9–46, esp. pp. 19–38.

54 Michael Krepon, 'Can Deterrence Ever be Stable?' *Survival* 57:3 (2015), pp. 111–132.

55 Norman Friedman, *The Fifty-Year War: Conflict and Strategy in the Cold War* (Annapolis, MD: Naval Institute Press, 2000), p. 207.

56 Alastair Macdonald, 'As Russia Growls, EU Goes Cool on Eastern Promises', *Reuters*, 24 May 2015; Theresa Fallon, 'Is the EU on the Same Page as the United States on China?' *The Asan Forum*, 30 June 2016.

57 Federal Chancellor, 'Policy Statement by Federal Chancellor Angela Merkel on the Situation in Ukraine', 2014, in Ian Ferguson and Susanna Hast, 'Introduction: The Return of Spheres of Influence?', *Geopolitics* 23:2 (2018), pp. 277–284: p. 277.

58 *Association Agreement Between the European Union and its Member States, of the one part, and Ukraine, of the other part*, 29

May 2014 (*Official Journal of the European Union* L161/3) Title II Article 4:1, p. 5; Article 10:1, p. 7.

59 Daniel Triesman, 'Why Putin Took Crimea: The Gambler in the Kremlin', *Foreign Affairs* 95:3 (2016), pp. 47–54: p. 50.

60 Dexter Filkins, 'On the Warpath: Can John Bolton Sell an Isolationist President on Military Force?' *The New Yorker*, 6 May 2019, pp. 32–45: p. 45.

61 Michael Howard, *Captain Professor: A Life in War and Peace* (New York: Continuum, 2006), p. 230.

62 Colum Lynch, 'Exclusive: US Boycotts UN Drone Talks', *Foreign Policy*, 14 March 2014.

63 Eric Posner, 'Obama's Drone Dilemma', *Slate*, 12 October 2012.

64 *The 9/11 Commission Report: Final Report of the National Commission on Terrorist Attacks Upon the United States* (New York: Norton, 2004), p. 362.

65 Marc Trachtenberg, *A Constructed Peace: The Making of the European Settlement 1945–1963* (Princeton, NJ: Princeton University Press, 1999), pp. 12–13, 14, 15, 27–28.

66 Forrestal Diaries, 28 July 1945, vol. 2, p. 75.

67 *Foreign Relations of the United States 1961–1963* 14:87–98 (4 June 1961); cited in Marc Trachtenberg, *A Constructed Peace: The Making of the European Settlement 1945–1963* (Princeton, NJ: Princeton University Press, 1999), p. 283.

68 G. John Ikenberry, *Liberal Leviathan: The Origins, Crisis and Transformation of the American World Order* (Princeton, NJ: Princeton University Press, 2011), p. 27, n. 35.

69 Nuno Monteiro, 'Unrest Assured: Why Unipolarity Is Not Peaceful', *International Security* 36:3 (2011/2012), pp. 9–40.

70 Philip Stephens, 'Peace and Prosperity: It is Worth Saving the Liberal Order', *Financial Times*, 9 February 2017.

71 Tanisha Fazal, 'Dead Wrong? Battle Deaths, Military Medicine, and Exaggerated Reports of War's Demise', *International Security* 39:1 (2014), pp. 95–125: p. 116.

72 Gary L. Bass, *The Blood Telegram: Nixon, Kissinger and a Forgotten Genocide* (New York: Alfred Knopf, 2013).

73 Michael Mann, 'Have Wars and Violence Declined?' *Theory and Society* 47 (2018), pp. 37-60: pp. 54-55.

74 William D. Hartung and Bridget Moix, 'Deadly Legacy: US Arms to Africa and the Congo War', *World Policy Institute*, 3 February 2000, pp. 2-3.

75 Michael Fullilove, 'We Must Find a New Asia Focus as World Order Changes', *The Australian*, 10 May 2019.

76 I am grateful to Daniel Immerwahr for creating and supplying this image.

77 Paul T. Chamberlin, *The Cold War's Killing Fields: Rethinking the Long Peace* (New York: Harper Collins, 2018), p. 1.

78 Conrad C. Crane, *American Airpower Strategy in Korea, 1950–1953* (Lawrence: University Press of Kansas, 2000), p. 8; John Tirman, *The Deaths of Others: The Fate of Civilians in America's Wars* (New York: Oxford University Press, 2011), p. 92.

79 Secretary of State Dean Acheson to Ambassador Alan Kirk, 28 June 1950, in William Stueck, 'The Korean War', in Melvyn P. Leffer and Odd Arne Westad, eds., *The Cambridge History of the Cold War, Volume 1: Origins* (Cambridge: Cambridge University Press, 2010), p. 276.

80 Michael Lind, *Vietnam: The Necessary War: A Reinterpretation of America's Most Disastrous Military Conflict* (New York: Touchstone, 1999), pp. 31-76.

81 Fredrik Logevall, *Choosing War: The Lost Chance for Peace and the Escalation of War in Vietnam* (Berkeley, CA: University of California Press, 1998).

82 John McNaughton, 'Proposed Course of Action re Vietnam', 24 March 1965, in George C. Herring, ed., *The Pentagon Papers*, abridged edn (New York: McGraw-Hill, 1993), pp. 115-118.

83 Henry Kissinger, 'The Viet Nam Negotiations', *Foreign Affairs* 47:2 (1969), pp. 211-234: pp. 218-219.

84 Statement of Principles, *Project of the New American Century*, 3 June 1997, at http://www.newamericancentury.org/statementof-principles.htm; letter to President Clinton, 26 January 1998, at http://www.newamericancentury.org/iraqclintonletter.htm.

85 Michael J. Mazarr, *Leap of Faith: Hubris, Negligence, and America's Greatest Foreign Policy Tragedy* (New York: Public Affairs, 2019), pp. 149, 179, 192–193; Patrick Porter, *Blunder: Britain's War in Iraq* (Oxford: Oxford University Press, 2018), pp. 72–132; Ahsan I. Butt, 'Why Did the United States Invade Iraq in 2003?' *Security Studies*, 4 January 2019, pp. 2–21.

86 Quoted in Nicholas Lemann, 'The Next World Order', *The New Yorker* 24 March 2002.

87 Thomas E. Ricks, 'Briefing Depicted Saudis as Enemies', *Washington Post*, 6 August 2002.

88 George Packer, 'The Liberal Quandary over Iraq', *New York Times Magazine*, 8 December 2002, pp. 104–7.

89 'Principles for Iraq – Policy Guidelines', 13 May 2003, Donald Rumsfeld Papers, at http://papers.rumsfeld.com/library/default. asp?zoom_sort=0&zoom_query=principles+for+iraq&zoom_per_ page=10&zoom_and=0&Tag+Level+1=-1%7E0&Tag+Level+2=- 1%7E0.

90 Bob Woodward, *State of Denial* (London: Pocket Books, 2006), pp. 83–85; Wolfowitz, cited in T. Ricks, *Fiasco: The American Military Adventure in Iraq* (New York: Penguin, 2006), p. 30.

91 See Eliot A. Cohen, 'Iraq Can't Resist Us', *Wall Street Journal*, 23 December 2001.

92 'White House Says Iraq Sovereignty Could Be Limited', *New York Times*, 22 April 2004.

93 Quoted in John A. Tirpak, 'The Air Force's "Forever War" Is Its Toughest Pill to Swallow', *Air Force Magazine*, March 2018.

94 Shawn Snow, 'Esper Says US Forces Combating ISIS in Libya "Continue to Mow the Lawn"', *Military Times*, 15 November 2019.

95 Letter, Syria Study Group to Senate Majority Leader and Speaker of the House of Representatives, 1 May 2019, 'Key Findings', p. 1, at https://static.politico.com/5c/d9/9f55a18c44 f9905ac21fa772a198/syria-study-group-interim-assessment-and-recommendations.pdf.

96 Micah Zenko, *Reforming US Drone Strike Policies* (Council on

Foreign Relations, Special Report no. 65, January 2013), pp. 12–14; Greg Miller, 'CIA Seeks New Authority to Expand Yemen Drone Campaign', *Washington Post*, 18 April 2012.

97 Kurt Volker, 'What the US Risks by Relying on Drones', *Washington Post*, 27 October 2012.
98 See David H. Petraeus, 'America Must Stand Tall', *Politico*, 7 February 2017; Ben Glaze, 'Fight Against ISIS a "Generational Struggle", Warns Former Top US Army Chief General Petraeus', *Mirror*, 22 November 2017; 'Petraeus: We Went to Afghanistan for a Reason, and We Need to Stay', 16 June 2017, at https://www.pbs.org/newshour/show/petraeus-went-afghanistan-reason-need-stay.
99 Remarks by Lieutenant-General H. R. McMaster at the Munich Security Conference, 22 February 2018, at https://www.whitehouse.gov/briefings-statements/remarks-ltg-h-r-mcmaster-munich-security-conference/. Kyle Rempfer, 'H. R. McMaster Says the Public Is Fed a "War-Weariness" Narrative that Hurts US Strategy', *Military Times*, 8 May 2019.
100 Paul D. Miller, *American Power and Liberal Order: A Conservative Internationalist Grand Strategy* (Washington, DC: Georgetown University Press, 2016); 'Critics Should Stop Declaring Defeat in Afghanistan', *Foreign Policy*, 12 April 2019.
101 Robert J. Lieber, *Retreat and Its Consequences: American Foreign Policy and the Problem of World Order* (New York: Cambridge University Press, 2016); 'Foreign Policy Realists are Unrealistic on Iraq', *The Chronicle Review*, 18 October 2002; 'The Folly of Containment', *Commentary*, 7 March 2003, pp. 15–21; 'Rethinking America's Grand Strategy', *Chronicle of Higher Education*, 4 June 2004.
102 'War with Iraq Is Not in America's National Interest', *New York Times*, 26 September 2002.
103 Kori Schake, 'The Trump Doctrine Is Winning and the World Is Losing', *New York Times*, 15 June 2018.
104 E. H. Carr, *The Twenty Years' Crisis 1919–1939: An Introduction to the Study of International Relations* (London: Palgrave Macmillan, 2001 [1939]), pp. 42–62, 80.

105 Nicholas Redman, 'Moscow Rules', *Survival* 61:3 (2019), pp. 247–254: p. 249.

106 Andrew J. Nathan and Andrew Scobell, 'How China Sees America: The Sum of Beijing's Fears', *Foreign Affairs* 91:5 (2012), pp. 32–47; Ian Easton, 'How China's Military Really Sees America', *The National Interest*, 16 April 2018, also the source of quotations from Chinese authors that follow.

107 The following quotations are from Andrew J. Nathan and Andrew Scobell, 'How China Sees America: The Sum of Beijing's Fears', *Foreign Affairs* 91:5 (2012), pp. 32–47.

108 Peter Conradi, *Who Lost Russia? How the World Entered a New Cold War* (London: Oneworld, 2017), pp. 152–207; Andrew Monaghan, *Russian State Mobilisation: Moving the Country onto a War Footing* (Chatham House: Russia and Eurasia Programme, May 2016), pp. 7–14;

109 'The President's News Conference with President Vladimir V. Putin of Russia in Strelna, Russia', 15 July 2006, *Public Papers of the Presidents of the United States: George W. Bush*, vol. 2 (Washington, DC: US Government Printing Office, 2010), pp. 1394–1401: p. 1401.

110 Keith Gessen, 'The Quiet Americans Behind the US–Russia Imbroglio', *New York Times Magazine*, 8 May 2018.

111 Joshua R. Itzkowitz Shifrinson, 'Deal or No Deal? The End of the Cold War and the US Offer to Limit NATO Expansion', *International Security* 40:4 (2016), pp. 7–44.

112 NSC Paper, 'Moving Toward NATO Expansion', 4 October 1994, Clinton Presidential Library, pp. 2016–2140.

113 President Bill Clinton to Strobe Talbott, *The Russia Hand: A Memoir of Presidential Diplomacy* (New York: Random House, 2002), p. 202.

114 Ivan Krastev and Leonard Benardo, 'No Reset: The Unquiet American', *The American Interest*, 4 February 2019.

Chapter 3 Rough Beast: How the Order Made Trump

1 Stephen Chaudoin, Helen V. Milner and Dustin Tingley, 'Down But Not Out: Liberal International American Foreign Policy', in Robert Jervis, Francis J. Gavin, Joshua Rovner and Diane N. Labrosse, *Chaos in the Liberal Order: The Trump Presidency And International Politics in the Twenty-First Century* (New York: Columbia University Press, 2018), pp. 62, 83.

2 Michael Fullilove, 'We Must Find a New Asia Focus as World Order Changes', *The Australian*, 10 May 2019.

3 Philip Bump, 'Donald Trump Will be President Thanks to 80,000 People in Three States', *The Washington Post*, 1 December 2016.

4 Pew Research Centre, *2016 Campaign: Strong Interest, Widespread Dissatisfaction* (7 July 2016), p. 32.

5 Neta C. Crawford, 'The Pentagon Emits More Greenhouse Gases Than Any Other Part of the US Government', *Live Science*, 12 June 2019.

6 On the transnational quality of the crisis, see Adam Tooze, *Crashed: How a Decade of Financial Crises Changed the World* (New York: Allen Lane, 2018), pp. 9, 19; on the 'interlocking matrix', see H. S. Shin, 'Globalization: Real and Financial', BIS 87th Annual General Meeting, cited in Tooze, *Crashed*, p. 618, n. 22.

7 Rosella Capella Zielinski, 'US Wars Abroad Increase Inequality at Home', *Foreign Affairs* 95:5 (2018).

8 Jonathan D. Caverley, *Democratic Militarism: Voting, Wealth, and War* (Cambridge: Cambridge University Press, 2014).

9 The linkages between Trump's rise and the preceding order are the basis for both of the most provocative diagnoses, one Marxist and one conservative: Perry Anderson, 'Passing the Baton', *New Left Review* (2017), pp. 41–64; Victor Davis Hanson, *The Case for Trump* (New York: Basic Books, 2018).

10 Aziz Rana, 'Decolonizing Obama', *N + 1* (Winter 2017), pp. 22–27: p. 22.

11 As Roger Eatwell and Matthew Goodwin argue, in *National*

Populism: The Revolt Against Liberal Democracy (Milton Keynes: Random House, 2018), pp. 265–266.

12 Douglas L. Kriner and Francis X. Shen, 'Battlefield Casualties and Ballot Box Defeat: Did the Bush-Obama Wars Cost Clinton the White House?' 20 June 2017, at http://www.forschungsnetzwerk. at/downloadpub/2017_SSRN-id2989040_usa.pdf.

13 See Robert D. Kaplan, 'Trump's Budget Is American Caesarism', *Foreign Policy*, 26 May 2017.

14 See Matthew Fay, 'Libertarians, Donald Trump, and War' *Niskanan Center*, 30 March 2017, at https://niskanencenter.org/ blog/libertarians-donald-trump-war/.

15 Tal Copan and Eugene Scott, 'Trump Touts "Militaristic" Policies, Gets Panned by General', *CNN*, 13 August 2015.

16 Lauren Caroll, 'Super PAC Ad Says Trump Likes War, Even Nuclear, but that Needs Context', *Politifact*, 19 June 2016.

17 'Bush-era Officials Reshape Trump Administration; US Troops in the Middle East Reportedly Rise 33%', *Hareetz and the Associated Press*, 20 November 2017.

18 'Contractor Support of US Operations in the U.S. CENTCOM Area of Responsibility', January 2019, at https://www.acq.osd.mil/log/ ps/.CENTCOM_reports.html/5A_January_2019_Final.pdf.

19 Yahel Arnon and Yoel Guzansky, 'A Conventional Arms Race', *INSS Insight* 1074, 11 July 2018.

20 'Trump Tells Pentagon "to top" France Military Parade', *BBC*, 7 February 2018.

21 Peter Beinart, 'Why Trump Can't Handle the Costs of War', *The Atlantic*, 20 October 2017.

22 'The Secret Death Toll of America's Drones', *New York Times*, 30 March 2019.

23 As I demonstrate elsewhere: 'Why American Grand Strategy Has Not Changed: Power, Habit and the US Foreign Policy Establishment', *International Security*, 42:4 (2018), pp. 9–46.

24 'Remarks by the President in Conversation on Poverty at Georgetown University', 12 May 2015, at https://obamawhite house.archives.gov/the-press-office/2015/05/12/remarks-presi

dent-conversation-poverty-georgetown-university; Jeffrey Gold-berg, 'The Obama Doctrine: The US President Talks Through His Hardest Decisions about America's Role in the World', *The Atlantic Monthly*, 317:3 (2016), pp. 70–90.

25 Andrew Bacevich, *The New American Militarism: How Americans Are Seduced by War* (New York: Oxford University Press, 2005).

26 Christopher J. Coyne and Abigail R. Hall, *Tyranny Comes Home: The Domestic Fate of US Militarism* (Stanford, CA: Stanford University Press, 2018).

27 Michael J. Glennon, *National Security and Double Government* (Oxford: Oxford University Press, 2015), pp. 39–65.

28 Robert Myers, 'The "Warspeak" Permeating Everyday Language Puts Us All in the Trenches', *The Conversation*, 6 August 2019.

29 Stephen Baele, 'The Real Problem: The Militarization of the NFL', *The American Conservative*, 27 September 2017; Sen. John McCain and Sen. Jeff Flake, *Tackling Paid Patriotism: A Joint Oversight Report* (2015), at http://www.documentcloud.org/documents/2506099-tackling-paid-patriotism-oversight-report.html.

30 Philip Gourevitch, 'Bushspeak', *The New Yorker*, 13 September 2004, pp. 36–41.

31 Alex Ward, 'How the Trump Administration Is Using 9/11 to Build a Case for War with Iran', *Vox*, 14 June 2019.

32 Zachary Zeck, 'South Korea Extends Ballistic Missile Range', *The Diplomat*, 4 April 2014.

33 As Chris Preble argues, in *Peace, War and Liberty: Understanding US Foreign Policy* (Washington, DC: Cato Institute, 2019), p. 121.

34 Andrew Sullivan, 'The Limits of My Conservatism', *Intelligencer*, 16 August 2019.

35 https://twitter.com/SenTomCotton/status/1144295494073618432; for the DoD's response, see letter, Under Secretary of Defense John C. Rood to the Honourable James M. Inhofe, Chairman, Committee on Armed Services, 26 June 2019, at https://twitter.com/AlexEmmons/status/1144633957683777536.

36 Jeff D. Colgan and Robert O. Keohane, 'The Liberal Order Is

Rigged: Fix It Now or Watch It Whither', *Foreign Affairs* 96:3 (2017), pp. 36–44.

37 Russ Feingold, 'US Campaign Finance Laws Resemble Legalized Bribery. We Must Reform Them', *Guardian*, 8 November 2017.

38 See https://www.transparency.org/country/USA.

39 David Klion, 'American Empire Is the Sick Man of the 21st Century', *Foreign Policy*, 2 April 2019.

40 David Barstow, Susanne Craig and Russ Beutner, 'Trump Engaged in Suspect Tax Schemes as He Reaped Riches from His Father', *New York Times*, 2 October 2018.

41 Marc Jones, 'World Has Racked Up 7,000 Protectionist Measures since Crisis: Study', *Reuters*, 14 November 2017.

42 Bill Clinton, 'Expanding Trade, Protecting Values: Why I'll Fight to Make China's Trade Status Permanent', *The New Democrat*, 12:1 (2000), pp. 9–11.

43 George H. W. Bush and Brent Scowcroft, *A World Transformed* (New York: Random Books, 1999), p. 89.

44 See Michael Lind, 'The Cost of Free Trade', *The American Prospect*, 1 December 2011.

45 Robert Gilpin, *War and Change in World Politics* (Cambridge: Cambridge University Press, 1981), pp. 166–167.

Chapter 4 A Machiavellian Moment: Roads Ahead

1 Elisabeth Bumiller and Norimitsu Onishi, 'US Lifts Ban on Contact with Indonesia's Kopassus Special Forces', *New York Times*, 22 July 2010; Philip Dorling and Nick McKenzie, 'Obama Caved In on Kopassus', *Sydney Morning Herald*, 17 December 2010.

2 Graham Allison, 'What Should Be the Purpose of American Power?', *The National Interest*, 19 August 2015.

3 As J. G. A. Pocock argued, in *The Machiavellian Moment: Florentine Political Thought and the Atlantic Republican Tradition* (Princeton, NJ: Princeton University Press, 1975), pp. 31–49, 156–183; see also Robert Kagan, *The Return of History and the End of Dreams* (New York: Atlantic, 2008).

4 Michael Ignatieff, 'Machiavelli Was Right', *Atlantic Monthly* 312:5 (2013), pp. 40–44.

5 See Jonathan Haslam, *No Virtue Like Necessity: Realist Thought in International Relations since Machiavelli* (New Haven, CT: Yale University Press, 2002) – 'counterblast' quotes in the following paragraphs are from p. 36.

6 Niccolò Machiavelli, *The Prince*, trans. Tim Parks (London: Penguin, 2009), esp. ch. 15, p. 60.

7 Woodrow Wilson, An Address to the Senate, 22 January 1917, *The Papers of Woodrow Wilson*, vol. 40 (Princeton, NJ: Princeton University Press, 1966–94), p. 536.

8 See John A. Thompson, 'Woodrow Wilson and Peace without Victory: Interpreting the Reversal of 1917', *Federal History* (2018), pp. 9–25.

9 John A. Thompson, 'Wilsonianism: The Dynamics of a Conflicted Concept', *International Affairs* 86:1 (2010), pp. 27–48.

10 Ross A. Kennedy, *The Will to Believe: Woodrow Wilson, World War I, and America's Strategy for Peace and Security* (Kent, OH: Kent State University Press, 2009), p. 102.

11 For this argument in greater depth, see Michael C. Desch, 'America's Liberal Illiberalism: The Ideological Origins of Overreaction in US Foreign Policy', *International Security* 32:3 (Winter 2007/2008), pp. 7–43; on the linkages between liberalism and imperialism, see also L. E. Ambrosius, 'Woodrow Wilson and George W. Bush: Historical Comparisons of Ends and Means in Their Foreign Policies', *Diplomatic History* 30 (2005), pp. 509–543; David M. Kennedy, 'What "W" owes to "WW"', *The Atlantic* 30:5 (2005), pp. 36–40.

12 I adapt this audit from Hugh White, 'What's So Great About American World Leadership?', *The Atlantic*, 23 November 2016.

13 As John A. Thompson argues in *A Sense of Power: The Roots of America's Global Role* (Ithaca, NY: Cornell University, 2015), pp. 25–56.

14 Daniel Yergin, *Shattered Peace: The Origins of the Cold War and the National Security State* (New York: Penguin, 1978), p. 197.

15 See further Paul Kennedy, *The Rise and Fall of Great Powers* (New York: Random House, 1989), pp. 357–60.

16 Mike Patton, 'US Role in Global Economy Declines Nearly 50%', *Forbes*, 29 February 2016, at https://www.statista.com/statis tics/270267/united-states-share-of-global-gross-domestic-prod uct-gdp/.

17 The estimate of Joseph M. Parent and Paul K. MacDonald, 'The Road to Recovery: How Once Great Powers Became Great Again', *Washington Quarterly* 41:3 (2018), pp. 21–39, n. 2.

18 Steven Van Evera, 'A Farewell to Geopolitics', in Melvyn Leffer and Jeffrey W. Legro, eds., *To Lead the World: American Strategy after the Bush Doctrine* (Oxford: Oxford University Press, 2008), pp. 11–30; and my own work, *The Global Village Myth: Distance, War and the Limits of Power* (Washington, DC: Georgetown University Press, 2015), pp. 148–194.

19 See Michael J. Mazarr, 'The Risks of Ignoring Strategic Insolvency', *Washington Quarterly* 35:4 (2012), pp. 7–22.

20 Walter Lippmann, *US Foreign Policy: Shield of the Republic* (Boston, MA: Little, Brown, 1943), pp. 69-70; Samuel P. Huntington, 'Coping with the Lippmann Gap', *Foreign Affairs* 66:3 (1988), pp. 453–477; Patrick Porter, 'Beyond the American Century: Walter Lippmann and American Grand Strategy, 1943–1950', *Diplomacy and Statecraft* 22 (2011), pp. 557–577.

21 Congressional Budget Office, *The 2018 Long-Term Budget Outlook*, p. 1.

22 Congressional Budget Office, *The 2017 Long-Term Budget Outlook*, p. 39, at https://www.cbo.gov/ publication/52480; Joseph Lawler, 'Budget Office: Debt on Track to Double in Next 30 Years, Substantial Risks for the Nation', *Washington Examiner*, 26 June 2018; Doug Bandow, 'The One Reason America Can't Police the World Anymore: Washington is Broke', *The National Interest*, 26 December 2018.

23 Manmohan S. Kumar and Jaejoon Woo, 'Public Debt and Growth', IMF Working Paper, WP/10/74, July 2010, at http://www.imf.org/ external/pubs/ft/wp/2010/wp10174.pdf; and Carmen M. Reinhart

and Kenneth S. Rogoff, 'Growth in a Time of Debt', *American Economic Review* 100:2 (May 2010), pp. 573–578, at http://www. ycsg.yale.edu/center/forms/growth-debt.pdf; discussed also in Salim Furth, 'High Debt is a Real Drag', *Heritage Foundation Issue Brief* No. 3859, 22 February 2013.

24 Jonathan Kirshner, 'Dollar Primacy and American Power: What's at Stake?', *Review of International Political Economy* 15:3 (2008), pp. 418–438; Christopher Layne, 'This Time It's Real: The End of Unipolarity and the *Pax Americana*', *International Studies Quarterly* 56:1 (2012), pp. 203–213.

25 Cited in *Foreign Affairs* 98:2 (2019): 'Should Washington Not Worry about the Budget Deficit?', at https://www.foreignaf fairs.com/ask-the-experts/2019-04-16/should-washington-not -worry-about-budget-deficit.

26 Max Boot, 'Why Winning and Losing Are Irrelevant', *Washington Post*, 30 January 2019.

27 Nikki Wentling, 'VA Reveals Its Veteran Suicide Statistic Included Active-Duty Troops', *Stars and Stripes*, 20 June 2018, at https:// www.stripes.com/news/us/va-reveals-its-veteran-suicide-stat istic-included-active-duty-troops-1.533992; Neta C. Crawford, 'United States Budgetary Costs of the Post-9/11 Wars Through FY2019: $5.9 Trillion Spent and Obligated', 14 November 2018, at https://watson.brown.edu/costsofwar/files/cow/imce/papers/ 2018/Crawford_Costs%20of%20War%20Estimates%20Through% 20FY2019.pdf. pp. 23–29.

28 Bryan Dorries, *The Theatre of War: What Ancient Tragedies Can Teach Us Today* (New York: Random House, 2016).

29 Pew Research Center, *Public Uncertain, Divided over America's Place in the World*, 5 May 2016, pp. 11–19, at https://www.pewre search.org/wp-content/uploads/sites/4/2016/05/05-05-2016-For eign-policy-APW-release.pdf.

30 President of the United States, *National Security Strategy of the United States of America* (2017), pp. 2–3; US Department of Defense, *Summary of the 2018 National Defense Strategy of the United States of America: Sharpening the American Military's*

Competitive Edge (2018), pp. 1–3; Secretary of Defense James N. Mattis, 'Remarks by Secretary Mattis on the National Defense Strategy', 19 January 2018, at https://dod.defense.gov/ News/Transcripts/Transcript-View/Article/1420042/remarks -by-secretary-mattis-on-the-national-defense-strategy/.

31 'Remarks by Vice President Pence at the West Point Graduation Ceremony', 25 May 2019, at https://www.whitehouse.gov/brief ings-statements/remarks-vice-president-pence-west-point-gra duation-ceremony/.

32 'Remarks by the Vice President Aboard USS *Ronald Reagan*', 19 April 2019, at https://www.whitehouse.gov/briefings-statements/ remarks-vice-president-aboard-uss-ronald-reagan/.

33 Van Jackson, 'Power, Trust, and Network Complexity: Three Logics of Hedging in Asian Security', *International Relations of the Asia-Pacific* 14: 3 (2014), pp. 331–56; Leonid Bershidsky, 'Reality Check: Europe Won't Roll Over on Iran', *Bloomberg*, 10 May 2018.

34 Atman Trivedi and Aparna Pande, 'India is Getting Cold Feet about Trump's America', *Foreign Policy*, 30 August 2018.

35 As Paul Kennedy notes in regard to Philip II or Louis XIV, 'American Power Is On the Wane', *Wall Street Journal*, 14 January 2009.

36 According to an assessment by Neta C. Crawford of all war-related spending, including but beyond appropriations to the Department of Defense, including the separate fund 'Overseas Contingency Operations', interest on borrowing, veterans' benefits and disability spending: 'United States Budgetary Costs of the Post-9/11 Wars Through FY2019:$5.9 Trillion Spent and Obligated', 14 November 2018, p. 2, at https://watson.brown.edu/ costsofwar/files/cow/imce/papers/2018/Crawford_Costs%20of% 20War%20Estimates%20Through%20FY2019.pdf.

37 See William D. Hartung and Mandy Smithberger, 'America's Defense Budget Is Bigger than You Think', *The Nation*, 7 May 2019; Jeff Stein, 'US Military Budget Inches Closer to $1 Trillion Mark, as Concerns Grow over Federal Budget', *Washington Post*, 19 June 2018; Craig Whitlock and Bob Woodward, 'Pentagon Buries

Evidence of $125 Billion in Bureaucratic Waste', *Washington Post*, 5 December 2016.

38 President Dwight Eisenhower, 'The Chance for Peace', speech given to the American Society of Newspaper Editors, 16 April 1953.

39 Thomas Oatley, *A Political Economy of American Hegemony: Buildups, Booms and Busts* (New York: Cambridge University Press, 2015).

40 On the employment effects of defence spending, see Robert Pollin and Heidi Garrett-Peltier, *The US Employment Effects of Military and Domestic Spending Priorities*, Political Economy Research Institute University of Massachusetts, Amherst, December 2011, at https://www.peri.umass.edu/fileadmin/pdf/published_study/ PERI_military_spending_2011.pdf.

41 'Trump Budget Request Takes Military Share of Spending to Historic Levels', 15 February 2018, *National Priorities Project*, at https://www.nationalpriorities.org/analysis/2018/trump-bud get-request-takes-military-share-spending-historic-levels/.

42 Jeffrey D. Sachs, 'The Fatal Expense of American Imperialism', *Boston Globe*, 30 October 2016.

43 Joseph S. Nye Jr, 'Will the Liberal Order Survive?' *Foreign Affairs* 96:1 (2017), pp. 10–16: p. 10.

44 NSC 68, 'A Report to the National Security Council', Executive Secretary, 14 April 1950, *Naval War College Review* 27:6 (1975):, pp. 51–108, Section B.

45 Hal Brands and Charles Edel, *The Lessons of Tragedy: Statecraft and World Order* (New Haven, CT: Yale University Press, 2019), pp. 62, 140.

46 Barbara Cosette, 'A Political Diplomat: Madeleine Korbel Albright', *New York Times*, 6 December 1998.

47 Jonathan Chait, '61 Times Bill Kristol Was Reminded of Hitler and Churchill', *The National Interest*, 29 April 2015.

48 See Gerhard L. Weinberg, 'No Road from Munich to Baghdad', *Washington Post*, 3 November 2002; Christopher Layne, 'Security Studies and the Use of History: Neville Chamberlain's Grand

Strategy Revisited', *Security Studies* 17 (2008), pp. 397–437; Norrin Ripsman and Jack S. Levy, 'Wishful Thinking or Buying Time? The Logic of British Appeasement in the 1930s', *International Security* 33:2 (2008), pp. 148–181; David A. Bell, 'The Sound of Munich', *The National Interest*, 25 April 2016.

49 See Scott A. Silverstone, *From Hitler's Germany to Saddam's Iraq: The Enduring False Promise of Preventive War* (London: Rowman & Littlefield, 2019), p. 259.

50 See Dale C. Copeland, *The Origin of Major Wars* (Ithaca, NY: Cornell University Press, 2000).

51 Jonathan Kirshner, 'Gilpin Approaches War and Change: A Classical Realist in Structural Drag', in G. John Ikenberry, *Power, Order and Change in World Politics* (Cambridge: Cambridge University Press, 2014), pp. 131–161.

52 Paul K. MacDonald and Joseph M. Parent, 'Graceful Decline? The Surprising Success of Great Power Retrenchment', *International Security* 35:4 (Spring 2011), pp. 7–44; T. V. Paul, ed., *Accommodating Rising Powers: Past, Present, and Future* (New York: Cambridge University Press, 2016), p. 21.

53 Michael O'Hanlon, 'Farewell to General Mattis', *The Hill*, 21 December 2018.

54 Margaret MacMillan, 'Warnings from Versailles', *Foreign Affairs* 98:1 (2019), at https://www.foreignaffairs.com/articles/europe/2019-01-08/warnings-versailles.

55 Nicholas K. Gvosdev, 'US–Russia Relations Are Stuck on Repeat', *The National Interest*, 16 July 2018; Joshua R. Itzkowitz Shifrinson, 'Trump and NATO: Old Wine in Gold Bottles?' *H-Diplo*, 29 September 2017.

56 See Yuen Foong Khong, *Analogies at War: Korea, Munich, Dien Bien Phu, and the Vietnam Decisions of 1965* (Princeton, NJ: Princeton University Press, 1992).

57 Eugene Gholz, Daryl G. Press and Harvey M. Sapolsky, 'Come Home America: The Strategy of Restraint in the Face of Temptation', *International Security* 21:4 (Spring 1997), pp. 5–48; Barry R. Posen, *Restraint: A New Foundation for US Grand*

Strategy (Ithaca, NY: Cornell University Press, 2014); Christopher Layne, *The Peace of Illusions: American Grand Strategy from 1940 to the Present* (Ithaca, NY: Cornell University Press, 2006); John J. Mearsheimer and Stephen M. Walt, 'The Case for Offshore Balancing', *Foreign Affairs* 95:4 (2016), pp. 70–83; Christopher A. Preble, *The Power Problem* (Ithaca, NY: Cornell University Press, 2009).

58 Steven Van Evera, 'A Farewell to Geopolitics', in Melvyn Leffer and Jeffrey W. Legro, eds., *To Lead the World: American Strategy after the Bush Doctrine* (Oxford: Oxford University Press, 2008), pp. 11–30.

59 Chalmers Johnson, *Dismantling the Empire: America's Last Best Hope* (New York: Henry Holt 2010); Stephen Wertheim, 'Is It Too Late to Stop a Cold War with China?', *New York Times*, 8 June 2019.

60 Cited in Greil Marcus, *The Shape of Things to Come: Prophecy and the American Voice* (New York: Faber, 2006), pp. 8–9.

61 On the two traditions, see Michael J. Hogan, *A Cross of Iron: Harry S. Truman and the Origins of the National Security State 1945–1954* (Cambridge: Cambridge University Press, 1998), pp. 463–465; Michael Lind, *The American Way of Strategy: US Foreign Policy and the American Way of Life* (Oxford: Oxford University Press, 2006), pp. 3–43; Robert J. Art, 'The United States, The Balance of Power, and World War II: Was Spykman Right?', *Security Studies* 14:3 (2005), pp. 365–406.

62 See David Kang, 'Power Transitions: Thucydides Didn't Live in East Asia', *Washington Quarterly* 41:1 (2018) pp. 137–154; Paul Schroeder, 'Historical Reality vs. Neo-Realist Theory', *International Security* 19:1 (1994), pp. 108–148.

63 China's GDP is already bigger vis-à-vis America's than the USSR's ever was, for example – so in terms of latent potential, it is already a 'pole' – while Russia, for all its internal weaknesses, still has a nuclear arsenal capable of coercing any actor on the planet, a PPP GDP approximately equal to that of Germany, and a demonstrated willingness to use all levers of national power (even at

risk of escalation), while bearing domestic privations to defend threatened interests.

64 Aaron L. Friedberg, 'Competing with China', *Survival* 60:3 (2018), pp. 7-64: pp. 22-23; Howard W. French, *Everything Under the Heavens: How the Past Helps Shape China's Push for Global Power* (New York: Random House, 2017), pp. 89-127.

65 Andrew Monaghan, *Russian State Mobilisation: Moving the Country onto a War Footing* (Chatham House: Russia and Eurasia Programme, May 2016), pp. 7-14.

66 Ely Ratner, 'There is No Grand Bargain with China', *Foreign Affairs* 97:6 (2018); Michael McFaul, 'Russia As It Is', *Foreign Affairs* 97:4 (2018), pp. 82-91; Eric Brewer, 'Can the US Reinstate Maximum Pressure on North Korea?' *Foreign Affairs* 97:6 (2018).

67 Alexander Gabuev, 'Why Russia and China Are Strengthening Security Ties', *Foreign Affairs* 97:5 (2018).

68 Jamil Anderlini, 'China and Russia's Dangerous Liaison', *Financial Times*, 9 August 2018.

69 Jack S. Levy and William R. Thompson, 'Balancing on Land and Sea: Do States Ally Against the Leading Global Power?' *International Security* 35:1 (2010), pp. 7-43: p. 33.

70 Robert David English, 'Russia, Trump and the New Détente: Fixing US-Russian Relations', *Foreign Affairs* 96:2 (2017); Graham Allison and Dimitri K. Symes, 'A Blueprint for Donald Trump to Fix Relations with Russia', *The National Interest*, 18 December 2016.

71 Peter Beinart, 'America Needs an Entirely New Foreign Policy for the Trump Age', *The Atlantic*, 16 September 2018.

72 In this way, I depart from the recent 'accommodationist' literature; see Jonathan Kirshner, 'The Tragedy of Offensive Realism: Classical Realism and the Rise of China', *European Journal of International Relations* 18:1 (2010), pp. 53-75; Hugh White, *The China Choice: Why We Should Share Power* (Melbourne: Black Ink, 2012); Charles Glaser, 'A US-China Grand Bargain? The Hard Choice Between Military Competition and Bargaining', *International Security* 39:4 (2015), pp. 49-90; Graham T. Allison,

Destined for War: Can America and China Escape the Thucydides Trap (New York: Houghton Mifflin, 2017); Lyle J. Goldstein, *Meeting China Halfway: How to Defuse the Emerging US–China Rivalry* (Washington, DC: Georgetown University Press, 2015).

73 John Hemmings, *Safeguarding our Systems: Managing Chinese Investment into the UK's Digital and Critical National Infrastructure* (London: Henry Jackson Society, 2017); Francine Kiefer and Jack Destch, 'What Congress is Doing to Stop Russian Hackers Next Time', *Christian Science Monitor*, 5 June 2017.

74 As Eric Heginbotham and Jacob L. Heim argue, in 'Deterring without Dominance: Discouraging Chinese Adventurism under Austerity', *Washington Quarterly* 38:1 (2015), pp. 185–199; see also Michael Beckley, 'The Emerging Military Balance in Asia: How China's Neighbours Can Check China's Expansion', *International Security* 42:2 (2017), pp. 78–119.

75 Sebastian Rosato and John Schuessler, 'A Realist Foreign Policy for the United States', *Perspectives on Politics* 9:4 (2011), p. 807.

76 Jeffrey Record, *Beating Goliath: Why Insurgencies Win* (Washington, DC: Potomac Books, 2007).

77 Stephen Biddle, 'Afghanistan's Legacy: Emerging Lessons of an Ongoing War', *Washington Quarterly* 37:2 (2014), pp. 80–81; Alexander Downes and Jonathan Monten, 'Forced to be Free? Why Foreign-imposed Regime Change Rarely Leads to Democratization', *International Security* 37:4 (2013), pp. 90–131.

78 Robert Jervis, 'Domino Beliefs and Strategic Behaviour', in Robert Jervis and Jack Snyder, eds., *Dominoes and Bandwagons: Strategic Beliefs and Great Power Competition in the Eurasian Rimland* (New York: Oxford University Press, 1990), p. 43.

79 National Defense Strategy Commission, *Providing for the Common Defense: The Assessment and Recommendations of the National Defense Strategy Commission* (2018), pp. vi, 6, 25.

80 Janan Ganesh, 'Washington's Consensus is Dangerously Interventionist', *Financial Times*, 6 February 2019.

81 Elbridge Colby, 'How to Win America's Next War', *Foreign Policy*, 5 May 2019.

82 Samuel P. Huntington, 'Coping with the Lippmann Gap', *Foreign Affairs* 66:3 (1988), pp. 453–477.

Afterword: Before Our Eyes

1 Amaani Lyle, 'DOD Must Meet New Challenges with Smaller Force, Fox Says', US Department of Defense, American Forces Press Service, 7 April 2014, at http://archive.defense.gov/news/newsarticle.aspx?id=122001.
2 Rupert Brooke, 'Peace', 1914, at http://ww1lit.nsms.ox.ac.uk/ww1lit/education/tutorials/intro/brooke/ipeace.
3 Peter Wiseman, 'Domitian and the Dynamics of Terror in Classical Rome', *History Today* 46:9 (1996), pp. 19–24.

Index

McMaster, H. R., 118
MacMillan, Margaret, 176–7, 178–9
McNaughton, John, 111
Madison, James, 145
Maidan revolution, 100
Maier, Charles, 38
Malaysia, 191
Mao Zedong, 106
Marshall Islands, 57
Marshall Plan, 41
Mauritius, 57
mental health, and the military, 166
Merkel, Angela, 43, 77, 99
Middle East
    conflict overview, 9
    in the future, 184, 195–6
    place in the liberal order, 60
    US failures in, 160–1
    see also individual countries by
        name
militarism see war and militarism
Miller, Paul, 118
missile control, 144, 161
monarchism, 65–8
monetary policy see economics and
    finance
Montenegro, 178
Morefield, Jeanne, 25, 72
Morgenthau, Hans, 75
Mozambique, 109
Munich agreement (1938), 171–2
Munich Security Conference (2019),
    8, 10
Muslim Brotherhood, 52, 77

NAFTA see North American Free
    Trade Agreement
Napoleon Bonaparte, French
    emperor, 27
nationalism, 9, 71, 143–4
NATO
    anniversary, 42
    and authoritarian regimes, 46
    and Balkans, 46, 80, 82
    Chinese attitude to, 124
    enlargement into Russian spheres
        of influence, 100, 187
    founding principles, 31, 32

in the future, 187
and the liberal order, 41, 66
and liberal values, 46
and Libya, 71
modern containment of Russia,
    178
and peace, 107
reasons for creation, 100
Trump's attitude to, 140
US relations with, 43–7, 120
Nazis
    potential containment by pre-
        emptive strike, 173–5
    potential containment without
        war, 171–3, 176–7
    US help for former, 86
Netanyahu, Benjamin, 42
New Zealand, 163
Newfoundland Declaration (1941),
    31
Nicaragua, 41, 82
9/11, 112, 144
Nixon, Richard, 43, 106–7, 198
non-intervention, 58–9
North American Free Trade
    Agreement (NAFTA), 32, 93
North Korea
    in the future, 167, 184, 191, 194
    as illiberal state, 36
    nuclear programme, 9, 79–80, 191,
        194
    Trump's attitude to, 139, 140
    US relations with, 79–80, 160
Northern Mariana Islands, 57
nostalgia, 17–18, 25
NSC 68 (Cold War strategy
    document), 50, 85, 170–1
nuclear weapons
    in the future, 167–8
    liberal attitude to, 56
    near misses, 98
    non-proliferation regime, 35, 44,
        97, 160
    North Korean programme, 9,
        79–80, 191, 194
    nuclear deterrence, 41, 56, 94–9,
        180
    Russian arsenal, 239